WHICH WAY NIGERIA?

Selected Speeches

Jerome Udoji

Spectrum Books Limited
Ibadan
Benin-City • Kaduna • Lagos • Owerri

Published by
Spectrum Books Limited
Spectrum House
Ring Road
PMB 5612
Ibadan, Nigeria

in association with
Safari Books (Export) Limited
1st Floor
17 Bond Street
St. Helier
Jersey JE2 3NP
Channel Islands
United Kingdom

Europe and USA Distributor
African Books Collective Ltd.
The Jam Factory
27 Park End Street
Oxford OX1, 1HU, UK

© Jerome Udoji, 1999

First Published, 1999

ISBN: 978-029-085-0

Printed by Polygraphics Venture Limited Ibadan

DEDICATION

To my mother
IKPOAKU OLININE

Contents

Foreword

In this book, *Which Way Nigeria*, Chief Jerome Oputa Udoji, a doyen of the Nigerian Civil Service and a trail blazer in the search for new directions for Nigeria's industrial development, has left for posterity his thoughts on burning issues of national unity and social and economic progress. A selection of speeches on topical issues of the moment during the heydays of his diverse roles in Nigeria's public administration and economic management, his views are still relevant today as the problems focused in the book remain critical pre-occupations for public administrators and managers of the Nigerian economy.

The author set the stage by suggesting practical ways of achieving national unity and securing the citizen's loyalty to the Nigerian nation, in his contribution at the deliberations of the 1979 Constituent Assembly that produced the 1979 Constitution. Thereafter, he touched on other wide-ranging issues of interest including civil service administration; appropriate political structure for the governance of Nigeria; the need for a strong local government with more powers, and effective mechanisms for the industrial and overall development of the Nigerian economy.

A strong advocate of the private sector as the engine of growth, the author argues against government involvement in economic activities. In the same vein, he made a foray into the controversial question of religion in education, arguing strongly that it (religion) is central to character formation and provides a guide to man in his life's journey. He then concludes that religion should be a major concern of our educational endeavours. Emphasizing the importance of education in the formation of the individual, the author looks at the equally controversial issue of the role of government and the private sector in education. Reflecting his liberal mind, he questions the propriety of government monopoly of education. One reads with nostalgia the result of the take-over of schools by the government as represented by an educational system that today appears impersonal and indifferent to the type and character of the products of our educational institutions, who are lacking in all-round development that was the quintessence of the legacy of the erstwhile voluntary agencies.

Those who have not been privileged to read the Report of the 1970-74 Public Service Review Commission (popularly known as the Udoji Report), will in this book come into intimate acquaintance with most important aspects of that Report on civil service reforms, which the country is still grappling with today. After reading through it, one will come out with no doubt that if the recommendations of the Report had been faithfully implemented, the nation's bureaucracy would have been better motivated, more efficient and effective. But because the reforms were half-heartedly implemented and even completely neglected in some parts, the civil service has remained highly demoralised, de-motivated, less efficient and insufficiently productive.

Policy makers, research institutes, educational administrators, especially at the tertiary level, and industrial managers will find in the book interesting and useful suggestions on how to make the products of the educational institutions relevant to industry. Here, dialogue, co-operation and co-ordination among the various parties are considered necessary to fashion out appropriate curriculum and focused research.

In the copious pages devoted to public and/or civil service, the author renders revolutionary views, borne of his experience in public administration, on such issues as political neutrality of the civil servant, the tenure of office of top civil servants, and the public servant as a policy maker. The general perception of the civil servant as a policy maker and the practice of career civil service for all officers are rigorously challenged in the book. The arguments for this position are stimulating and present challenging reading for all.

Beyond concerns of civil service reform and public administration, the author shows his versatility by dwelling on such issues as economic and business management. Among subjects of discourse in the book are entrepreneurship development in Africa, privatisation of public enterprises, the private sector as the engine of growth, as well as the relationship between productivity and the reward for labour.

These are topical issues in today's search for efficient mechanisms for the management of the Nigerian economy in general and industrial business in particular. An advocate of a strong private sector, the author opines without equivocation that for privatisation to be a viable option to public enterprise, government must be prepared to give up control and management, since "in business, government's hand is a dead hand". In recognition of the active and substantial role the indigenous private sector should play inthe privatisation process, the book underscores the overriding need for African entrepreneurship development.

The travails of the Nigerian economy since the early 1980s and the declining fortunes of the manufacturing sector over the years received the author's attention. Here, the failure of the structural adjustment programme (SAP) to restore life to the manufacturing sector, because of inappropriate policies; the problems and prospects of the Nigerian manufacturing sector; and the whole question of backward integration/local sourcing of raw materials are issues that are lucidly discussed in the book. The views expressed on these issues are still valid today, and therefore represent necessary readings for government policy makers and planners.

As I commend this book to the general public, I strongly believe that economic managers in both the private and public sector will find it a useful reference partner. I cannot but conclude with an invitation to everyone to read Chapter 22, dealing with an interview of the author by Business Contact Magazine. The young generation will particularly find the chapter a compulsory reading for lessons on personal development and self-actualisation.

Chief (Dr) R.F. Giwa
President
Manufacturers
Association of Nigeria
January 4, 1999.

Preface

Chief J.O. Udoji is the quintessential man of many parts—moralist, Papal Knight of St Gregory the Great, farmer, ex-chief secretary and head of service, former chairman of the Public Service Review Commission, former member of the 1978 Constituent Assembly, former president of the Manufacturers Association of Nigeria, ex-president of the Nigerian Stock Exchange, one-time board chairman of a number of multinational corporations, and so on and so forth. One of the results of his life of active engagement is a frightening accumulation of heaps of speeches on various subjects. This, good as it may be, presents particular difficulties and challenges when these speeches are to be collected into a book form for posterity. The first challenge is: How many of these speeches should be selected bearing in mind that many readers are easily intimidated by very voluminous books, and that the cost of producing a book is often dependent on the book's size? Second, is the question of focus. Since these speeches cut across different spheres of life, which ones should be selected without the resulting book losing focus and perspective? Third, is the question of time span. Given that some of the speeches were made a long time ago, and knowing that societies and the problems they confront are often dynamic, which year should we use as the cut-off year in the selection process? Fourth, is the problem of arranging the selected speeches even after they have been sorted into one of two categories — should they be arranged chronologically or in terms of thematic relatedness?

We decided to select only speeches which fit into one of the two sections that this collection is divided, and then used other sub-criteria to tighten the selection process. Within each section, thematic relationship rather than chronology is used in determining the order of arrangement. The speeches selected were those made between the early seventies and the mid nineties. One thing that will immediately strike the reader is how topical the problems the speeches addressed remain today, and how some of the apparently new challenges facing the country are mere mutations of old problems which were not conclusively resolved in the past. The reader is then given an opportunity to compare the solutions proffered in the speeches with some of the solutions being peddled for similar problems today. In this lies some of the main justifications for publishing this collection.

This collection, as mentioned earlier, is divided into two sections: *Section 1* is made up of speeches dealing with various aspects of the public sector. The first speech in this section gives us a summary of the author's opinions on the elements of an ideal constitution for a plural country like Nigeria. There are also speeches on the thorny questions of government take-over of schools, the often acrimonious relationship between universities and the government, and the uneasy co-existence of church and politics. Most of the speeches, however, deal with various aspects of the civil service. In the section, we get highly informed speeches on such problems as the institutional means of improving the public service, the question of the political neutrality of civil servants, the African civil servant as a policy-maker, and the issue of the tenure of office of top civil servants. This section also includes speeches which elaborate on and defend the Public Service Review Commission's recommendations. It is expected that the section will be of special interest to public servants, students of management, public administration, and, of course, the government.

Section 2 is made up of speeches on the private sector. Some of the crucial questions that the speeches in this section try to answer are: How have certain macroeconomic policies of the government affected the private sector? Are trade fairs really necessary in a country that virtually has no technology of its own to exhibit? How should local raw materials be developed? What kind of problems do agro-based industries face in Nigeria? What are the roles, problems and achievements of the Manufacturers Association of Nigeria? What kind of problems do manufacturers in Nigeria face? What is the importance of limited liability companies and the Stock Exchange? What should be the ideal relationship between the organised private sector and the government?

It is very much hoped that this section will especially appeal to private sector operators, students of business administration, as well as the government.

It is recommended that these speeches be read contextually,

that is, bearing in mind the kind of structure the country had when they were made, the policy environments in which they were made, the kind of debates that were current, the kind of prognoses that were being proffered for those problems, and so on and so forth. By reading them this way, and linking them to the way similar issues are debated today, one will also be able to see how those debates have evolved over time, and how some have transformed into what will appear to be completely new problems. This, for us, is another reason why these speeches deserve to be published.

It will, perhaps, be necessary to underline that this is a collection of speeches and not a book in the traditional sense of the word. Because of this, certain arguments, phrases or even passages are sometimes repeated *verbatim* in a number of the speeches. We do not consider this a weakness. If anything, it is more a reflection of Chief Udoji's belief that when one is called upon to make a public speech, the critical challenge is not how pedantic or bombastic one sounds, but how to deliver one's message clearly, simply and logically. This probably explains his preference for the colloquial style of writing. In fact, he often regards undue attention to the elegance of language or the arcane vocabularies of the *literati* as an unnecessary showmanship. We feel that this ability to use everyday language to explain even technical issues makes these speeches highly accessible, irrespective of one's academic background.

Patrick Adibe

xiii

Introduction

The common comment of readers of *Under Three Masters* is that I did not say enough, that after whetting the appetite of readers, I left them hungry. To quote one of such comments: "I read the book in one sitting. Fascinating. Your observations struck a series of responsive cords. Books like this are very important. They help people and students to understand what texts don't say." I have therefore decided to publish these speeches which were made during my public and private sector careers, with the hope that they will fill the gaps left in *Under Three Masters*.

It is surprising, and a matter of regret, that most of the speeches made more than ten, and in some cases twenty, years ago are still relevant and topical today! It is a sad reflection that relatively little or no progress has been made in about two or more decades.

The book is in two sections. *Section 1* contains speeches on the public sector. It contains, among others, speeches made on Nigerian civil service structure, its management, public enterprises and privatisation. The sector also contains speeches made in Zimbabwe, to the country's top civil servants on her independence, a speech made in Seychelles to members of the African Association for Public Administration and Management (AAPAM). It also includes a speech at the 1979 Constituent Assembly, and one made at Ahmadu Bello University on the relationship between universities and government.

Section 2 covers speeches on the private sector. The speeches were mostly addressed to the government in order to acquaint it with the problem facing the private sector, in general, and the manufacturing industry in particular. Most of the speeches in the section were made in the eighties.

Jerome Udoji

Section 1: The Public Sector

Mr. Chairman, the surest way to give every Nigerian a sense of belonging, and thereby forge national unity and loyalty is the pursuit of even and balanced development throughout the country. In this regard, I recommend that we borrow a leaf from the Swiss model of how to achieve unity in a multi-ethnic society. For example, what is wrong with the specifying in an appropriate legislation that every child before leaving school should learn at least one Nigerian language other than his or hers? What is wrong in specifying that the premier secondary school in each local government headquarter should contain a certain percentage, no matter how low, of students from other ethnic and linguistic groups? What is wrong in specifying that in the allocation of state lands in the capital of every state a certain percentage should go to people of other ethnic groups?

— From contributions made as a member of the Constitutional Assembly which produced the draft of the 1979 Constitution.

Civil servants, no matter how highly placed, should resist the temptation of arrogating to themselves a role that does not properly and legitimately belong to them. They must not allow the abnormal circumstances of colonialism and militarism to delude them into believing that they have a decisive role in policymaking. Nor should they be so naive as to interpret their important supportive role of assembling, collating and interpreting data and suggesting alternative policy implementation options, as policy-making."

— From a paper presented to a roundtable conference on "African Public Services and Public Policy-Making in the 1980s, Mahe, Seychelles, September 22-29, 1980.

The Making of a Nation ✦

"Uncompromising statements and threats do not help those who are anxious to find a solution that would be acceptable to all concerned. Those who threaten us with irreducible minimum and religion being more important to them than the unity of this country should know that some of us love our religion as dearly as they do even though we do not make any noise about it."

Introduction

The Chairman: The Honourable Chief J.O.Udoji.

Chief J.O. Udoji (Ihiala/Nnewi/Idemili): My name is Jerome Oputa Udoji. I represent Ihiala/Nnewi/Idemili Constituency of Anambra State.

Mr. Chairman, Sir, I support the second reading of the Federal Republic of Nigeria Constitution Bill. I do so with mixed feelings, for this is the third time in the past twenty years that I am participating, directly or indirectly, in the task of making a constitution for Nigeria. History has recorded the first two attempts as failures. I pray that we do not fail a third time. It will be a great shame if we do, for never in the history of this country, or of any black African country for that matter, has there been such a formidable assemblage of talents that I see around me— university dons and professors, legal giants and medical wizards, renowned economists and accountants, industrialists and technocrats from various disciplines, administrators and managers of great experience, skilful trade union leaders, women talent and student talent, and, last but not the least, political timbers of all sizes.

An Honourable Member: What of the Military?

Chief Udoji: Military talent also.

✦   Contributions made as a member of the 1979 Constituent Assembly which produced the 1979 constitution.

Unity is vital

Mr. Chairman, permit me to join previous speakers in complimenting the Constitution Drafting Committee, CDC, especially its chairman, and members of the draft sub-committee for the hard work and mental discipline with which they produced the Draft Bill within the specified time limit. We all know that completing programmes, projects and assignments in time is not a common feature of Nigerian public life. I hope that we in this house will not only follow their example, but will beat their record.

I will now go to the report and the draft constitution. The one theme which runs through the report, and which finds expression in several sections of the Bill is the need for unity and national loyalty among Nigerians. This is not surprising, for the one great problem facing Nigeria today is UNITY, in capital letters. It is how to weld the various ethnic, linguistic and religious communities into an integrated nation. We all know, even though at times we are ashamed to admit it, that the average Nigerian has yet to grow out of his clan and ethnic group in order to cultivate a Nigerian-wide outlook. For this reason, he tends to give more loyalty to his group than he is prepared to give to the Nigerian nation. The CDC itself was very conscious of this, and so tried very hard to make provisions that would enhance unity and national loyalty. These provisions are contained in Sections 8(2), 9(1), 36(1), 170-176 and 210(1) of the Bill. They are important, and, with your permission Mr. Chairman, I would like to quote just a few of them.

Section 8 (2) provides that:

> The composition of the federal government or any of its agencies, and the conduct of their affairs shall be carried out in such manner as to recognise the federal character of Nigeria and the need to promote national unity and to command national loyalty. Accordingly, the predominance in that Government or in its agencies or persons from a few states, or from a few ethnic or other sectional groups, shall be avoided.

Section 9(1) stipulates thus:

National integration shall be actively encouraged whilst discrimination on the grounds of place of origin, religion, sex, status, ethnic or linguistic association or ties shall be prohibited.

This section goes on to list various ways of promoting national integration. These include free mobility, full residence rights, intermarriage, and associations that cut across ethnic barriers. Section 36(1) provides for the right to property in any part of the country. Sections 170 - 176 require political parties to be open to all citizens, and their executives to reflect the federal character of Nigeria. Section 210 (1) defined the expression *Federal Character of Nigeria* in these words:

Federal Character of Nigeria refers to the distinctive desire of the peoples of Nigeria to promote national unity, foster national loyalty and give every citizen of Nigeria a sense of belonging notwithstanding the diversities of ethnic origin, culture, language or religion which may exist and which it is their desire to nourish and harness to the enrichment of the Federal Republic of Nigeria.

Mr. Chairman, the CDC should be praised for their laudable and patriotic intentions. But, unfortunately, the provisions are not good enough. They are vague, imprecise and capable of manipulation in view of the ambiguous and ambivalent language in which they are couched. Mr. Chairman, I am thinking of the words like *to know, how much is encouraged, how far is promoted* and *by how much do you foster?*

I am sure that past and present Nigerian governments will swear that they have been conducting their affairs in the spirit of these provisions even though these provisions did not exist in those days. But we all know that all along, there has been murmuring here and there. Before the civil war, the regional leader whose party was not in control of the federal government was loud in his complaint that his people were not having their fair share of the national cake. I think that was the first time the expression *fair share of the national cake* came into the political dictionary of the country. Today, other Nigerians complain that they do not belong. They point at blind spots and pockets of neglect around them. They refer to appointments to high offices of State, the distribution of some federal government grants, the location of industries and government-sponsored modernisation projects, which seem to be concentrated in a few favoured areas.

Mr. Chairman, the surest way to give every Nigerian a sense of belonging, and thereby forge national unity and loyalty, is the pursuit of an even and balanced development throughout the country. In this regard, I recommend that we borrow a leaf from the Swiss model of how to achieve unity in a multi-ethnic society. For example, what is wrong with specifying in an appropriate legislation that every child before leaving school should learn at least one Nigerian language other than his or hers? What is wrong in specifying that the premier secondary school in each local government headquarter should contain a certain percentage, no matter how low, of students from other ethnic and linguistic groups? What is wrong in specifying that in the allocation of state lands in the capital of every state a certain percentage should go to people of other ethnic groups? What is wrong in specifying that at the senior intake level, every federal government establishment should contain, at least, a certain percentage of persons from other ethnic groups?

The need for equitable revenue allocation formula

Whilst on this matter, Mr. Chairman, I would like to comment on the role of an equitable system of revenue allocation as an instrument of forging national unity. An equitable system is, of course, one that is designed to ensure even and balanced development. To achieve this, those designing the formula will have to bear in mind that the exercise is not being conducted in a vacuum or on a clean slate; that already the federal government has, in some states, made substantial investments which can be quantified in revenue terms. Any allocation that fails to take such investments into account will only succeed in aggravating present imbalances and make nonsense of the theories of need and even development.

The need for a sound economic policy

I now turn to the directive principles and objectives of economic policy. The CDC rightly rejected the socialist ideology of state ownership and control of all the means of production and distribution, in favour of the mixed economy system of partnership between the state and the citizen. The rejection, Mr. Chairman, the report tells us, is contained in Section 10(1) (b) of the Bill which reads as follows:

The State shall, without prejudice to its right to participate or operate in other areas of the economy, manage and operate the major sectors of the economy.

And major sectors of the economy is defined as:

The economic activities that are operated exclusively by the Federal Government on the day the Constitution comes into force and any other economic activity that the National Assembly may declare from time to time.

In my view, this provision reflects not a rejection, but a prospective adoption of the socialist ideology, because it gives the State not only the powers to intervene in all areas of the economy but also the power to exclude private initiative in such areas. One is tempted to ask: Where then is the mixed economy system, if no area of the economy, no matter how lowly, is reserved for the private sector?

Already we know that some states are competing with their citizens in such areas as inter-state passenger transport, dry-cleaning, and retail trade. Again, both the federal and state governments are competing with Nigerian citizens in the purchase of shares of commercial companies and banks. We seem to have lost our sense of economic priorities, for I cannot see the sense of spending millions of naira to buy into vulnerable commercial companies when millions of Nigerians in rural areas are going without roads, water, electricity and proper communication facilities. I might in this regard refer to projects like the trade fair. What is the point of spending ₦90 million (we are told for the first phase) to host an international trade fair when we have very little export to exhibit except crude oil and cocoa. It means we

have embarked on the unusual and uncommercial practice of the
buyer paying for the advert of the goods he wants to buy. Also,
what is the point of spending millions of naira to host FESTAC
when that money could have been used in providing a first class
hospital for every division in the federation? There is also the
propriety of providing a colour T.V. in a country that cannot boast
of an efficient and reliable telephone system. I am told that the
German engineer installing the colour T.V. complained about his
inability to ring his wife in Hamburg.

Mr. Chairman, we are told that the reason for government
intervention in areas like banks is for purposes of control. I am
sure that financial and banking experts here will agree that no
amount of shares in a commercial bank will provide as effective a
control as that provided by a vigilant Central Bank. In other
words, there is no need for further control when the Central Bank
is there to do so.

The strongest argument, however, against excessive
government intervention, is the unsatisfactory performance record
of the enterprises that are already exclusively managed by
government, namely, National Electric Power Authority (NEPA),
the Nigeria Airways, Railways, Ports Authority and the Posts
and Telecommunications. If after a decade of monopoly
government is still unable to manage the post offices efficiently,
what guarantee is there that it can efficiently manage complex
and sophisticated commercial and industrial enterprises the
socialists would want the government to take over?

Mr. Chairman, the failures of government enterprises are due
to two main causes. The first is the lack of technical and
managerial capabilities. The second is that even where the
necessary expertise exists in the management of an enterprise,
the boss complex and the bureaucratic control process at present
operating in the ministries, are such that enterprise managers are
denied operational autonomy and financial flexibility essential
for their success. This denial is at the root of the failure of many
government enterprises. Until the civil service, which at present
is overburdened, can develop a versatile and efficient bureaucratic

machine to back-up government intervention in business, the State should content itself with overall control of the economy through appropriate legislation, development plan and economic guidelines. It should, however, complement and supplement the efforts of the private sector, particularly in areas where the private sector is hesitant to venture, either because of the strategic nature of the activity or the amount of investment involved, or the low rate of return. When we get to the committee stage, I shall propose amendments which will, as suggested by my friend from Gusau (Alhaji Yahaya Gusau), make it possible for private enterprises to participate in the major sectors of the economy; and also remove economic activities from the major sectors of the economy when it is in the interest of the public to do so.

Policy on education

I support the educational objectives and directive principles enunciated in Section 12 of the Bill. There is, however, a very serious omission; no mention is made of religious education. Here, I am in complete agreement with the member for Bodinga (Alhaji Ibrahim Dasuki), who said that we shouldn't ignore religion in our educational system. Mr. Chairman, we can only do so at our peril, for religion is central in character formation. It provides a set of do's and don'ts which act as beacons to guide a man in his journey through life. I am one of those who believe that the present wave of crime and indiscipline in schools, including examination leakages, is traceable to the absence of religious education in schools. I shall, at the appropriate time, propose an amendment that religious education be included in Section 12 of the Bill.

Press freedom

Before declaring my stand on this controversial question, I would like to explain what I understand by press freedom. To me, it means nothing more than freedom of access to any information of public interest. It is essentially a matter of communication between the press and government. The press complains that government operations are surrounded by excessive secrecy, and that it cannot discharge its responsibilities to the public if it is denied access to information that the citizen has a right to know. Government, on the other hand, maintains that there are certain information that cannot be released to the press without embarrassment to itself or to some persons or institutions. Having once, as head of the civil service, been in charge of government's classified documents, I agree with the press that there is excessive secrecy in government operations. With the exception of matters of State security and matters concerning personnel and annual budget, very few others need to be classified as secret and confidential. Many a time, a file remains on the secret and confidential list when the reason for such classification has ceased.

We must admit that the press in a developing country like Nigeria has special responsibilities. These include public enlightenment, upholding the constitution and freedoms embodied in it, keeping the conscience of the nation and guarding its morals (this is very important). This is with particular reference to the *Lagos Weekend*, because the press has responsibility to guard the morals of the nation and be the keeper of its conscience, and also act as a watchdog of the doctrine of accountability. If the press is to discharge these educative and investigative functions, its hands must be strengthened by an appropriate provision in the constitution. Mr. Chairman, I support such a provision that will give freedom of access to such information that the citizen has a right to know.

Local government

I support those who advocate more powers for local government councils. In this regard, it appears that the much advertised local government reform is, as far as some areas in the south are concerned, mere reform in form and not in functions. In fact, the reform has adversely affected the powers that local governments enjoyed twenty years before.

In the 1957 Local Government Law in Western Nigeria (I use Western Nigeria as an example because I was a District Officer [D. O.] there), the councils had powers over natural resources, public health and housing, roads, transport, lighting and public enlightenment. Details of these powers included improvement of agriculture and livestock, control of erosion, hospitals, maternity homes and dispensaries, public water supply, public roads, lighting of public places, transport by land and water, information and publicity. None of these powers are included in the reformed powers of local government contained in Schedule 3 of the Bill. The question, therefore, is: Is this a reform or a downgrading of local governments?

In the past, one of the main complaints against local governments was the poor quality of the councillors and their staff. Today, there is a great improvement in both, particularly in the quality of councillors. Among the councillors in my own constituency, we have former permanent secretaries, principals of secondary schools, lawyers, engineers, architects and statisticians. We even have a former chief secretary and a former acting president of the federation; I am sure that this improvement is not restricted to my area. One, therefore, expects that advantage should be taken of this general improvement to make the work of local governments more meaningful and challenging. Unless this is done, the councillors will get frustrated, and very soon local governments will once again degenerate to the business of semi-illiterate farmers and traders with a sprinkling of a few school master sons of the soil. Now that we have the best opportunity to bring development to rural areas, we must not allow the opportunity to slip. At the committee stage, I shall propose additions to the subjects listed in Schedule 3 of the Bill.

The presidential versus parliamentary system of government

Mr. Chairman, I now turn briefly to the executive. The pros and cons of the presidential versus parliamentary system have been ably argued by the protagonists of each system. The important issue, to my mind, is not so much the system but the stature, quality and character of the men and women who operate the system. In this regard, I do not agree with those who condemn

the 1963 constitution as the cause of the demise of the first republic.
I maintain that the constitution is not as bad as it is being painted.
If it were, the CDC would not have lifted so many sections from
it. If that constitution had been given to another set of people,
say the British or Germans, they would have made a success of
it. It failed because of ourselves.

Several Honourable Members: No! No! No!

Chief Udoji: Mr. Chairman, it failed because of our deficiencies
in terms of:

❑ what it takes to forge national unity and loyalty;
❑ our conception of power;
❑ our lack of the spirit of public service;
❑ the absence of self-imposed discipline; and a
❑ code of conduct in office holders.

In spite of what I have said, I believe that given the right type
of persons, the presidential system is better for Nigeria in her
present stage of national development when she is in dire need
of a national symbol that could well be provided by a candidate
acceptable to the generality of the Nigerian people. Another
advantage of the presidential system is that it gives the people a
chance of making a direct popular choice of their leader, rather
than the indirect and uncertain choice emanating from the
parliamentary system where a person may become a leader or
prime minister without winning the majority of the votes cast.
The parliamentary system, in a way, is like an electoral college
system of elections.

Referring to the functions of the president, I am in support of
what my friend, Chief Adebo, said about ensuring that we do
not over-burden the president with responsibilities. This could
be averted by the constitution making it mandatory on the
president to assign certain specific functions to the vice-president.
I am not, however, in support of an expendable and disposable
vice-president, for in a situation such as ours his removal might
lead to instability.

The Public Service

Mr. Chairman, I shall now say a few words on the public service. *The Chairman:* Very few.

Chief Udoji: I am surprised that neither the sub-committee on the public service nor the CDC considered the desirability of bringing the structure of the Service in line with the recommended presidential system. Under a presidential system, there are two categories of public servants. The career cadre, who form about ninety-nine per cent of the Service; they are appointed and are removable by an independent public service commission.They enjoy security of tenure including permanency, pensionability and anonymity The remaining one per cent non-career officers are politically appointed to hold top sensitive positions. Their appointments are based on their commitment to the political programme of the president and their ability to deliver his election promises. Permanent secretaries and heads of non-ministerial departments come under this category.

Already, this categorisation has started to develop in the Nigerian public service since the present administration introduced the purge, and all that is required is to formalise and regularise what is almost a *de facto* situation. The formalisation will take the form of declaring posts below that of permanent secretaries the end of the career cadre. Any appointments above that level will be on mutually agreed contract terms, the duration of which will normally not exceed the term of office of a particular president. This distinction will provide a convenient safety valve to the parties concerned. It will enable the government to remove honourably and without bitterness obsolescent top officials. On the other hand, it will save top officers the embarrassment of being kicked around or accused of disloyalty or lack of commitment, or being made to take a second oath of office. Such politically appointed non-career officers should be distinguished from the career officers by an appropriate designation. I suggest that of deputy minister.

The issue of Sharia Court

I shall finally touch on the Federal Sharia Court of Appeal. Mr. Chairman, I am not a Muslim and I do not live in the North. Therefore, my views will be qualified by these two facts. I have, however, listened carefully to the arguments for and against the establishment of a Federal Sharia Court of Appeal.

There are two arguments for it. The first is the legal argument put forward by Chief Rotimi Williams (CDC). To him it is a simple and straightforward matter of providing a court which will exercise appellate jurisdiction over the various existing state Courts of Appeal. The second argument is that put forward by the Honourable Member for Fika-Fune (Alhaji Ciroma), that Sharia is a matter of religion. He said and I quote:

> If we agreed to the freedom of religion, there is no need to truncate my freedom. I must be given the chance to do it fully. If I am not subject to Sharia, I will regard myself as not having the freedom of religion.

Again, those who oppose the establishment of Federal Sharia Court of Appeal do so both on legal and religious grounds. The lawyers say that Chief Williams, in his very able and convincing arguments about the need for an avenue of appeal from existing Sharia Courts, failed to tell the House that at present, appeals from the state Sharia Courts lie to the Supreme Court. This avenue of appeal is illustrated diagrammatically at page 106 of vol. II of the report. I feel that it would have been more helpful if Chief Williams told us what is wrong with the present system of appeal, and why it is better to establish a separate Federal Sharia Court of Appeal. Also, lawyers would like to be convinced that the establishment of such a separate court would not offend Section II (1) of the constitution which provides for equality of rights and opportunities and Sections 9 (1) and 35 (1) which provide against discrimination on grounds of religion.

Those who oppose the court on religious ground argue that to establish on a national level and with national funds, a court which will only deal with the laws of a particular religion, is not only giving that religion preferential treatment but it is tantamount to making that religion a State religion. They say that already the federal government is discriminating against other religions in matters such as pilgrims' welfare. A priest complained that two years ago, whilst organising a pilgrimage to the holy land, the federal government did not agree to let him have one of the Nigerian planes, even on hire.

Mr. Chairman, the problem before us is how to ensure that our Moslem brothers have an avenue of appeal in such a way that we do not offend other fundamental sections of the constitution, and without giving other religious groups the impression that their religion is inferior or that the government is giving state recognition to a particular religion. The answer appears to be that appeals should lie to the existing Federal Court of Appeal and that when cases do come before the court, the president should empanel Moslem members of the court to deal with the matter.

Mr. Chairman, may I conclude by appealing to those who speak on this sensitive matter to do so with restraint and tolerance. Uncompromising statements and threats do not help those who are anxious to find a solution that would be acceptable to all concerned. Those who threaten us with irreducible minimum and religion, being more important to them than the unity of this country, should know that some of us love our religion as dearly as they do, even though we do not make any noise about it. Again, those who threaten us with the situation in Lebanon and Ireland should remember that Nigeria does not belong to them alone. It belongs also to some of us, and particularly to millions of Nigerians who have not the privilege of being heard in this House.

Thank you, Mr. Chairman.

(2)

Rural Development should be given a Priority ✦

" Without a stable and progressive local government there can be no stable and progressive nation. But we are yet to be convinced that the authorities appreciate this basic and catalytic potentiality of local governments."

Introduction

We, the Obis, Elders, development unions and self-help societies in Ozubulu welcome you to our town. We welcome you, in particular, to Ekwusigo, the site of the much-talked about spare parts and machine tools industry. It is also the site of our latest self-help project — the Ekwusigo Modern Market and Shopping Centre.

We would like to begin this address by congratulating you on your re-appointment as Commissioner for Local Government, Rural Development and Chieftaincy Affairs. It is an important and all-embracing ministry. The present state of economic emergency and the declared rural development priority by both the federal and state governments make it one of the most important ministries.

Local government is the basic unit of government. It is government at the grassroots, the government that affects the life of a citizen from the cradle to the grave. Without a stable and progressive local government, there can be no stable and progressive nation. But we are yet to be convinced that the authorities appreciate this basic and catalytic potentiality of local governments. If they do, they will not starve local governments of funds or control them so rigidly as they do at present. Our

---

✦ An address presented to the Anambra State Commissioner for Local Government, Rural Development and Chieftaincy Matters at the official opening of the Ekwusigo Market and Shopping Centre at Ozubulu, October 19, 1985. The Ekwusigo Market and Shopping Centre was built by the Ozubulu community as a self-help project. The author is an indigene of this community.

16

plea, therefore, is that local governments be given financial flexibility and management autonomy especially now that many enlightened men and women are retiring to rural areas and can participate in the running of efficient local government councils. A government that has no autonomy is no government at all.

Rural development

We congratulate the new state government for making rural development its priority. This is how it should be, for after all, in our country, the natural resources — land, vegetation, animal and minerals which are the objects of development are in the rural areas. And it is their utilisation that brings development and consequent improvement in the quality of life in rural areas.

Ozubulu is a typical rural area. At present, mainly old men, women and children inhabit it. The young men have all gone to Onitsha, Aba, Enugu, and other urban areas where they are either trading or seeking for non-existent jobs. We want them back, and one of the quickest ways of attracting them is the speedy execution of the metallurgical industry, which has been on the drawing board of the state government for the past ten years. It is in anticipation of the take-off of that industry that this market was planned.

We request you to pass our appeal for the early establishment of the industry to both the government and your colleagues, especially the commissioner for industries. If finance is the stumbling block, we are prepared to assist in mobilising the necessary capital both locally and in the capital market. A group of young Ozubulu businessmen have asked me to announce their pledge of one million naira towards the project. When established, the industry will provide employment to thousands of people, and kick-start the industrialisation of not only Anambra State but the whole of the former Eastern Region. A machine tool industry is a catalyst industry. It will provide essential spare parts now in need all over the country. It will, in particular, produce capital goods for the establishment of several new industries. It is in this regard a basic industry which, together with the proposed petrochemical industry, can provide the manufacturing sector with at least 40% of the machinery and the materials, which are at present being imported from abroad.

One cannot discuss rural development in Ozubulu without mentioning her famous kaolin deposits. Mr. Moukhouse, a geologist, first discovered these deposits in the colonial days. Again, recently, another geologist, Dr. Beltaro, drew attention to the deposits. Also, the feasibility study by Scoup Consultants for the Anambra State government recommended their exploitation for both ceramics and refractory bricks. The effect of such exploitation in stemming unemployment and urban migration cannot be over-emphasised.

Another effective means of improving rural life is to increase the productivity and earning capacity of peasant farmers. This can be done by providing farmers with improved seed yams and cassava cuttings now available at the International Institute for Tropical Agriculture, Ibadan. Also, such inputs as fertilisers, pesticides and herbicides will boost production. Assistance to peasant farmers should be supplemented by incentives to companies and individuals capable of large scale mechanised farming. It is only by such a combined effort that we can be able to feed the ever-growing population of Nigeria. In this connection, mention should be made of the 2000 hectares of land which the Anambra State government recently provided in this area for a joint venture enterprise of Nigerians and expatriates anxious to go into large scale cultivation of irrigated rice. The project is being frustrated by the delay by the Federal Ministry of Commerce in issuing licence for the importation of necessary irrigation machineries. Whatever further assistance the state government can render in this regard will be highly appreciated especially now that the importation of rice is prohibited.

Honourable commissioner, none of the projects mentioned above — metallurgical industry, ceramics, or mechanised rice farming, can be established without the basic infrastructure of road, water and electricity. Fortunately, skeletal forms of these utilities are already in existence in Ozubulu. What they require is maintenance and expansion, in view of the developmental needs of today. In particular, the pipe-borne water supply system needs revamping as the high tank built over twenty years ago is still without a drop of water. As a result, water does not get to all parts of the town including hospitals and schools. We implore that these urgent requests be referred to the appropriate ministries.

Self-help projects

Having dwelt on rural development, we will now address you, Sir, on the market. We said in the beginning that the Ekwusigo Market and Shopping Centre is our latest self-help project. Others include the present joint hospital, the post office, three secondary schools, and a number of civic centres. We invite you to visit and see them for yourself.

The market is a 4 million naira project. So far we have spent 1.8 million naira in building lock-up shops and open sheds. Both the sole administrator and secretary of Nnewi Local Government Area[1] attend our meetings regularly and give valuable advice, but they have not given us any material or financial assistance. We need such encouragement at least in the construction of internal market roads and such public facilities as incinerator, toilets and offices. Permit us to observe that the state government has not been encouraging us. Almost every amenity in Ozubulu has been through the combined efforts of the people, and the time has come to give us concrete encouragement. We intend, therefore, to present the account of the present market to your ministry, on completion, for reimbursement. We will, however, welcome reimbursement either in cash or in kind. Completion of those remaining open sheds, improved and expanded rural water supply, as well as improved rural electrification will be acceptable reimbursements in kind.

We cannot end this address without paying tribute to the landowners who donated the land. Incidentally they are also the landowners of the site of the metallurgical industry. Because of their generosity, we appeal to you to consider some tangible compensation for them. We would also like to take this

---

[1] At the time the speech was made, Ozubulu was under Nnewi Local Government Area. Now, it is the headquarter of Ekwusigo Local Government Area.

opportunity to thank Mr. Linus Mbaso and Chief Jerome Udoji who initiated the project during their tenures as councillors at the Nnewi Local Government.

Finally, we ask that you use your good offices to persuade the commissioner for works to speed up the declaration of Ekwusigo and its environs as a planning area. This will obviate the present unplanned haphazard development going on in the area. We end by pledging our loyalty and support to the present military administration. We support, in particular, the ban on the importation of rice and maize and urge government to take all necessary measures, no matter how unpleasant, which in their opinion will bring about a speedy recovery of the economy.

3

Government should not Monopolise Education✦

"Many Nigerians believe that the present widespread decline in morals, evidenced from the increase in armed robbery, to cheating in examinations, is traceable to government take-over of schools and the consequent indiscipline resulting from lack of appreciation that character formation is the most vital element in a child's education."

Introduction

We are gathered here to celebrate the 50th anniversary of the founding of our college. I wonder how many of you have thought of the significance of this occasion. For me, it is an important landmark, an occasion for stocktaking and drawing the balance sheet, not only of our selves as individuals, but more importantly of the institution that launched us into the world. Yes, it is this institution that is mainly responsible for whatever each and every one of us is today.

I do not think that any of us will dispute the fact that secondary education is probably the most important education that prepares one for adult life. Primary education is rudimentary education that provides a child with the basic tools of communication, literacy and numeracy. Secondary education, on the other hand, equips a youth with a variety of skills and environmental knowledge with which he can blaze his individual trail in the uncharted sea of life. This education also comes at such an impressionable age in one's life that both the knowledge and contacts made at the time often last throughout one's life. Hence, most people tend to refer more to their secondary school ties and friends than to their university connections.

If our secondary school plays such a dominant and important

✦ Address delivered as president of St. Charles Old Boys' Association on the occasion of the 50th anniversary of the college, at Onitsha, November 4, 1978.

role in our lives, what then are our responsibilities to her? In other words, how do we show our appreciation? I think we can do this by upholding the objectives and traditions of our great college, and it is with reference to such objectives and traditions that we can properly conduct the stocktaking exercise in order to determine whether we and our institution are on debit or credit side.

Traditions of St. Charles College, Onitsha

What then are the objectives and traditions of St. Charles College? The founding fathers of the college did not bother to make their intentions public, and the college did not have a coat of arms with its motto inscribed on it. It was not until after the war that a shield was devised consisting of white and green stripes on a red background with the letters SCCO[1] superimposed. The shield did not give any clue to the objectives of the college, and I assume that the white and green stripes refer to the colours of the national flag and the red background, a reminder of the civil war.

There is no doubt, however, that when Bishop Shanahan founded the college in 1928, his main purpose was the regular supply of better educated and qualified teachers who would carry out his philosophy of evangelisation through education. Bishop Shanahan believed that the surest and most effective method of bringing the message of Christ and Christianity was not to preach them in isolation but to do so through education, that is, through the development of the whole person, physically, mentally and spiritually. It is important, however, to bear in mind that the grand strategy was evangelisation, but the vehicle was education through teachers who are well-grounded in the doctrines and ethos of the Roman Catholic Church.

How far has this objective been achieved? There is no doubt that until the civil war the objective was being achieved in that the college produced about 3,000 well-educated men who spread

---

[1] St. Charles College, Onitsha.

the message of Christianity not only in the classrooms, but also to the public at large. I am afraid that since the civil war and the take-over of the college by government, no one can, in all honesty, say that the original objective is being pursued. The take-over shattered the very foundations and ideals of the institution, and changed its character. It ceased to be a privately owned and managed missionary institution and became a public, impersonal and indifferent college. The priorities were also reversed; education became the principal objective while the objectives of evangelisation and character formation were abandoned.

Government take-over of schools

We were told that the primary reason for the take-over was to enable government control education. I feel this is a very specious argument because government had always controlled education. The education laws, from the Education Ordinance of 1916 through the Order-in-Council No. 16 of 1952, the Western Region Education Law of 1955, the Eastern Region Education Law of 1956, and the Northern Region Law of 1963, gave those governments power to control every aspect of education — from who can teach, (qualifications of teachers), to who to be taught (pupils and their numbers), what to teach (syllabus) and when to teach (time-table and school hours). These education laws and regulations made under them were so extensive in their control coverage that they prescribed even the size of classrooms, as well as ventilation, and the size of blackboards. One is, therefore, tempted to ask: What else do those who talk of control of education want?

I would concede that what the education laws failed to provide adequately for, was the financing of education. This was done through the system of grants-in-aid, which led to abuses in the hands of some unscrupulous persons. Apart from that, the system of control and management through voluntary agencies produced satisfactory results in terms of the efficiency of individual schools and colleges, discipline, dedication to duty, and the standard and quality of education. If anything went wrong, it was not because of the absence of powers of control on the part of government, but because of the laxity of those responsible for enforcing the law, namely, the inspectorate divisions of the ministries of education.

I am of the opinion that the areas that need the urgent attention of state and federal governments is not the ownership of schools and colleges but:

1. Proper financing of education to ensure adequate accommodation of pupils and students, adequate equipment and teaching aids, and last but not the least, salaries and conditions of service for teachers which are not less favourable than those prevailing in the civil service.
2. Improvement in the content of education on a continuing basis, to ensure its relevance in a dynamic and technological age. This will be achieved through curriculum development, rewriting of syllabi and retraining of teachers.
3. Ensuring the efficiency and effectiveness of the system by regular inspection and research.

If the above conditions are met, it will be in the best interests of all concerned if the management of schools and colleges is left in the hands of recognised voluntary agencies. I will, however, not object if government retained the ownership and management of a few schools and colleges for purposes of comparing standards. *By all means, let the government control education but it should not monopolise it.*

Education is a co-operative effort in which the State, the teacher (including teachers of religion), and the parents, have vital roles to play. The State discharges its role by ensuring adequate and non-discriminatory facilities for the education of every child. Parents discharge theirs mostly by example and discipline in the home. Teachers do theirs mostly through the instructions they provide in schools.

Many Nigerians believe that the present widespread decline in morals — evidenced from the increase in armed robbery, to cheating in examinations — is traceable to government take-over of schools, and the consequent indiscipline resulting from lack of appreciation that character formation is the most vital element in a child's education. This lack of appreciation is clearly illustrated by the neglect of religious and moral instructions in schools. Both are absolutely necessary in character formation. Religion, of whatever denomination or creed, imparts beliefs and principles which act as beacons that guide a child in his perilous journey through life. Moral instructions, on the other hand, provide the norms for the regulation of the relationship between man and man. These are the foundations of citizenship, for a nation that believes in God cannot produce God-fearing and law-abiding citizens unless the character of her youth is properly formed through family example and regular religious and moral instructions in schools. It is only under these circumstances that St. Charles College could be expected to play a role consistent with the aims and objectives of its founders.

Our responsibilities as old boys are two-fold: the first and foremost is to fight for the restoration of the independence and religious integrity of our *alma mater*. This we can do by joining forces with the growing number of Nigerians who are disenchanted with the present standard of education and are advocating the return of schools and colleges to their original owners. This is a very appropriate time to make our views known on the matter since a new government is about to be installed and political parties are formulating their manifestos. I must say in this regard that Nigerians in general appear to be good at complaining but not good at planning. They sit back and expect things to happen by chance. If you want something to happen, or if you want something to change, you have to plan and work for it. That is the only way to achieve objectives. But if you fold your arms and expect manna to fall again from heaven, I am afraid, you may have to wait till doomsday.

Our second responsibility to our *alma mater* is not different from that of other products of catholic institutions. It is, in the words of the Gospel, to be the light of the world. We can do this by being good witnesses of Christ in all the different theatres of life in which we operate — the home, the farm, the office, the market, the town union, the local government council, the political party, the professional association, the trade union, etc. In these forums, we must have courage and not hesitate to stand up for truth and justice even if it is unpopular or inconvenient to do so.

I started by referring to this occasion as one of stocktaking. I will end by saying that whatever the present balance sheet may be, we have the consolation that it is only an interim balance sheet. What is important is the final stocktaking which, for some of us, is no longer far removed. I pray that when that time comes and the balance sheet is drawn, we will be found to be heavily on the credit side.

4

Relationship between Universities and the Government✦

> *"In the circumstances of the complex and great problems of development facing the country, it seems that Nigerian universities should actively support the economic and social development of the country. This would be their best assurance of both academic freedom and institutional autonomy."*

Introduction

Honourable Chancellor, the Pro-Chancellor, the Vice-Chancellor, Your Excellencies, Emirs and Chiefs, Ladies and Gentlemen. On behalf of the honorary graduates and myself, I thank all those who, in one way or another, have been associated with the great honour that was conferred on us today. We thank in particular the backroom officials who are mainly responsible for the excellent administrative arrangements of both the convocation and luncheon. We also thank the public orator for the compliments and tributes of praise, which are embodied in his citations. We pledge our loyalty to the university, and promise not only to uphold its motto and abide by the ideals that motivated its founding fathers, but also to do nothing that is capable of tarnishing its good image.

When the vice-chancellor requested that I make a speech of thanks on behalf of the honorary graduates, he suggested that I might use the opportunity to expand on my defence of the Public Service Review Commission's report. I am also not unaware that some of you expect me to speak on some aspects of *Udoji*.[1] I am afraid that I am going to disappoint you because *Udoji* is no longer

---

✦ Address delivered on behalf of the honorary graduates of Ahmadu Bello University, December 6, 1975.

[1] Because he was the chairman of the Public Service Review Commission (September 1972– September 1974), the commission was often called the *Udoji Commission*, and its report, the *Udoji Report*.

27

a controversial issue. Thanks to the new military rulers who have not only adjusted the salary structure but have also started to implement the more important recommendations of the report. These include the reconstitution of the Supreme Court, the appointment of the ombudsman or public complaints commissioner, and the formulation of a code of conduct for public officers.

I must of course not forget to mention the recent purges in the public service. This is an exercise which I hope will only be a means to an end. The end should be effective and devoted service. To achieve these, vigorous steps should now be taken to effectively install the result-oriented new style of management and ensure, through continuous supervision, that it actually takes root. A vacuum after the present exercise will be a most dangerous thing. It could lead to a situation similar to the biblical parable of the man possessed by the devil. After the demon was driven out, because his mind remained vacant, it came to be occupied, not by one demon , but by seven others.

Honourable Chancellor, we have in the past two days heard a lot about the achievements of our university, the problems it has overcome, and its proposals for the future. Sir, permit me to speak briefly on a matter which I consider of primary importance to its future growth and development. It is on the thorny relationship between universities and the government.

Relationship between universities and the government

Since the past few years, the relationship between universities and the government has been strained to a point where both sides seem to have lost confidence in each other. One only has to listen to the remarks that university men and top civil servants make about each other to realise the extent of the estrangement. This seems to have led to some lack of co-ordination and differences of opinion on such vital matters as the role of the visitor, the powers of the council, the appointment of vice-chancellors, conditions of service, and interpretations of academic freedom. I strongly feel that it is the duty of all, especially those not directly involved in the friction, to see that it does not escalate to confrontation and conflict.

For me, the root cause of the friction is the different perceptions of the role of the university by the two groups: the universities seem to see their main role from that part of the law establishing them, which empowers them to "encourage the advancement of learning and to hold out to all persons without distinction of race, creed or sex, the opportunity of acquiring a liberal education." From this, university men and women often claim academic freedom for themselves as well as autonomy for their institution. Individual academicians often interpret this to mean freedom to teach and publish the truth as they see it, and to do research as they choose without being penalised either within the university or from outside, provided that they do not break the law.

The university as an institution often interprets autonomy to mean freedom to teach and examine students undisturbed, freedom to choose what to teach and how to teach them, freedom to do research, freedom to select students, and the freedom to appoint, promote or fire staff. In all these areas, universities claim the freedom to determine the criteria by which they will act. They also demand the freedom to apply those criteria without outside control or interference.

The government, on the other hand, has a different perception of the role of universities. To quote from the third National Development Plan, the major objective of universities should be "to create the capacity for training the much needed high level personnel for all sectors of the economy". In other words, the government expects the universities to be primarily responsible for the nation's high-level manpower needs.

I believe that the differences of interpretation between the universities and government are not irreconcilable. I see for instance no reason why the universities should not accept as their primary mission the training of the high-level manpower needs of the country. I do not think that accepting this mission will infringe on the autonomy of the universities. I actually believe that if this objective is well-performed by the universities, it would actually enhance their autonomy. In the circumstances of the complex and great problems of development facing the country, it seems that Nigerian universities should actively support the economic and social development of the country. This would be their best assurance of both academic freedom and institutional autonomy. I also feel that researches conducted by the universities should be directed towards national goals, that is, adapting worldwide store of knowledge and technologies to the solution of Nigeria's problems.

I am convinced that it is in this way that our universities can retain their relevance to their environments. I am not unaware that in recent years our universities have been making vigorous efforts to achieve greater relevance through curriculum adaptation. I believe, however, that relevance is much more than a mere adaptation of curriculum or courses to the local environment. I am of the opinion that relevance also involves dialogue and co-ordination with the government and with employment agencies. I believe that the present lack of dialogue and co-ordination is partly responsible for the current ugly situation of engineering graduates either being unemployed or teaching mathematics in secondary schools. What else, but lack of dialogue and co-ordination could be responsible for hiring foreign experts to do jobs which our universities, if adequately funded, could perform?

Another source of friction between the universities and government is in the area of university expansion and development. On the one hand, there is the enthusiasm of each university to offer as many courses as possible while the government would like to see some harmonisation, integration, co-ordination and balance among them. This involves the adoption of a master plan, and some measure of control in the establishment of faculties, which universities often oppose.

The lack of a clear-cut national policy on university education is also a source of friction. At present, the universities operate on an out-of-date policy which was formulated in 1959 by the Asby Commission. The commission recommended four universities for

---

[2]   This number has since increased by many folds. There are today about forty-two universities in the country.

Nigeria. Today, we have ten full-fledged universities[2] and three university colleges. The Ashby Commission estimated that by 1970, university enrolment in Nigeria would be about 7,500. But in 1970, actual university enrolment turned out to be 14,286. The commission also projected that the country should plan for a total university enrolment of about 10,000 between 1970 and 1980. Today, we already have 23,000, and plan for 53,000 by 1980.

I feel that it is important to remember that Ashby was in 1959 dealing with a country which was on the eve of independence, and there were, therefore, a number of variables which he could not properly take into account. Ashby was also at that time dealing with Nigeria which had a population of a mere 50 million and a development budget of 292 million naira as opposed to today's Nigeria which has an estimated population of 70 million, and a development budget of 3 billion naira.[3] In fact, government's current allocation for university education is more than the total budget for the whole country in 1959.

From the above, it is therefore very imperative that Nigeria should formulate a new policy for university education. For this, I suggest the setting up of a high-powered commission of renowned educators with wide terms of reference, which could include the following:

a. To review the whole system of higher education in Nigeria, and determine whether the universities are fulfilling their roles, taking into account the development needs of the nation.
b. To determine the priorities in the area of higher education as they affect the development needs of this nation.
c. In the light of the above, to formulate a national policy and programme for higher education in the next two decades.

I propose that the membership of such a commission should include representatives of the National Universities Commission, manpower experts, and academicians from both the developing and developed countries.

---

[3] Currently, the population is estimated at over 100 million. The development budget, in naira terms, has since passed the billion naira mark.

Just as the government needs to formulate a clear-cut policy on university education, it is similarly important for the universities to evaluate whether they have been pursuing the elitist idea of liberal education for the few, or the more practical open policy of public education for all citizens who qualify for it, and who through it can develop their innate potentials to the point where they can give their best in the service of the nation.

Honourable Chancellor, let me conclude by saying that in the circumstances of the urgent national development needs of the country, and the obvious educational imbalances among the various components of the federation, the problems of higher education centre primarily on the appropriateness of the principles of selection and admission of students; the relevance of curriculum and research, and the success with which they are adapted to national developmental goals. Universities should also be judged by how well they cater for the manpower needs of the nation, how effectively the graduates find appropriate employment within the economy, and how cost effective the universities are compared with the rest of the economy.

5

Church and Politics in Nigeria ✢

"Fortunately or unfortunately, the controversy on the role of the Church in politics does not only exist between people of different religious beliefs such as Moslems and Christians. It also exists between Christians and Moslems of different denominations, and sometimes even between adherents of the same religious denomination."

Introduction

Thank you, Mr. Chairman, for your introduction. Thank you also for inviting me to participate in a symposium marking the federation week of your organisation. The subject, *Church and Politics*, is both topical and controversial. It is topical for, since the publication of the draft constitution[1], no other subject has dominated the media in the way Sharia has done. And the question raised by Sharia is essentially that of the place of the Church and Mosque, in other words, religion, in the constitution and government of the country.

We all know that religion is a very subjective and emotive subject about which it is almost impossible to be exact or scientific. You cannot prove it altogether on the natural plane. It begins where science ends and that is why it contains mysteries. It is a matter of conscience and belief. This being the case, I propose in this brief presentation, to adopt an analytical and historical approach, leaving it to each of you to make your own conclusions in accordance with your faith and conscience. This is of course partly why the subject is controversial. The danger, however, is that the controversy invariably involves those in positions of power and prestige and whose opposing views are capable of rocking the ship of state as is the case in Lebanon and Ireland.

✢ An address delivered to the Nigerian Federation of Catholic Students at the University of Nigeria, Enugu Campus, February 4, 1978.

[1] Draft of the 1979 constitution.

33

Fortunately or unfortunately, the controversy surrounding the role of the Church in politics does not only exist between people of different religious beliefs such as Moslems and Christians. It also exists between Christians and Moslems of different denominations, and sometimes even between adherents of the same religious denomination.

Forty years ago, William Temple, the archbishop of Canterbury, advocated Christian responsibility for politics and economics. For him, the church had the right and duty to declare the principles which should govern the ordering of society. While there seems to be a consensus that the Church should lay down the moral principles for the conduct of individuals, the right of the church to lay down principles for trade unions, employers associations, or governments, has often been questioned. For William Temple, this type of distinction was unacceptable. He believed that the nature and destiny of man gave the church the qualification for deciding what kind of structure of society was wholesome or unwholesome for man. Temple did not stop there. He proceeded to criticise the profit motive, the unrestricted private ownership of land, as well as monopolies. But William Temple was taken to task by many critics, including members of his own Church such as the Dean of St. Paul's, the Rev. Mr. Inge, who warned against ecclesiastical interference in politics. Temple's critics maintained that the gospel contained no social programme, and that its business was to convert individuals and not to reconstruct society.

The Catholic Church and politics

In the Catholic Church, opinions are divided on what should be the proper relationship between Church and State. For instance, Paul Nitta, a Catholic theologian, is of the view that the church does not have a mission to establish social justice in the world. He supports this by citing John 13: 36, where Christ said His kingdom is not of this world; and Luke 12: 13, where Christ explicitly refused to be made a judge and promoter of human justice. The occasion was when one of the crowd said to Jesus,

"Master, tell my brother to divide the inheritance with me." But Jesus replied, "Man, who has appointed me a judge or arbitrator over you." The Church, according to Nitta, "must resist any attempt to be used for earthly goals, however lofty they may be. She must also avoid even the appearance of being an ideological and temporal pressure group, or of taking sides with party solutions."

On the other hand, the synod of the American Catholic Bishops recently declared that any action on behalf of justice is a "constitutive dimension" of the Church's ministry, and that the Church has the right and duty to proclaim justice on the social, national and international levels, and to denounce instances of injustice when the fundamental rights of man and his salvation demand it. This view of the Church's mission requires the Church to relate positively to the political order since social injustice and the denial of human rights can often be remedied only through governmental action. The synod believes that if world concern for social justice and human development is to be effective, persons and organisations must participate in the political process in accordance with their own responsibilities and roles.

Coming nearer home, let us examine the position in our own country and in our own Church. Until recently, the attitude of the Roman Catholic Church in Nigeria was that the Church, and its adherents, should have little to do with government and politics. These were considered either too worldly or too protestant - dominated for catholic participation. For this reason, Catholics were discouraged from taking appointments in government and commercial houses. My father-in-law, the late Mr. William Onuchukwu, a headmaster with a flair for sports, was invited in the twenties to become an Inspector of Police but was discouraged from taking up the position by Bishop Shanahan[2]. Similarly, I was, in 1936, offered a clerical appointment at the secretariat of Southern Nigeria at Enugu, but I could not take it up because my school manager refused to give me a testimonial or a letter of

---

[2] The Catholic Bishop of Onitsha

release from my teaching job.

This policy of Catholics not being allowed to participate in politics and government was sometimes carried a little too far. It was, for example, largely responsible for the late start of secondary grammar schools by Catholics. At that time, the normal qualification for standard government jobs was Class IV Secondary or the School Certificate, and these were obtainable only from secondary grammar schools. Any Catholic young man aspiring to government employment had, therefore, to go to either the Dennis Memorial Grammar School at Onitsha or the Hope Waddel Training Institute at Calabar. Unfortunately, some of the people in this group never returned to their Catholic faith, and it was to stem the exodus that Christ the King College, Onitsha, was founded in 1932.

Today, the Catholic Church is less conservative in its attitude towards government and politics. It no longer has any reservations about its adherents participating in both politics and government. It, however, still has reservations when it comes to members of the clergy doing so. I know that certain government appointments have been turned down by the clergy, and for good reasons. The one or two isolated examples of acceptance must, therefore, be regarded as exceptions.

Reasons for the change of attitude by the Catholic Church

Several factors were responsible for the change of attitude. The first was the good account which Catholics who had either left Catholic schools or taken up public appointments rendered of themselves. This was particularly noticeable in the case of Catholic students in non-Catholic institutions. They were found to be more serious in the practice of their religion than those in Catholic institutions where things were often taken for granted.

The second factor was independence, which accelerated the assumption of high offices of State by available qualified Nigerians. This made the Catholic missionaries to realise the shortsightedness of their erstwhile policy.

The third factor was the expansion of missionary activities in education and health. This brought Church leaders in contact with government officials, some of who appeared unappreciative of their zeal and services.

Four, was party politics, which exploited every possible human sentiment, including religion.

The fifth factor, which is by far the most important, is Sharia. It introduced an entirely new dimension to the whole question of Church and politics. Sharia is the Koran-based religious law which governs the personal life of Moslems in matters such as marriage, divorce and inheritance. Moslems maintain that Sharia is the law revealed by God for the governance of their lives from sunrise to sunset, and that it is a way of life for them from the cradle to the grave. The question arises: Which religion is not a way of life? Is Christianity not a way of life? Is Hinduism not a way of life? Is it not the way of life laid down by traditional religions that Christianity and Islam condemn?

The point at issue, however, is not whether or not Islam is a way of life. It is also not whether Moslems are free to follow that way of life in the practice of their religion. The issue is the demand by Moslems for the establishment of a Moslem or Sharia legal code parallel to the existing legal system, which they describe as Christian. They base their arguments on two main grounds. The first is that the present legal system was imposed by the British, and since we have now attained independence, it should be discarded in favour of an indigenous system. The second argument is that if Moslems were not allowed to practice Sharia up to the highest courts in the land, it would amount to a denial of religious freedom.

Christians replied that the civil courts are not Christian courts but national courts established by the Nigerian Parliament to enforce laws made by the Parliament in which Moslems, Christians and worshippers of traditional religion are members. They point out that the best evidence that civil courts are not Christian courts is the fact that they approve of divorce, which some Christian or ecclesiastical courts do not entertain. Christians also argue that to allow Sharia courts to be established at the federal level would result in a parallel legal system, which would

be detrimental to the unity of the country. They also contend that
the proposals that such courts would be established with federal
funds, but manned exclusively by Moslems, would offend the
constitutional provisions against discrimination on grounds of
religion, as well as the provision that Nigeria will be a secular
state. A secular state, we should remember, is one which has no
State religion, and which treats all religions alike.

It would, however, appear that the demand of our Moslem
brothers and sisters for the introduction of Sharia, and the recent
activities of Moslem students of Ahmadu Bello University, is part
of an international Islamic revival which was referred to in a recent
article in *American Newsweek* as "Islam on the March". The
article reported that at a recent conference in Cairo, leading
Moslem scholars urged all Moslem States to scrap their western
style legal codes and return to the Sharia. The conference also
sanctioned greater missionary efforts in the West and warned
Moslem politicians to counter intellectual invasions, which are
capable of undermining Moslem beliefs. The article went further
to say that the result of the conference was that fanatical student
groups, and outright terrorists, were fomenting civil uprisings,
and toppling governments in the name of Mohammed's holy
word.

To get the complete picture, one should add the recent
warnings to Christians by Idi Amin[3], and the statement credited
to Dr. Aliyu, head of the Department of Research, Ahmadu Bello
University, at page 24 of the January 13 issue of *New Nigeria*. I
quote: "I have no doubt in my mind that if we are honestly and
objectively searching for a permanent and enduring solution to
our problems, it is to Islam that Africa must turn, for it is the only
system that is timeless."

Let me say in conclusion that the controversy over the role of
the Church in politics is as old as history. It existed in biblical
days, and throughout the Middle Ages. Older European countries

---

[3] Idi Amin, a Moslem, was the president of Uganda at that time. As he became more and
more isolated by Western countries, he forged closer ties with the Arab world.

have been through the phenomenon, which is now rearing its ugly head in the new African States. I hope we will have the wisdom of learning from history. We cannot be wiser than the accumulated knowledge and solution of older nations. Thank you.

6

Management by Objectives ✦

"Often, ... managers fail to have a holistic view. In instances like this, they may behave like the proverbial three blind men who met an elephant on the road: one touched the elephant's leg and swore that a tree was on his way; another touched the elephant's trunk and was convinced that a snake was barring his way; the third blind man felt the elephant's belly and proclaimed that he was up against a landslide."

Introduction

One of the key statements of the president, Major-General Ibrahim Babangida[1], on taking over power on August 27, 1985, was that the civil service would be made more responsible and accountable for their advice and actions. Barely five weeks after he made this statement, he posted military personnel as chief executives to all federal government parastatals. Since then, the military chief executive of one of the parastatals, the National Shipping Line, has openly indicted the management of the company for being responsible for the heavy financial losses sustained by the shipping line. Again, on October 25, the president in an address delivered at the Institute of Strategic Studies, Jos, warned that he would meet officials of the nation's public institutions to "lay bare what his administration requires of them".

At the state level, several governors have also complained about the ineffectiveness of civil servants. A few days ago, the governor of Kwara State, whilst inaugurating a street light project, repeated the president's warning about holding individual civil servants personally responsible for the success or failure of projects. He said he would not tolerate any "dead woods".

Let me say immediately that I strongly feel that the posting

✦ Keynote address delivered at a Workshop on *Management by Objectives* organised for permanent secretaries and chief executives at the Federal Agricultural and Rural Management Training Institute, Ilorin, November 4, 1985.

[1] Babangida, who came to power through a military coup on August 27, 1985, gave himself the title of President. His regime lasted until August 1993.

of military chief executives to parastatals is a very ominous signal. Are the positions of permanent secretaries and managing directors not being compromised and rendered redundant by this action? They had better watch out.

Reasons for the ineffectiveness of the civil service

There are, of course, many reasons why the civil service is not as effective as it should be. One of the main reasons, in my opinion, is that the service is completely incompatible and out-of-tune with the present political system in the country. For example, while our political system has long moved away from the Westminster parliamentary system of government, our civil service is still cherishing the traditions, and observing the modalities of the discarded system. Our last attempt at civil rule was run on the lines of the presidential system of government without our civil service being restructured to harmonise with the new system. Naturally, there will be problems of incompatibility. I don't think that any one can efficiently run a presidential system with a parliamentary type of civil service. White House is a long way from Whitehall.

It is unfortunate that many top civil servants still regard themselves as *independent* and *neutral* advisers to ministers and commissioners; *independent* and *neutral* in the sense that it is not they, but the minister/commissioner who is wholly responsible for the success or failure of ministerial programmes. I think that such a belief may be true in a parliamentary system, but not under a presidential system of government. A parliamentary system seems to be more suited for developed economies. Under such a system, often the main job of a top civil servant (i.e., permanent secretary or head of department) is to assist his or her minister in piloting legislation through parliament. In a developing country like Nigeria on the other hand, government is the catalyst and the prime mover of development. As such, top civil servants who work closely with ministers are much more than their Whitehall counterparts. They are not advisers, but colleagues, partners and active participants with the ministers. Often, their main job is to make things happen and to bring about change and development on the ground.

The introduction of the presidential system brings into proper focus this participatory role of top civil servants. Unlike in the parliamentary system where ministers are elected parliamentarians and can therefore rightly claim superiority and authority to speak for the people (their constituency), under the presidential system, only the president can claim such authority and superiority. He alone goes round the country and gets the mandate to rule for a specified period. All others, ministers, aides, top civil servants and others who are appointed at the president's pleasure, are there to help him carry out his mandate. They are, presumably, each appointed by virtue of their individual talents especially with respect to the overall programme of the president. Once appointed, each has his definite and specific task, and should perform at the level of responsibility assigned to him. In such a situation, those assigned to any department or ministry, be they ministers, aides, or top civil servants, share success or failure jointly and severally. Obviously, top civil servants when appointed to such high sensitive political positions lose permanency in the particular post but not in their civil service grade. They also lose anonymity. Such top officers are therefore easily distinguished from other senior and junior officers who are appointed and removed by an independent public service commission. It is this latter group that rightly deserve permanency of tenure and anonymity. Their job is the execution of programmes under the direction and supervision of the president's men.

Another reason why I feel that the civil service is performing poorly is that it seems to be suffering from acute obsolescence. It is using antiquated tools to manage a modern government, and a relatively modern economy. It is like a general medical practitioner trying to use simple antibiotics to cure cancer, or a farmer trying to clear a thick bush with a hoe and a machete instead of using a tractor and a bulldozer.

Let me say clearly that the management of the modern public service is big business and requires big business methods. Today the public services of Nigeria are involved in affairs that were beyond the imagination of civil servants thirty years ago. Government is now selling insurance, and minting coins; it is sailing ships and refining oil; it is into banking, and it is communicating with all parts of the world. It is also forging steel and producing paper. Tomorrow it may be producing machine tools and petrochemicals. All these are in addition to the regular works of government which are also expanding.

Management by objectives

I am convinced that once top civil servants accept their new roles, and adopt up-to-date methods of management, they will not fail to achieve the goals and targets of their departmental programmes. One of such up-to-date methods is *Management by Objective* (MBO). It is a process of identifying goals and objectives, defining responsibilities of officers in terms of expected results, and measuring performance against those goals and objectives. The process unites the goals and targets of the department or organisation with those of the officers.

The introduction of the practice of MBO requires major efforts and special instruments for, in a business enterprise or an organisation, officers are not automatically directed towards a common goal. On the contrary, several factors militate against the pursuance of a common goal. Some of these factors are the different viewpoints from which managers in different functional areas, and at different levels of management, perceive their work. The production man may see his job purely in terms of production, the marketing manager may be narrowly concerned with marketing, and the personnel man may see his job as only ensuring smooth personnel management. Often, these managers fail to have a holistic view. In instances like this, they may behave like the proverbial three blind men who met an elephant on the road: one touched the elephant's leg and swore that a tree was on his way; another touched the elephant's trunk and was convinced that a snake was barring his way; the third blind man felt the elephant's belly and proclaimed that he was up against a landslide.

All these blind men were talking about the same elephant in the same way as the functional managers — production, finance and personnel — are talking about the same business enterprise. Even where the managers are performing the same functional jobs, their visions about their work may be different. Again there is the story of three stone cutters employed by a builder. They were asked individually what they were doing. The first replied, "I am earning my daily bread." The second kept on hammering while he said, "I am doing the best job of stone cutting in the entire country." The third man looked up, and as if he was seeing a vision, said, "I am building a cathedral." Which of the three men is a true manager? The first man knows what he wants to get out of his work, a living; he wants a fair day's pay for a fair day's work. He is not a manager. The second man is a real problem. He is after workmanship. He is a dedicated and committed professional, but he wears blinkers and thinks of nothing but being the best stone cutter in the country. Workmanship is good but it must be directed to the overall objective, i.e, building the cathedral. The third man is a true manager. He is working for a predetermined purpose, a precise objective, i.e., building a cathedral.

To overcome the obstacles described above requires more than good intentions, sermons and exhortations. It requires policy and structure. It requires that management by objectives be purposely organised and made a living law of the entire management group. First of all, everyone in the organisation or enterprise must be properly educated about the objective of the enterprise, and what it sets out to achieve. This should form part of the training of workers. Unfortunately, many employers concentrate on functional training of workers and ignore their education. But there is a big difference between the two. Training is instruction on how to perform functional jobs such as how to grow tobacco, how to make cigarettes and how to package them. But education is instruction about the aims and objectives of the company, what, in specific and quantifiable terms, the company sets out to achieve within specific periods; the company's ethos, culture and traditions. Education also includes a clear knowledge and understanding of departmental and individual roles in the achievement of the overall objectives of the organisation.

The first step, therefore, in the adoption of MBO methods is knowledge of the overall aims and objectives of the enterprise or parastatal. Then comes knowledge of the particular objectives and responsibilities of the various departments in the achievement of these objectives. Finally, very important is the responsibility of individual managers in the whole exercise.

It is not enough for individual managers to know what is expected of them, they must also know its time frame. This is not a one-way traffic where the superior officer hands down to his subordinate his work programme. The superior and subordinate officers must agree on the assignment as well as on its timing. They both must set the performance standard for acceptable work. They are then in a good position to measure actual results achieved against the projected plans and standards. In a situation like this, the performance of the manager is carefully linked to the objectives of his unit or section, and through them to the overall or corporate goals of the organisation. In this way, all the managers in the organisation are working towards the same objectives because their activities are designed, directed, and monitored towards meeting common goals and objectives.

An important element of MBO is work measurement and timing. Every manager must know in clear and quantifiable terms what results are expected from him and when. MBO does not mean common goals for all managers. It is specific targets for individual managers within specific periods. MBO goes beyond knowing what to do and how to do it to actually doing it correctly and on time. MBO translates paper plans into actual achievements on the ground.

Another aspect of MBO is evaluation, feedback, and redirection of efforts to meet predetermined work assignments. It means a continual appraisal of how the manager is meeting his projected targets. The feedback to the supervisor helps to ensure his full understanding and support, and corrective action if need be. The performance evaluation is for the purpose of helping the manager achieve his target. It is supportive and not faultfinding.

It is based on measurable results and not on personality traits. It is to solve problems, not to place blame. It is an open report and evaluation system.

MBO also ensures the proper utilisation of manpower and, therefore, helps to eliminate waste. It tolerates no passengers, for everyone has a definite job or work. It also identifies training needs to enable workers achieve their targets.

It is impossible to present a complete picture of MBO in a single session. All I have tried to do is to emphasise how it can foster such aspects of management as goal setting, timed targets, performance evaluation, manpower utilisation, and training. In a nutshell, I consider MBO as one of the indispensable methods of a result-oriented management. The only way in which the service can earn the respect of political leaders and the public, is by producing the desired result on time. In this respect, the technique of MBO will be highly valuable.

Mr. Chairman, what I have been saying so far is not new. We said them ten years ago in the report we submitted to the government on the management of government business. The recommendations were accepted but were not fully implemented. But those were the days when the oil money was flowing and the nation could afford to be careless and inefficient. Today the oil money is no longer flowing as before. It is now a mere trickle. As a result, austerity abounds everywhere. The country can, therefore, ill-afford an ineffective and unproductive public service. The time has therefore come, in fact it is long overdue, when all those management practices which are capable of pulling the country out of its present economic distress should be harnessed and implemented. It is now, or never!

7

Under Three Masters ✥

"What matters is not who you are, or what qualification you have, but what you can achieve. This is what interests the politician and it is this sort of man that he wants and will respect and retain. He will respect the officer who finds ways and means of accomplishing a task and not one who gives half a dozen reasons why the task cannot be accomplished."

Introduction

I am pleased to be associated, once again, with this premier institute in the field of public administration. My last address to the institute was during the celebrations of its tenth anniversary. On that occasion, I congratulated the director and his staff for their pioneer work and outstanding contribution in providing Nigeria with competent administrators during the independence decade. I concluded with the hope that the institute would again take the lead in providing the country with equally competent managers needed in the present decade. To emphasise my point regarding the changed role, I suggested that the institute might consider changing its name to the *Institute of Management and Development*.

When I made that suggestion, I looked around for reactions but not a word was breathed and I wondered whether the silence meant approval or utter disapproval. I had, therefore, wanted on this occasion to take up that suggestion again and force a discussion on it but your director told me that the majority of the audience today would be young graduates in the early years of their career, and that they would prefer to hear how another old foggy fumbled his way through the service under three masters — the colonial, the political, and the military masters.

✥   Speech delivered at the 4th Annual Re-Union Dinner, Institute of Administration, University of Ife, June 27, 1974. This is also the title of the author's memoirs. See, Jerome Udoji, 1995: *Under Three Masters. Memoirs of an African Administrator* (Ibadan, Spectrum Books Limited).

The unwanted child

Let me warn you that although Chief Adebo[1] and I are colleagues and friends, our stories are very different. His is the success story of a wanted child. Mine is that of an unwanted child and his frustrations. I know you will be wondering why I describe my story as that of an unwanted child. I will illustrate this by telling you a few stories of actual events during my career.

The first story is that of my interview at the colonial office. I took an unusual step in my application. I applied to join the Colonial Administrative Service as a secretary of state appointment. Before then, the Africans in the Service were recruited locally as clerks, typists and interpreters. The outstanding ones among them were promoted to such positions as administrative assistants, and later as assistant secretaries. This was the case of my friend, Simeon Adebo, and others like S. Ade Ojo and Mr. McEwen. They all had their careers mostly in the Nigerian secretariat. If you are a direct secretary of state appointment, you come in a senior level, and are normally posted to the field to enable you learn the local language, fly the union jack, represent the Crown, particularly on Empire Days, among other duties. The local language is important for your confirmation.

The first question I was asked at the interview was why I wanted to join the Colonial Administrative Service, and whether I did not realise that it was a scaffolding which would be cast away as soon as the permanent structure was up. My reply was that I believed that a Nigerian material in the scaffolding would eventually have a place either in the main building or in the outer structures around it. Although I was eventually appointed, this indication of not being wanted did not end with the colonial office.

My first posting was to Ado-Ekiti, which was then in Ondo Province. Six months after my arrival, the Oba, the Ewi of Ado, threw a party in my honour, and during the reception he revealed that before my posting a letter had gone to some of the Obas

---

[1]   Chief Adebo at the time the paper was presented, was Nigeria's ambassador to the United Nations.

enquiring if they would welcome an African administrative officer. Apparently some of them had reservations, but he decided to give the experiment a trial. But that was not the end of the reservations. The next was during my posting as the only African permanent secretary among eleven others to serve the newly appointed ministers in 1954. Most of the ministers preferred European permanent secretaries but one of them agreed to give me a trial. Maybe he believed I could not do much harm since it was a professional ministry[2] where both the minister and the chief professional officer belonged to the same profession.

I am happy to recollect that subsequent events proved that those who agreed to try the experiment did not regret their decision. I left Ado-Ekiti for Ilaro and was succeeded by an African. When I left Ilaro, an African also succeeded me. In the same way, after about a year in the ministry, the minister and his colleagues became the greatest advocates for the Nigerianisation of the post of permanent secretary.

The one lesson from these stories is the importance of establishing one's acceptability. It is not something that we can lay claim to, no matter how erudite and eminent we may be. It is something that has to be earned and demonstrated. It happens, not only with individuals, but also with organisations. Take the example of the Ministry of Economic Planning. When this ministry was about to be created, there was a strong resistance from officials of the Ministry of Finance who argued that there was no need for such a ministry because planning was inherent in all that it did. The ministry was eventually created and it has justified its existence such that today it has become one of the most important ministries of government. In some countries it has swallowed the Ministry of Finance. The same, I hope, is true of the Ministry of Establishment, which today is looked upon as a poor relation of both the Public Service Commission and the office of the military governor. If the Ministry of Establishment would move away from preoccupation with staff complements and negative and protective rules and concentrate on

---

[2] The Ministry of Health.

management, i.e., managing people so that they can achieve objectives with minimum expenditure of resources, then it would be easier for it to earn its due respect. After all, human resources are the greatest asset of any organisation, and he who manages it must be a key man in the organisation. But to be accepted as such, the manager must demonstrate his importance and value to the organisation.

Lessons learnt from serving three masters

I shall now devote the remaining time to discussing the lessons under each of my three masters:

My colonial masters

First is the colonial master under whom I served for ten years. The one lesson I have continued to remember is the efficiency of that service. That efficiency was mostly due to three factors. The first was that there was a clear understanding of what the colonial policy was, and every officer knew exactly what he was expected to do towards its achievement. Second, there was a clear delegation of power and authority over a short span of control. The span of control was from the divisional officer to the resident, and from the resident to the chief commissioner, and through him to the governor. Third, the officers were loyal, dedicated, and totally committed. It did not mean that the officers had no personal ambitions and objectives. But it meant that every officer reconciled his personal objectives with the overall organisational objectives. Officers sought the fulfilment of their ambitions through the service, with the service and in the service of the overall objectives of the colonial office. No one had any ambitions or objectives outside the service.

Can we say that of the service today? How many senior officers today are conversant with the policy plans of their ministries? I understand that a recent progress report by the Ministry of Economic Development revealed that some permanent secretaries appeared to be ignorant of the contents of the second four-year development plan. If this is so, what then do you expect from such officers? There is a saying that if you do not know where you are going, you cannot be lost. The inference is that you are already lost before you even took the first step.

My political masters

Now what about the lessons from my service under political masters? The one great lesson from that period is the need for professionalism. By this I mean every public officer must be an expert in his own chosen field. There must be a body of skills over which he and members of his profession can claim exclusive knowledge of. It might be engineering, medicine, financial management, personnel management, or economic analysis. The officer must constantly keep himself up-to-date with the latest advances in his profession. Because of the advances in technology, people often lag behind developments in their fields in a very short time. I read in one of my journals that there is great unemployment in America, among engineers aged thirty-five years and above. This is largely due to obsolescence as a result of rapid advances in the field of engineering and technology. As long as a civil servant knows his stuff, he has nothing to fear from a political master. I believe that in the much talked of friction between civil servants and politicians, the civil servants are more to blame. The only way to win the respect of the politician is to prove to him that he cannot do without you. Even if he hates your guts, he will respect and retain you. To him you will be a necessary evil. Chief Awolowo, as premier of Western Nigeria, was reported to have described administrative officers as necessary evils. If a politician discovers that you are not much better than he is, he will begin to treat you as one does an expendable material.

Let us take the example of a permanent secretary in a ministry. His main jobs as the head of the ministry are those of management, namely:

Planning: This means developing the objectives of the ministry in clear quantifiable terms and over specific periods.

Organising: This means structuring and arranging resources in order to achieve the targets set in the plan. These resources are men, money and materials. To organise well requires creativity, decision-making and leadership.

Controlling: This means maintaining adherence to the plan.

Tell me which politician will not hold fast to and respect such an officer who helps him to achieve results. The trouble is that many officers are very input-oriented, instead of being output-oriented. What matters is not who you are, or what qualification you have, but what you can achieve. This is what interests the politician, and it is this sort of man that he wants and will respect and retain. He will respect the officer who finds ways and means of accomplishing a task and not one who gives half a dozen reasons why the task cannot be accomplished.

My military masters

For two reasons, I will not discuss any lessons from my service with the military. The first is that my service under them was a very short one, only seven months. The second reason is that one does not normally comment on the performance of actors whilst they are still on the stage. Until the final act, they may still spring surprises which may invalidate earlier assessments. So, one has to wait until the play is over and one is safely on his way home.

In conclusion, let me warn you that listening to the experience of an old foggy is not good enough. The experience may be as antiquated as the man himself. If you want to succeed you must first of all be a professional or a specialist in your own chosen field. You must keep abreast of the developments in that field by exposing yourself to new ideas, and by joining the relevant professional associations, subscribing and contributing to professional journals, and participating in professional seminars. Secondly, you must use your expertise to achieve the objective of the ministry. It is by so doing that you will retain the confidence of your colleagues and earn the respect of your masters whoever they may be.

8

Institutional Means of Improving the Public Services ✥

"A major problem in the relationship between the central and local governments is how to reconcile the central government's responsibility for policy direction and assessment of performance with the desirability for efficient popular participation at the local level."

Introduction: Framework of authority within which the civil service operates — the position in developed countries

Originally the civil servant was a servant of the Crown or Emperor. This was the position in Rome, and later in England. As a servant and member of the royal household, he derived his authority not from any imperial statute but from the discretionary prerogative of the sovereign. To question his actions would therefore be tantamount to questioning the authority of his master — the sovereign. It was not until the development of Parliament that the actions of the servants of the Crown (ministers and civil servants) began to be questioned, first by parliament and later by the public. And with the development of ministerial government, and the expansion of governmental activities, some of the duties imposed on ministers and civil servants began to appear on statutes.

Even in a relatively new country like the United States of America, the constitution does not directly provide for the civil service. It does so indirectly where it gives the president the power of appointing, and the Senate the power of confirming officers of the United States. Another reference in the American constitution

---

✥ An address delivered in Nairobi, in December 1968, at a seminar for top civil servants from East, West and South Africa.

is where it refers to "all other officers of the United States, which shall be established by law". It follows that in the United States, as in England, the civil servant derives his authority either from the head of state or from the Legislature.

Such statutory provisions as there are in Britain and the United States are isolated cases where specific duties are imposed on civil servants. In other words, there is no comprehensive civil service law under which the structure and conditions of employment are legally defined and made subject to the interpretation of the courts of law. An attempt was made in England after the Trevelyan and Northcote Report of 1854 to embody the civil service reform proposals in an Act of Parliament, but the government of the day opposed it and decided to legislate for the civil service by Order-in-Council under the royal prerogative. In 1920, an Order-in-Council gave the treasury the power to make regulations for the civil service.

The absence of a civil service law in both the United Kingdom and the United States was largely responsible for the late introduction of a civil service career which was based on merit in both countries. In the United Kingdom, the patronage system (by which offices were openly for sale or were granted as rewards for services to the Crown) operated until the Trevelyan and Northoote Reforms of 1854. This reform introduced merit as the criterion for appointment. In America, the spoils system by which civil servants were regarded as political agents of the political faction in power continued until the Pendleton Act of 1883. This Act brought into operation a career system based on merit and fitness for appointment after a competitive examination.

Corruption, inefficiency and other abuses of the patronage, and spoils system must have been some of the reasons that forced upon France and some other European countries the concept of a non-political civil service. To ensure such a politically neutral public service, the conditions of service of public officers are contained in a statute and subject to interpretation by the courts. In France, it is the *Statut General de la Fonction Publique* of 1946; in Germany it is the *Bundesbeamtengesetz* of 1953; in Switzerland the federal officials come under the Federal Statute of Public

Officials of 1927 which was amended in 1949. In Sweden, the. civil service is covered by constitutional provisions. In countries like Spain, the provisions of the civil service law are so detailed that they contain such details as hours of work and procedures for dealing with correspondence. Although the legal provisions may vary from constitutional clauses to legislative enactment, the problem which these countries are trying to solve is similar: to have a self-governing and self-administering service which is insulated from outside interference, whether social, political or judicial. In the fields of recruitment, discipline and promotion a group of officials is generally responsible, not an outside body. This is particularly true of France, Germany and Italy.

The situation in Africa

In the new African countries the idea of a Civil Service Act is a recent innovation. The independence constitutions of the early African countries (Ghana and Nigeria) were silent on the civil service. The only civil service posts mentioned in such constitutions were those of attorney-general, permanent secretary, director of public prosecutions and director of audit. There were, however, provisions for the establishment of a Public Service Commission, the purpose of which was the insulation of the civil service from political control. It is, however, arguable whether such purposes were achieved, or were capable of being achieved. It may be the arguments about the desirability of the independence of the civil service that made countries like Ghana, Tanzania and Uganda introduce Civil Service Acts.

The arguments in favour of a Civil Service Act are that: such an Act embodying the duties, responsibilities and functions of the civil service will give the civil service a legal identity and also enhance the status and prestige of the civil servant. But this view is not universally accepted. Some people are sceptical of the merits of a Civil Service Act vis-a-vis the public service of a developing country. They argue that such an Act may produce the opposite effects in many African countries; that given the present level of understanding and relationship, the introduction of such an Act will be drawing attention to what may be considered in certain quarters as excessive and bureaucratic powers of the public servant, and the legislature might end up curtailing instead of enhancing the status and prestige of the public servant. In these circumstances, it is argued, it might be wiser to rely on the provisions of the constitution and the guarantees contained therein since these override legislative enactment. The current experience is that Public Service Act could be used as levers for removing the independence guaranteed the public service in the constitution.

I would argue that before introducing a Public Service Act, the wisdom of emphasising the special features of the public service should be considered. The concept of an official who is subject to special regulations and privileges may give rise to a tendency for civil servants to turn themselves into a special class. In other words, to unduly enhance the prestige and status of civil servants may result in turning the service into a privileged caste of bureaucrats and technocrats with undesirable social, economic and even political consequences. This, in turn, can be dangerous for the relations between the public servant and the community.

I feel that the peculiar conditions of a developing country like Nigeria demand that the conditions of service of civil servants, including their autonomy, should be flexible and constantly under review. This will not be the case if the conditions are enshrined in a statute. Most African countries are made up of ethnic groups at varying levels of economic and educational developments. Therefore, to enshrine in a statute a merit system based on fitness for appointment after a competitive examination may be socially unfair and politically disruptive. In many African countries, there may often be the need to vary the qualifications (in conjunction with upgrading courses) in the case of educationally backward groups. A quota system may even be desirable in certain classes of appointment.

The concept of a civil service law was a concept born out of the philosophies of the nineteenth century Europe — a period of rapid all-round development. Many African countries have yet to reach that stage. Without an enlightened and articulate public opinion, and the correct political, social and economic environments, the chances of a civil service law guaranteeing an independent career merit system will be very slender indeed. As far as the service itself is concerned, there is no doubt that a body of laws which defines the functions, duties, responsibilities, as well as the rights of a public servant will make for certainty and good working morale. But it does not necessarily require an Act to achieve this. By tradition, general orders and financial instructions are regarded as authoritative and of compelling, if not legal, validity.

Before leaving the subject of the source of authority within which civil servants function, a distinction may be made between civil service law and administrative law. A civil service law is a law dealing with the structure, organisation, powers, duties and procedures of civil servants. Administrative law on the other hand deals with delegated legislation, administrative tribunals and the exercise of powers by central, local and statutory bodies. In France, unlike in England, administrative law is administered in separate administrative courts. These courts ensure that both the civil servant and public authorities observe the law. In this way, these courts which were originally designed to protect public officers have come to assume the role of the protector of the citizen against the "tyranny" of the administration. There is no need, particularly in a developing country, for the law to give more protection to a civil servant than it gives to ordinary citizens. Such a protection may divorce him from the people. With regards to the protection that administrative courts offer to the citizen, I will argue that greater and more flexible protection is offered him by other forms of control of the public servant, namely, ministerial, treasury, parliamentary, professional and work controls.

Legal relationships between the central government and statutory bodies such as local governments and corporations

Local governments

Local governments are the creation of the central government.

They are created by a statute which give them their powers and functions. The functions are generally considered to relate to matters of local interest such as:

i.   the maintenance of law and order;
ii. the maintenance of local roads;
iii. the running of local primary schools; and
iv. the collection of rates and taxes.

Usually, the statute that grants these powers to a local government body also provides safeguards for their proper exercise. This is done by giving the central government powers of direction and control. The most important of these is the power of suspension or dissolution by the appropriate central minister if he thinks that the local government body is not performing its functions satisfactorily. Next in importance is the financial control which is exercised through the approval of annual estimates, the making of grants and loans, and the auditing of accounts.

In recent years, many African governments have been embarking on ambitious economic policies and programmes. Confronted with the totality and enormity of development challenges, they find that matters such as roads and education, which were formerly considered of local interest, have acquired national importance in the context of economic development and planning. They find that in order to succeed they have to encroach on the independence and autonomy of local governments as well as on the liberty and property of individuals. They find also that local governments do not have the resources, men, or organisation to cope with development demands. The result is often lack of interest, frustration and inefficiency at the local government, and the concentration of powers in the central government which is able to assemble both the resources and men who understand and can more effectively solve these problems of development.

Proponents of centralisation argue that decentralisation is much more attuned to a developed economy with a strong nationally conscious central government anxious to hive off matters of local interest to capable and locally elected citizens, and that to advocate decentralisation for emergent African countries would be to ignore the twin problems facing African governments: fostering national unity and rapid economic growth, neither of which may be solved quickly enough in a decentralised or plural structure. In addition, it is argued that centralisation will ensure easy mobilisation and mobility of scarce resources such as funds and trained personnel.

Opponents of centralisation, on the other hand, argue that the politicians and civil servants who run central governments are increasingly out of touch with the wishes and aspirations of the people, that the party system and the use of party whips make the centralised government ineffective in representing the wishes of the people, and that a gap is developing between the government and the governed. They further argue that there is a growing desire for participation at all levels, that local governments have an important role in fostering rapid economic growth, that it will also decongest government at the centre. Proponents of decentralisation equally argue that local governments free national leaders from onerous details, help bring the government closer to the people, increase the people's understanding and support of social and economic development activities, and facilitate personal and group adjustments to needed changes.

A major problem in the relationship between the central and local governments is how to reconcile the central government's responsibility for policy direction and assessment of performance with the desirability of efficient popular participation at the local level. It would seem that there are two possible courses of action:

The first is to leave the local government structure as it is now but to drastically reduce their functions only to such matters as they are capable of discharging effectively. Such functions would probably be limited to matters as:

- liquor licensing;
- recreational Facilities;
- minor health matters;
- collection of rates and taxes; etc.

This option may be more acceptable to the people in that it leaves room for some participation.

The second course would be to abolish the present fragmented and incompetent local governments and replace them with new authorities which are bigger and more capable of fulfilling the tasks of management and development. This course of action was recommended by a recent commission which considered organisational and structural reforms in the machinery of the government of Ghana. The commission condemned centralisation as slow and inefficient and recommended the creation of plural authorities in the form of district regional authorities comprising representative councils with clearly defined responsibilities. The district authorities would elect self-accounting and rating authorities with responsibility for the comprehensive development of their areas. In particular, they would be responsible for:

- ❑ roads and buildings;
- ❑ health (excluding large hospitals);
- ❑ land administration;
- ❑ social services and community development;
- ❑ agricultural extension services;
- ❑ primary or middle schools;
- ❑ fire fighting;
- ❑ general amenities; etc.

Regional authorities on the other hand, would be composed of representatives of district councils and senior officials of regional authorities. Regional authorities would have direct responsibility in the management of large regional hospitals, secondary schools, teacher-training colleges, nurses' training schools and major workshops. They would approve district authority estimates and negotiate on their behalf with the treasury for annual subventions.

These recommendations go beyond mere delegations of authority to regional and district authorities. They are creations of separate and independent legal institutions outside the ministries and have clearly defined functions. The recommendations, in my opinion, seem more like the creation of regional governments instead of regional policies. Regional policy means regional plans, regional development, and/or strong regional arms of the central government, but not necessarily regional governments in the sense of regional representative councils. Representative councils will not be satisfied with being consultative and deliberative but would also want to be executive. The experience in Nigeria with deliberative provincial councils was that they constantly demanded executive powers, a desire not altogether unconnected with separatist tendencies.

On the whole, the choice between centralisation and decentralisation will depend on the circumstances of a country, particularly its level of political and economic development. For an undeveloped country, centralisation may be necessary if initial progress is to be made in economic development, and if there is to be a substantial rise in general social and economic efficiency. But as effective development proceeds and the general level of technical efficiency rises, new problems may begin to emerge. The number of units will increase, not only in the economic system but also in public administration. At this point, the central authority may become inefficient because its control becomes increasingly difficult. This may then be the ideal time for powers of decision-making in economic and social matters to be decentralised. In other words, the need for decentralisation does not suddenly arise. It is a gradual process.

Public corporations

One of the results of the expansion of governmental activities is the growth of public corporations. Like local governments, corporations are creations of central statutes and instruments of decentralisation, but unlike them, they are created to perform specific functions of a commercial or industrial nature. Unlike local governments, they are better equipped technologically and financially for performing their functions and are not hampered by the effects of elected membership. In a way, the growth of public corporations in recent years is a reflection of the weakness of local governments and their inability to cope with the increasing demands of development. It may be that in future, and unless the system of local governments becomes more successful, more and more of the functions of local governments may be taken over by corporations.

In view of the differences between local governments and corporations, the problem of their relationship with the central government is also different. Here the main problem is how to reconcile the need for operational efficiency and financial flexibility with the necessity to conform to the overall policy of the central government. Corporations are constituted by law to achieve a public purpose, and as such, it is incumbent on the government to ensure that they accomplish the purposes for which they are created. What corporations should therefore seek is not freedom from government control but freedom from those restrictions which are unsuited to a business operation.

Corporations should also not insist on organisational autonomy for that will exclude them from participating in the formulation of public policies affecting their spheres of activity. The ideal of autonomous corporations has not been realised in practice in most African countries. In West Africa, the record is that governments are bringing them under stricter government control by the appointment of full-time civil servants as chairmen or directors of many of these corporations. Furthermore, steps are also taken to bring the wage structure of corporations in line with that of the civil service. The present trend is towards integration with the government in everything except perhaps what is unsuited to a business operation. One advantage of this tendency is that it may facilitate the interchange of staff between the various agencies of government, and might eventually lead to a unified public service for all persons engaged in public duties.

Internal organisation of government

The requirements of rapid economic growth have made co-ordination and the assessment of performances of great importance. The traditional practice is to use the Ministry of

Finance for the control of personnel, the surveillance of common practices and procedures, and the co-ordination of economic policies. This is still the practice in western Nigeria.

Since economic development is now the major concern of most African governments, there is an increasing awareness of the need for co-ordinated efforts in the sphere of economic planning. Most African countries have, therefore, introduced planning ministries. Ministries of Finance are considered too negative, cautious and unimaginative for bold and positive planning. The new ministries of planning have, in several cases, started with the usual difficulties of shortage of staff, absence of statistical data, uncertain status in the government, and resentment from the strongly entrenched Ministry of Finance, which regards the new ministry as a rival institution. This makes institutional liaison between the planning ministry and the other ministries weak. One of the results is that programmes are honoured more in breach than in their observance. Priorities are ignored, and there have been instances where later budget decisions distorted the decisions of the planning ministry. To remedy this situation, some countries have strengthened the planning ministry with an economic committee at which the head of government presides. Such a committee is usually made up of the economic ministries — finance, commerce, agriculture and economic planning.

The main function of the committee is to approve the recommendations of the planning ministry before it goes to the cabinet. Where there is a Ministry of Planning, the Ministry of Finance is often restricted to:

1. securing funds necessary for government's current expenditure;
2. securing enough additional funds for government's investment outlays;
3. pursuing a functional tax policy in place of the traditional policy of taxing for a balanced budget. Such a policy will stimulate private savings and encourage their flow to productive fields.

Ministries of finance, however, resist such limitations of their functions and argue that there is an element of planning in all their activities.

The other ministry which has invaded the controlling influence of the Ministry of Finance is the Ministry of Establishments, sometimes known as the Ministry of Public Service Matters. This ministry arose out of the need for an organisation or authority to supervise the Africanisation of the service, and to bring pre-independence practices and procedures in line with the status and aspirations of the new governments. In recent years, the ministry has been concerned more with personnel administration and the general management of the service. This includes identifying and developing management talent, career planning, and training in management techniques. In some countries, these functions are performed, not by a ministry, but by a department in the office of the president or prime minister. This is because at independence, the management and control of the service became a matter of public and political interest.

In the last few years, there have been a lot of structural and organisational reforms aimed at improving the effectiveness of the public service in many African countries. In spite of these reforms, there is still a clamour for more reforms. Critics of the public service draw attention to the structure and procedures of private industrial and commercial firms, and urge the government to adopt such practices and procedures. It is, however, believed that there is a limit to management practices which the government can adopt. For example, the management of private firms usually want to discipline and dismiss employees without having to defend its action before an appeal body. It wants to promote workers on the basis of its own standards of merit. It wants a flexible working load with layoff based on merit. It also wants to pay individuals on the basis of its own assessment of their merit and not according to a uniform scale which regards everyone alike.

But because the objectives of government are often different from those of private enterprises, the extent and level of their accountability also differ. In the nature of things, and in view of their different roles, government methods are bound to be different from those of private enterprises.

9

Administrative Reform in Emergent African Countries ✥

"The old-fashioned idea that administrators are born and not made no longer holds true. Administration is now becoming a science, which can be learnt in the classroom. In fact, today, administrators and managers can be trained to use the tools of their trade in much the same way as a craftsman can be trained to use the tools of his craft."

Introduction

Thank you, Mr. Chairman, for your introduction. Thank you also for inviting me to participate in this month's session of the Public Service Forum. I must warn that I have not come to make any leaks of the report of the commission. It will take another eighteen months before that can be done. I have, however, come to discuss with you some of the suggestions that are put forward for our consideration. The subject I have chosen is "Administrative Reform." I chose it because it is the most important and probably most difficult problem facing emergent African countries in the field of public administration. I intend to deal with the subject under four headings:

First, I will explain what I mean by administrative reform. Second, I will outline the reasons for administrative reforms. Third, I will discuss the urgent areas for administrative reform. Finally, I will, if there is time, deal with some of the problems that confront those who initiate administrative reforms.

Meaning of administrative reform

By administrative reform, I mean the transformation of a pre-

---

✥ **Address delivered** to the former Mid-Western Public Service Forum, April 1973.

independence traditional and colonial bureaucracy into a dynamic national civil service which is development and achievement-oriented, and responsive not only to political leadership but also to modern techniques of management. The description of the pre-independence civil service as colonial requires no explanation. Everybody knows that the colonial service was responsible not to the people of the colonies but to the imperial power. It was traditional because it was resistant to change. It was bureaucratic because it was a government by civil servants who had great respect for rules, procedures and precedents. But it was an efficient civil service because it achieved the objectives for which it was established. This efficiency was the result of training and total commitment on the part of the members of that service. Every member of the service, from the district officer to the governor, knew what the colonial policy was, and what, at his level, he was expected to do towards its achievement. Every officer was also trained and retrained for his role. There was a pre-service training, a mid-career training, and even those at the top had regular training in the form of annual leave, part of which was spent in consultations with policy-makers in the colonial office. There was also a two-way traffic in communication from the district officer to the governor, and every officer participated fully in the formulation of policy. Responsibility for decision- making was also decentralised to the level of operation. Finally, the service was suitably motivated in that the service cared for the officers, and the officers cared for it: there were, for instance, good conditions of service including salary, allowances, housing and promotion prospects within and outside the colony of posting. It was a first-class service with first-class conditions.

The need for reform

One may ask, if the colonial service was so efficient, why then do we need to reform it? The need for reform arises primarily out of the challenges of independence. The challenge of independence is the challenge of development. During the agitational politics of the colonial days, the politicians made many promises, one of the most important of which was that independence would usher life more abundant. No sooner was independence achieved than the politicians realised that the economy was controlled by expatriates, namely, the British, Lebanese, French and Greeks, in that order. They also discovered that they could not fulfil the independence promises without controlling the commanding heights of the economy. To do this, they embarked on series of development programmes which were aimed at utilising the human, material and physical resources of the country for the benefit of the people. In pursuit of this, financial institutions, industries, transport and mining operations, to name just a few, were established. These enterprises expanded the public sector by encroaching into fields that were previously considered the preserve of the private sector.

The expansion created new tasks for the administration—tasks that required new men and new institutions; men with new orientations, new skills, new tools, and the technique for using them. Unfortunately, due to the political overtones of Nigerianisation, the need for the new crop of men was not realised early enough. The service continued, as it were, to harbour the old type of officers but in African garbs. It continued to recruit history and classics graduates and trained them in the pre-independence institutes of public administration, where the emphasis was on broadening the outlook of the recruits. We virtually replaced the expatriates with their prototype in black skins.

But what the new civil service needed most was no longer the jack-of-all trades type of officer but specialists in development administration, development economists, social scientists, physical planners, project evaluation experts, etc. Because of lack of appreciation of the importance of these specialists, the service was over-burdened with jobs and responsibilities for which it was not prepared or fitted for. Both the civil service machine and its operators were overloaded beyond their capabilities. It is, however, to the credit of that service that with minor reforms here and there it coped reasonably well with the burden. It is also to the credit of the service that it had the modesty to admit its inadequacies by calling for an overhaul of its structure, management and practices.

Another main reason for instituting administrative reforms is the advance in science and technology. We are all aware that our lives are now ruled by science, and that we live in an age of heart transplant moonflights, and jumbo jets. The advance in technology has affected even simple clerical works. When I joined the civil service in 1942, the preparation of salary vouchers was done manually by the simple process of mental arithmetic. Ten years later, it was done by adding machines. Later, the punch card replaced the adding machine, and today, the computer has replaced the punch card. I do not know how many of you are aware that in Britain and America, computers now sort letters by the use of code numbers. Also computers now do the booking of seats in airlines.

Some of you must have read recently in the Nigerian press that aircrafts, using electronic and magnetic devices, will now do prospecting for iron ore. The Nigerian Railways also uses computers to locate the position of locomotives and wagons as well as their contents. They also use computers for stock control, that is, to ascertain how much stock they carry, how much is used, and to whom it has been issued. Such changes require different methods of planning, different systems of accounting and different systems of auditing. What all these add up to is that if the service is to be efficient, it must keep abreast of changes by training and retraining its staff. This training is not only for general administrators. It is even more important for professionals. It is, for example, currently believed that an engineer who qualified thirty years ago is now thirty years out-of-date. Only the other day, I read in an American journal about the great unemployment among engineers aged forty and above. One of the explanations is that a few years after qualification, engineers become obsolescent because of the rapid advances in engineering technology. This means that we must not only keep our practices and procedures under constant review but that every officer must keep himself or herself up-to-date if he or she does not want to be swept into the limbo of obsolescence.

Urgent areas for administrative reform

I shall now turn to the question of areas for administrative reforms. Matters that call for administrative reform abound in the Service. They range from the structure of the Service to its management. I shall, however, list a few, which I feel require urgent action. Among these.are:

1. the multiplicity of classes, grade levels and salary scales;
2. the tension between the classes, in particular, between the administrators and professionals;
3. the lack of clear definition of authority and responsibility for the overall management of the civil service;
4. the lack of clear definition of individual tasks upon which to base recruitment, training , evaluation of performance and pay policies;
5. lack of professionalism, which results in the use of obsolete personnel and management practices.
   I shall now elaborate on each of the above points.

Multiplicity of classes and the tension between generalist administrators and professional officers

In the federal civil service, there are about 1,300 occupational groups often referred to as classes, or cadres. Each class has a number of grade levels and each grade level has its own salary scale. In some cases the scales overlap, in others the scales are common to more than one occupational group. Officers progress within their classes and hardly move from one class to another. When they do, they often do so with loss of seniority. This class system breeds class conflict and does not make for the best deployment and utilisation of available scarce manpower. It has caused great tensions between administrators and professionals. The tension has reached a stage at which it is affecting morale and productivity of the service generally. It has also reached a stage at which the classes call each other names. The administration is referred to as the "Elite Service", whilst the professionals are referred to as the "Second Class Service" Recently a new expression has appeared in the language of the classes: the professionals now refer to the permanent secretaries as the *New Super Homo Sapiens*.

The professionals are now demanding parallel structures with separate ministerial heads and their own heads of service. In a recent paper by Mr. Ige, federal permanent secretary, Ministry of Works , there is a statement which indicated that professional officers regard the secretary to the cabinet as head of the administrative class and not as head of the civil service. This is a very unhealthy situation which must not be allowed to deteriorate.

The complaints of professional officers seem to consist of the following arguments:

1. The boss complex of administrative officers (particularly young ones) in their relations with professional officers. Professional officers would like to receive directions only from their professional supervisors and not from administrative officers.

2. The promotion prospects, perquisites, status and prestige are far better in the administrative services than in the professional. Professional officers want conditions of service to be at par with the prevailing conditions for the administrative class, otherwise there will be serious loss of professional talent.

3. Professional advice should go directly to the decision-making level. It should not be subjected to quasi-professional criticism by administrative officers on its way up.

4. The management of professional work programmes, including postings and financial control, should be in the hands of the chief professional officer and should not be subject to direction from administrators.

Administrators, on the other hand, argue that starting salaries for professional officers are often higher than those for administrators, and that in some cases professional heads earn more than permanent secretaries; that the recent disparity in promotion rates is a temporary phenomenon due to the fact that the administrative service has been more rapidly Nigerianised than the professional service; that the highest posts in the service, including those of permanent secretaries, are now open to all officers who posses the required qualities and qualifications.

Professional officers have countered some of these points by arguing that while some professionals have risen to become permanent secretaries, those are exceptions rather than the rule. Administrators complain that professionals frequently find it difficult to remain detached in considering conflicting advice from two different professions because they have not been trained to see the whole picture; and that where a ministry comprises different professional advisers, it might be advisable to have an administrator at the head.

I feel that one of the main causes of the tension is not so much a matter of prospects but has also to do with status, power, prestige and recognition. One solution, which has been suggested, is the creation of a new class to be known as the senior management cadre which will consist of permanent secretaries and their deputies, heads of professional departments and their deputies, and general managers of corporations and their deputies. There will be conditions for entering the cadre, and such conditions will, among others, include selection after the successful completion of specialised management training courses. Provision should also be made for those who, because of their special professional competence, do not want to join the cadre to be retained as specialists and consultants. This suggestion of a new cadre will provide a machinery which will ensure that all existing classes are open-ended, and that the highest posts in the service are open to all classes.

An alternative suggestion is to merge all public officers into a single unified public service to be governed by standard practices in recruitment, promotion, a single superannuation scheme and a unified salary and grading structure, such that similar kinds of work, no matter where performed, will earn the same kind of remuneration. This option considers all government work as a single operation even though it may be carried out by a number of administrative and other agencies such as the civil service, the local government service, the teaching service, or boards and corporations.

Lack of clear definition of authority and responsibility for overall management of the civil service

At the moment, whatever management there is in the civil service is shared between three institutions — the public service commission, the head of the civil service and the Ministry of Establishments. Some responsibilities are also shared with the Ministry of Finance. A situation like this does not make for efficient management since it is difficult to determine which of them has the ultimate responsibility for the efficient performance and achievement of objectives. Solutions adopted in other countries may not necessarily suit the Nigerian situation. For example, in England, the control of the civil service is under the permanent secretary who is also the head of the civil service. He ranks equally with the head of the treasury and the secretary to the cabinet. In fact, they have another officer who, although not a civil servant, is the director-general of a team of experts who co-ordinate policy matters in the prime minister's office. Some countries have solved the problem by creating in the office of the president a Directorate of Personnel, which takes over appointments and promotions from the Public Service Commission leaving it with only an appellate jurisdiction.

Another model is to vest heads of ministries with the power of the Public Service Commission, again leaving to the latter only the hearing of appeals from aggrieved civil servants. Yet another system, which has been tried by at least one country, is to expand the Public Service Commission by transferring to it the functions of the Ministry of Establishment. I feel, however, that this is a problem to which Nigerians must find their own unique answer, taking into account their particular circumstances.

Lack of clear definition of individual tasks which should form the basis for formulating policies on recruitment, training, assessment of performance and pay

There is a saying that if you do not know where you are going you cannot be lost. The presumption is that you are lost already. The definition of individual tasks will depend on the objectives of the ministry as spelt out for the division or unit in which an officer is engaged. An officer must know what his unit is there to do, and how his work affects the achievement of those objectives. Individual tasks must be specified with reference to the time for their completion. It is on the requirement of the tasks to be done that recruitment and training should be based. Training should not be general, but must be geared to the performance of specific tasks, e.g., training for computer programming, training for programme budgeting, training for personnel officers, etc. Training should also be continuous from recruitment to retirement. The Service should borrow a leaf from the private sector where training is part of the total career development of an officer.

The tasks performed by an officer in the course of a year should be the basis on which his performance should be judged. The present system of confidential reports has been criticised as being outmoded. Originally conceived as a technique for staff training, staff development, and the achievement of greater efficiency, it has, it is alleged, become an instrument of nepotism and, at worst, of oppression and victimisation. The confidential report is essentially subjective and often not based on verifiable facts. It puts emphasis on personal traits rather than on job performance, on weaknesses or strengths rather than on potential? The reporting system is far from being standardised in that the words and expressions used may mean different things to different persons. Many a time, the reports are not honest because reporting officers do not want to get into trouble with their subordinates. The result is that everyone is rated alike, either very good or good.

It has been suggested in some quarters that the system of confidential reports should be abolished and replaced with appraisal interviews. These are interviews during which a senior officer discuses with his junior the work of the latter. This is not a casual discussion but a planned interview in which there is an opportunity to discuss the main assignments of junior officers, and how well he or she is meeting the requirements. The main advantage of the interview lies in its counselling effect. A lot, however, depends on the senior officer's approach. If he demonstrates that he wants to help, if he recognises the value and accomplishments of the junior officer, and if he shows that the purpose is to make the junior an even stronger officer, the interview will achieve the desired objectives.

Lastly, the tasks performed by an officer should form the basis of his total compensation — pay, allowances and pensions. These should be based on an analysis of the job and its evaluation in relation to other jobs.

Need for the professionalisation of administration and management

One of the complaints which professional officers level against administrative officers is that administration is not a profession, but an art, which any average intelligent person can easily acquire on the job. I think that this view could be true of the law and order administrator of days gone by, but it cannot be true of the present.day development administrator. Because of the demands and complexities of development, administration is no longer the job of the trial and error administrator. It is now a specialist and professional job. The old fashioned idea that administrators are born and not made no longer holds true. Administration is now becoming a science which can be learnt in the classroom. In fact, today, administrators and managers can be trained to use the tools of their trade in much the same way as a craftsman can be trained to use the tools of his craft.

It is the responsibility of administrators to fight for recognition as a profession. This they can do, not by staking a claim to professionalism, or by the mere occupation of administrative and managerial posts. To achieve recognition, they must satisfy the following conditions which are applicable to other professions:

First, there must be a body of knowledge and expertise over

which the members claim exclusive competence. We have noted that the tools of administration and management can now be learnt in the classroom. One of the tools is that of the behavioural sciences such as motivation, delegation and decision-making. Others are the management techniques of work study, operational research, critical path analysis, management by objectives, programme budgeting, management accounting, etc.

Second, the members of a profession must have a "corporate concern" for the advancement of this relevant body of knowledge and the techniques of its application. There should also be a close link between the practitioners and contemplative members of the profession. The practitioners must continually update their knowledge by reading professional journals, attending conferences, and by intellectual contacts with their colleagues.

Third, members must have self-discipline in the form of a code of conduct which the profession upholds. I am pleased to learn that the Institute of Public Administration of Ife University has attempted to formulate such a code of conduct. I recommend the Ife code for universal adoption but would like to amend code one thereof to read as follows:

> In the service of my country, I will put loyalty to the highest moral principles above all other loyalties, and I will at all times remember that the public is my client, and that it's good is my first duty.

Fourth, the profession must have a clientele. The clientele of professional administrators and managers range from government departments to private companies. In the case of administrators who are engaged in government departments, although they operate in a socio-political atmosphere, they must always bear in mind that the public, and not the minister or commissioner, is the clientele, and as such the interest of the public must always be paramount. Cases are bound to occur when the private interest of the minister or commissioner conflicts with those of the public. In such cases, the job of the administrator will be to put the case of the public as clearly and strongly as he can whilst allowing the minister or commissioner to pass a judgement on his assessment or recommendation. It may well be that the administrator is not in possession of all the facts — including political considerations.

I would like to conclude this discussion of the need for professionalism by saying that there is already an association with an aim of promoting the study, practice and status of the profession of administration and management as well as the adoption of adequate and up-to-date administrative and management practices. The name of this association is the African Association for Public Administration and Management, (AAPAM). It distributes management literature and organises annual seminars. This year, the association will hold a seminar in Nigeria on: *"The Management of Public Enterprises"*. More details about the association could be obtained on request from Professor Adebayo Adedeji, Mallam Mahud Tukur or myself. Professor Adedeji is one of the vice-presidents of the association, Mallam Tukur is a member of the executive, and I am the secretary-general.

Difficulties inherent in any reform exercise

The last problem I promised to discuss is the difficulties inherent in any reform exercise. Man is by nature resistant to change and no one wants to be told that he is not doing as well as he ought. Because of this resistance, we are not easily aware of the need for change. Even when there is this awareness, vested interests and human lethargy militate against any positive action on the part of politicians and civil servants.

Other factors which have blinded politicians and top civil servants to the need for reform were the overwhelming and pressing need to localise expatriate-held posts, and to fill the newly created positions as the civil service expanded to meet new goals. There was also the tendency to solve reform problems by the creation of new institutions rather than by the method of enquiring into management problems of existing organisations and ensuring that they functioned at maximum efficiency. Governments are yet to realise that most of the problems of administration emanate from human deficiencies, and that investment in improving administrative capability may be one of the most effective ways of achieving the goals of development.

10

Administrative Reforms in Nigeria since Independence ⬧

"Being usually resistant to change, governments often regard reforms as threats to its continued existence. This is why it requires not only an awareness but the commitment and courage of a political leader to carry through worthwhile reforms."

Introduction

Thank you, Mr. Chairman, for your introduction. Thank you also for the invitation to participate in your in-service course on modern management. You have asked me to speak on *Administrative Reforms Since Independence.* I propose to deal with the subject under four headings. First, I will explain what I understand by administrative reform. Second, I will argue the case for administrative reform. Third, I will comment on why there has been very few reforms, and finally, I will mention areas that I consider are in urgent need for administrative reform.

Meaning of administrative reform

The term administrative reform has been used so often in recent years that one is apt to take its meaning for granted. And yet it could convey different meanings to different people. This fact was brought home to me by a recent article in the *Quarterly Journal of Administration* by Professor Subramaniam on "The Zambian Administrative Experiment and Experience". In that article, the author argued persuasively that unless an administrative system has existed for "a long time" and has led to "mounting dissatisfaction" and a "deliberate investigation thereof" has been taken, any changes on the system cannot be

---

⬧ Speech delivered at the *Modern Management Seminar,* Ahmadu Bello University, Zaria, February, 1976.

properly labelled "administrative reform". Following from this, Professor Subramaniam did not consider the administrative changes that have taken place in Zambia since that country became independent in 1964 as administrative reform. However, he had no difficulty in using the term to describe the changes which took place in India on the recommendations of the Administrative Reform Commission of India and in Great Britain on the findings of the Fulton Committee. I do not know what he would label the changes which took place in Ghana as a result of the Mills Odoi Report , those in Kenya after the Ndegwa Report and in Nigeria after the Public Service Review Commission Report (1972-1974).

Followed to its logical conclusion, Subramaniam's definition means that we have to exclude virtually all African countries south of the Sahara from any talk of administrative reform. I am sure he did not intend this to result from his analysis. Be that as it may, for our purpose, I regard as administrative reform any systematic changes in the administrative system (no matter how old) designed to lead to more efficient, effective and responsive administration. By *responsive* I mean that the reforms must be geared towards the achievement of national objectives. One must, however, distinguish between large-scale administrative reforms and minor isolated administrative reforms. Examples of the latter include minor improvements, care or maintenance such as new leave rates, housing allowances, creation of new posts, etc. To qualify as reform, there must be an across-the-board change, the aim of which is the achievement of national objectives in the shortest possible time, and with the least expenditure in human and material resources.

The case for reform

At independence, Nigeria inherited an administration which was essentially designed for the maintenance of law and order in order to facilitate the exploitation of the natural resources of the country. Such an administrative system was highly centralised and undemocratic. One of the most important pre-independence promises of politicians was that independence would usher economic development, life more abundant, and a democratic and participatory government. As the new politically independent government embarked on economic development, government activities expanded, and it was impossible for the old system to cope with the increasing new demands on it. One of the results was that the gap between plans and performance grew wider through either administrative incompetence or the inadequacy of the institutional framework.

The need for reform resulting from these gaps was consistently highlighted in the report of international organisations especially the reports by the World Bank, the United Nations and the Ford Foundation. These organisations drew attention to the fact that one of the greatest obstacles to rapid economic development was not lack of finance, as was popularly believed, but lack of administrative capability to manage available resources.

Why there were very few reforms

One of the main reasons why there has been only very few reforms was because of the lack of awareness of the need for reform among the ruling elite. In spite of the gap between plans and performance, and in spite of the reports of international organisations, it took Nigeria twelve years before it took the first bold step to initiate reforms. I am referring to the establishment of the Public Service Review Commission[1]. Now I know that even that bold step was the brainchild of only a few members of the government who saw the need for that.[2] The majority of their colleagues thought that those arguing for reforms were only raising a false alarm, or crying wolf when none was in sight.

There is also a historical reason for the lack of interest in administrative reforms. During the agitation for independence,

---

[1] September 1972 to September 1974.
[2] Essentially Professor Adebayo Adedeji who was then the Federal Commissioner for Economic Development.

the politicians demanded and got political independence. They did not demand and, therefore, did not get administrative independence. By administrative independence, I mean a change in the style of managing government business so as to meet the expectations of the people. But failure to demand administrative independence might not have been an oversight. It seemed deliberate in the sense that both the politicians and top African civil servants appeared anxious to maintain the existing colonial administrative structures and practices in order to prove that they were not less competent than their erstwhile colonial masters. One of the results was that African civil servants became more British than the British, and proudly quoted British precedents and examples in the solution of essentially African problems. The interesting part of it all was that British practices continued to command respect in Nigeria long after such practices had been discarded as obsolete in Britain.

I will like to conclude this part of my address by admitting that it is not easy to initiate reforms. By nature, governments are bureaucratic institutions, and one of the attributes of a bureaucracy is a desire to perpetuate itself. Being usually resistant to change, governments often regard reforms as threats to its continued existence. This is why it requires not only an awareness but the commitment and courage of a political leader to carry through worthwhile reforms.

In this regard, Nigeria is a good lesson in administrative reform. The absence of reforms during the Balewa regime was essentially due to lack of awareness. But it must be conceded that the regime had to grapple with the highly demanding tasks of Africanising the Service and setting up the paraphernalia and apparatuses of independence such as a foreign ministry, formulating a foreign policy, representation at international bodies and setting up diplomatic missions abroad. That only few reforms took place during the Gowon regime was essentially due to lack of courage and bureaucratic resistance. I remember that some of the recommendations of the Public Service Review Commission were branded revolutionary and shelved. It was not until the advent of the Mohammed regime that several shelved recommendations were implemented. In that regard, the death of Mohammed is a particular loss to administrative reformers in Nigeria.

Areas of urgent administrative reform

I now come to areas of urgent administrative reform. Unfortunately, time will not permit their detailed discussion. I will list a few for further discussion in your future seminars. They are:

- The urgent need for enlightened administrative leadership.

- The need for the use of modern management methods such as scientific decision-making, management by objectives, performance budgeting, project management, cost benefit analysis, etc.

- The need for modern staff development policies including up-to-date selection methods, effective training and delegation of power, performance appraisal, and promotion based on proven performance.

- The need for clear definitions of objectives and targets for ministries and departments with time targets.

- The need for effective co-ordination of the various arms of government and its agencies towards the achievement of predetermined goals and objectives.

- The need for less rigid and less hierarchical structures in the Service.

- The need to encourage intra- and inter-sectoral mobility.

- The need to examine the role and tenure of office of public officers who hold sensitive and quasi- political appointments, especially with regards to the envisaged change from the parliamentary to the presidential system of government.

(11)

Political Neutrality of Civil Servants ✦

> *"The problem area is when we come to deal with officers whose jobs have policy contents, and whose conditions of service are neither strictly political nor strictly career. This is an area that calls for urgent examination and reform. Unfortunately, the area is manned by the mandarins of the civil service who by training and experience are resistant to change."*

Introduction

Some of the civil service legacies which were left by the British in their former colonies are now under attack as a result of developments and problems arising in those countries. Among these important changes are:

i.   The tradition of selfless service
ii. The concept of a career service
iii. The tradition of a politically neutral service.

I intend to deal briefly with the first legacy and then concentrate on the second because of its relevance to the third which is the subject-matter of this paper.

The principle of selfless service means that civil servants of all grades should display transparent honesty and integrity in the discharge of their duties. In particular, they should not use their public powers to enhance their private interests. Specific provisions prohibit engaging in any business, the management of which might conflict with official duties. This code of behaviour has come under much attack and abuse that one country — Kenya — had to lift the ban, not only to stop further abuses, but more importantly to enable Kenyan indigenes to participate in the economic development of their country which was dominated by foreigners. In many other African countries, the prohibition

---

✦ Address presented to a training workshop on public administration and management, Zimbabwe, April 1981.

has been rendered ineffective because the governments turned blind eyes to business activities run by the wives of public officers. There is, therefore, a need for a thorough re-examination of the rule with a view to either abrogating it as Kenya has done, or to strengthen it as it is the case in Nigeria where the 1979 constitution prescribed a stringent code of conduct for public officers. The 1979 constitution established a Code of Conduct Bureau before which public officers shall declare their assets on assuming and relinquishing office. An officer is obliged to declare in writing all his property, assets, and liabilities, including those of his spouse and unmarried children under the age of twenty-one years. The bureau is empowered to examine declarations and receive complaints about non-compliance. Members of the bureau are appointed by the president subject to the confirmation of the senate. But once appointed, they are directly responsible to the National Assembly.

One of the strictest codes of conduct is embodied in the Tanzanian Leadership Code which prohibits a holder of public office, either in the party, Parliament, or the civil service from having more than one source of income. This includes running a business and owning shares in a private company.

Career service[1]

The career service is a system by which a young man is recruited at an early age into the civil service, with an implied promise of a life career , during which he works his way up the hierarchy of the service. The promise of a career means the assurance of a life-long employment which can be terminated only by mental or physical incapacity or the commission of a criminal offence. The system is a closed one because it has no adequate provision for the admission of outsiders (older, qualified and experienced persons) into the higher grades of the hierarchy. When such persons are employed, they are on temporary and contractual

---

[1]   Some of the discussion here repeats the discussion on "The Tenure of Office of Top Civil Servants"

basis, and without the rights and privileges of the established permanent staff.

An important feature of the career system is the pension scheme which entitles an officer to additional remuneration on his retirement on grounds of age. This varies from one-third to half of the retiring salary, depending on the years of service.

Another feature of the system is the existence of a series of protective regulations against dismissal or termination of appointment. The regulations are so stringent that a doctor will, for example, find it very difficult to dismiss an incompetent or dishonest ward-servant, nor can a head of department easily terminate the services of a disobedient office messenger. In some countries, there is a convention which has almost the force of a regulation, and which says that at least two written warning notices should precede the termination of the appointment of an employee, no matter how lowly graded.

In Britain, the career system is so firmly established that it has not been easy to get rid of incompetent officers before their retiring age. It took an Act of Parliament[2] before the Foreign Office was able to retire members who though good subordinates were considered unfit for further promotion. Later, another Act of Parliament[3] made it possible for home civil servants to be retired after the age of fifty in the interest of efficiency. But these Acts were used sparingly. A minister once described the difficulties he had in pensioning off an inefficient officer in these words:

> Theoretically, it is now possible to retire an officer, with pension, at any time, after the age of fifty. On one occasion, I tried to do this. I aroused against myself all the camaraderie of the civil service and every obstacle was put in my way.[4]

Even the conviction for a criminal offence does not automatically result in a dismissal. Disciplinary proceedings will

---

[2]   See the Foreign Office Act of 1943.
[3]   See the Superannuation Act of 1949.
[4]   Quoted in an article written in *The New Statesman* of November 13, 1954, written by Mr. G.R. Stranss who was the minister of supply in the labour government of that time.

have to be initiated and this includes a review of the court's judgement. In the end, the disciplinary authority may impose a lesser punishment than dismissal such as reduction in rank or seniority, stoppage of increment, or ordinary reprimand. Sometimes, dismissal for a criminal offence does not affect the pension rights of the officer.

One of the results of such a career system supported by protective regulations is that almost every civil servant remains in his job until retiring age which varies between fifty and sixty. During the colonial era, the retirement age was optional at forty-five but compulsory at fifty-five. Some African countries have amended this. Nigeria, Ghana, Tanzania and Zambia have each raised the compulsory retiring age from fifty-five to sixty. Three reasons have been given for this:

The first is that colonial administrators put the retiring age low to enable them take up other jobs in their home country. Second, the control of malaria and other communicable diseases, and the rise in the general standard of living, have resulted in higher life expectancy. Third, is that in order to fill the gap left by the retirement of expatriate officers, the few experienced local officers are allowed to remain in the service for as long as they are able and willing to serve.

It is argued in some quarters that the career system, as described above, is unsuitable for the civil service of emergent African countries because ministers prefer and, in fact, want to work with people who share their dynamism and emotional commitment to the success of their policies and programmes; that the system operates best where civil servants have a tradition of competence, impartiality and dedicated service to the nation — qualities which are at the moment rare in African countries. It is further argued that the career system is expensive and should not, therefore, be continued in underdeveloped countries; that the system is bureaucratic, exclusive, stagnant and resistant to change, whilst what African countries need is the constant introduction of new talents and men with ideas who will be agents and catalysts for change. It is equally argued that the system creates an administrative elite, which leads to the widening of the gap between the 'government and the governed.

Political neutrality

Political neutrality means that a civil servant must give loyal service and support to the government of the day, irrespective of that government's political colour. He must also refrain from participating in political activities and controversies. This requirement is seen as a natural consequence, and a *quid pro quo* of the career system. Without a career system, political neutrality will have no base. It is the security and protection accorded civil servants under the rules of the career and merit systems that justify the restrictions imposed on them by the principles of neutrality. Unlike his minister, a civil servant cannot be removed from office at the will of the electorate. As we have seen earlier, a minister may even have a lot of difficulties in sacking a civil servant. For this, the civil servant must refrain from involving himself in politics.

Several arguments have been raised against this code of behaviour. In the first place, it is argued that the prohibitions in the ex-British colonies are more stringent and all embracing than they are in either Britain or the United States. In Nigeria, for example, the Civil Service Rules[5] prohibits an officer from.

a. holding any office, paid or unpaid, permanent or temporal, in any political organisation;
b. offering himself or nominating any one else as a candidate at an election of members of a local government council or a state or federal Legislature;
c. indicating publicly his support of, or opposition to, any party, candidate or policy;
d. engaging in canvassing support for political candidates.

These prohibitions apply to all officers irrespective of grade. In Britain, the rules divide civil servants into three groups for the purposes of political activities:[6]

---

[5] See the Federal Civil Service Rule 04213.

i. The "politically free" group, consisting of industrial and non-office grades who are free to engage in any political activity including standing for Parliament (although they would have to resign from the Service, if elected).

ii. The "politically restricted" group, consisting of all staff above the executive officer level, who are debarred from national political activities, but may apply for permission to take part in local political activities.

iii. The "intermediate" group, comprising all other staff — mainly members of the clerical and typing grades who may apply for permission to take part in national or local political activities apart from adoption as a parliamentary candidate. Recently, an independent committee of inquiry reported in favour of the retention of the rules but recommended the transfer of substantial number of staff from the "restricted" to the "intermediate" group. It also recommended an appeal body for staff who are refused permission.

In America, the Hatch Acts of 1939 and 1940 bar most civil servants in the national, state and local government services who are paid from federal funds from active participation in politics. Most governmental units with merit systems impose similar limitations on their civil servants. Because the American civil service is a mixture of the career and patronage systems, the doctrine of political neutrality does not apply to all public officers. It applies to only the 90% who come under the merit system, but not to the remaining 10% who are politically appointed. These are heads of agencies, and occupants of policy-making and confidential positions. The interesting thing in the American system is that some of the political appointments are made from career civil servants, but the majority of them are outsiders who combine professional expertise with sympathy for the policies and programmes of the party in power. The argument for bringing them in is that the career civil servant is by training neutral and

---

[6] See *Britain* 1980, p. 58.

anonymous, and cannot, therefore, be expected to advocate or implement government policies with the same dynamism, devotion and commitment as a political appointee. Furthermore, the patronage system is necessary for the survival of political parties. When a civil servant is appointed to a political position, he loses his tenure and neutrality while in the post. At the end of the administration, he may revert to his civil service post or retire if he is not assigned to a new job.

Another argument against the doctrine of political neutrality is a historical one. From the beginning, African civil servants have been involved in politics. They have identified themselves with the struggle for national independence. By training themselves to become efficient public servants, they have helped to make self-government possible, and they have been able to use their experience to further the national cause. One may, however, describe such involvement as national politics rather than party politics.

Opponents of neutrality also refer to the recent development in the African political scene, which points to its inappropriateness in the African situation. The first is the shift in the political power structure. Political power no longer has the demagogic agitational mass movement base it had in pre-independence days. It is fast acquiring a realistic and economic base. Anti-imperialist slogans, and promises of better days, are no longer sufficient to mobilise the populace. Political parties are now expected to present records of concrete achievements: the number of schools and hospitals built; the mileage of roads tarred; and the general rise in the level of consumption. Political leaders are, therefore, realising that their continuance in power is dependent on their ability to bring about rapid social and economic changes in order to satisfy the yearnings and aspirations of their supporters. This is one of the reasons for the various development plans and programmes which have become a common feature of every African government.

A natural concomitant of this desire for quick change and progress is the desire to ensure that the civil service is responsive to political leadership. Responsiveness is interpreted by politicians to mean the control of those civil servants whose jobs have considerable political content or extensive executive powers. They argue that they do not see how they can fulfil their promises to the electorate without controlling the civil servants who are responsible for the execution of their policies. They do not see how they are to be held responsible for the official actions and conducts of civil servants if they have no part in their appointment, deployment and discipline.

In their bid to gain control of the civil service, many governments took steps to amend the independence constitution that made public service commissions executive and independent of political control. The amendments either made the commission advisory, or vested the powers of appointments, promotions and discipline in the head of government. In 1970, Nigeria, Sierra Leone and Kenya were the few African countries that retained the executive public service commission. Tanzania and Uganda vested all powers of appointment in the head of government who could delegate his powers to a public service commission. Ghana and Botswana merged the public service commission with the central personnel agency. Sir Seretse Khama, president of Botswana, defended the transfer in these words:

> The view of the civil service as an independent political body, which is often used to justify the retention of such institutions as executive Public Service Commissions, can be qualified. In most African countries, the Public Service represents an important part, if not the major part of the best-paid and most influential group in the country. Given human frailty, there is no reason why public servants should be more immune to group interests than any other organised articulate group. Even in developed countries where public servants make up a much smaller percentage of higher income groups, they are inherently likely to reflect the values and prejudices of that group. But in developing societies, any in-built tendency there might be for public service to reflect sectional interests too closely is offset by the existence of other organised pressure groups such as trade unions, consumer groups and business and professional bodies. In many African countries, such pressure groups are often weak or altogether absent. Hence, the Public Service wields considerable influence.[7]

The second political development is that of one-party systems.

---

[7] Cited in the Report of the 9th Inter-African Public Administration Seminar, 1970, p. 4.

The only multiparty governments in black Africa, south of the Sahara, are Nigeria, Gambia, Mauritius, Ghana, Botswana and Zimbabwe.[8] The rest have one form or the other of one-party democracy. The one-party phenomenon started with Tanzania in the 1960s, where it was then argued that the multiparty system was alien to African political culture. It was also argued that the government of a typical traditional African village is made up of a village council which meets in the village square to deliberate on matters of common interest; that such a council does not resolve itself into opposing groups as if at war or in a football field. In any case, the present urgent and complex problems of forging national unity and bringing about rapid economic development cannot be solved through the wasteful, divisive and dilatory processes of the multiparty system. They require total mobilisation of all forces — economic, social, political, the civil service, and the bureaucracy.

There are still in Africa today, leaders who use the arguments of the 1960s to perpetuate themselves in power. In addition, these set of leaders now advance a new argument — the overriding importance of national security and stability. Consequently, opposition parties are often branded disruptive and destabilising, and their members are either detained or charged with treason. In the end, the opposition is either emasculated or outlawed. But this has proved short-sighted, at least in West Africa, where, in spite of the one-party system, the people of Ghana, Togo and Dahomey[9] resorted to *coups d'etat* as a means of changing their governments.

In one-party governments, like Tanzania[10], civil servants are completely politicised. They are encouraged to join the one political party and they can stand for parliamentary elections. They need not resign before doing so, for service in Parliament or service as minister is service to the nation, and qualifies one for

---

[8]   That is, 1981 when the author presented the paper.
[9]   Now called Benin Republic.
[10] Tanzania has since become a "multiparty democracy".

pension. This is also the practice in the United States where a civil servant appointed to a political office can count such service for pension purposes.

An often quoted advantage of a politicised civil service is that it makes civil servants to put their education and experience at the disposal of political parties, particularly during the formulation of strategic party policies.

Politics of appointment and of the role function

Another argument against political neutrality relate to the politics of appointment and the politics of the role function of certain grades of public officers, namely, permanent secretaries. There is no gainsaying the fact that there is politics in the appointment of top civil servants, particularly permanent secretaries. The constitution recognises this fact by vesting the powers of appointment, not on independent executive public service commissions, but on politicians — the prime minister or president.

That political considerations come into play is not in doubt because, at that level, loyalty, security and sympathy with the aspirations of political leadership outweigh considerations of merit and efficiency. Cases abound where obsolescent and incompetent officers are appointed permanent secretaries in order to reflect geographical spread in overall appointment, and to give the people of particular areas a feeling of belonging. The 1979 Nigerian constitution, section 5 (5) has given expression to this political fact of life by requiring the president, in the exercise of his powers of appointment (which includes the appointment of permanent secretaries), to have regards to the federal character of Nigeria and the need to promote national unity. Section 14 (3) of the same constitution explains the concept of *federal character* thus:

> The composition of the Government of the Federation or any of its agencies and the conduct of its affairs shall be carried out in such a manner as to reflect the federal character of Nigeria, and the need to promote national unity, and also to command the national loyalty, thereby ensuring that there shall be no predominance of persons

from a few states or from a few ethnic or sectional groups in that government or in any of its agencies.

A permanent secretary, by his role, is expected to advise his ministers on policy, and to supervise the execution of decided policies. Even where he does not agree with a certain line of policy, once a decision is taken, his job is to guide his minister to achieve his objectives with the least difficulty and delay. He is expected not only to be sympathetic but also to share the enthusiasm and commitment of his minister. Can any one in all honesty fulfil such a function without being involved with the politics of the matter? In view of the political considerations in the appointment of permanent secretaries, and taking into account their policy role functions, I submit that it is unrealistic, and a fiction, to expect political neutrality from officers at that level.

Conclusion

We have tried to show that the doctrine of political neutrality is one of the British legacies that have come under attack in several African countries. In one-party states, it is attacked as an exclusive and undesirable policy. In multiparty states, the attack is often against its wholesale application to all grades of public officers.

I feel that even in one-party states, the doctrine is still recommendable provided that its application is limited to civil servants whose jobs are essentially professional, executive and with little or no policy content— doctors in hospitals, lawyers in courts, teachers in schools, engineers at work sites, and architects at their drawing boards. These professionals normally come under the career system with all its characteristics of security of tenure, anonymity and pensionability.

The problem area is when we come to deal with officers whose jobs have policy contents, and whose conditions of service are neither strictly political nor strictly career. This is an area that calls for urgent examination and reform. Unfortunately, the area is manned by the mandarins of the civil service who by training and experience are resistant to change. I will like to believe that the reforms which I will recommend in this paper are in the best interests of all concerned. I believe that my suggestions will help to preserve the traditions of the service, its health, morale and integrity. Above all, it will improve the relationship between politicians and civil servants.

I propose that the Service should be restructured to reflect the realities of the present political situation. The new structure should distinguish and separate political appointments from career appointments, jobs with policy contents from those that are purely executive and professional; jobs that require security of tenure from those that should normally last for the duration of the appointing administrations, and jobs that demand political neutrality from those that do not. What is proposed is not much different from the age-long distinction between politics and administration.

The structure I am proposing is that the post of professional head of department should be the end of all career posts in the civil service. It should be the terminal post to which civil servants should normally aspire to reach before retirement. The post of permanent secretary does not, either by appointment or by function, belong to the career cadre. It should, therefore, be removed from that cadre and transferred to a ministerial cadre to which it rightly belongs. There is also a need to strengthen and deepen such a ministerial cadre in order to enable it cope with the increasing policy demands and complexities of modern governments.

The term "permanent secretary" becomes inappropriate in such a cadre, and should be dropped in favour of terms like assistant or deputy minister, which more correctly describes the functions. An enlarged political/ministerial cadre could consist of the following hierarchy: special adviser, assistant minister, deputy minister, and minister. Top civil servants of the grades of heads or deputy heads of departments could be appointed to the ministerial cadre, but such appointments should be in the nature of temporary assignments at the end of which the officers will again revert to their substantive career posts.

Let me again underline that these proposals are neither new nor original. They have been applied successfully in countries like France and the United States. In France, political appointments— whether from the civil service or from outside— form part of the extra-departmental group in every ministry, known as the *Mini Cabinet.* In the United States, the appointments are not so much an application of the patronage system. They are a means of mobilising the best-qualified and acceptable men to help the administration achieve its stated objectives. The success of the system in Africa will depend on the availability of the required number of men and women of the required calibre and expertise. But since the system is successful in former French territories, there is no reason why it should not succeed in Anglophone Africa.

Questions for discussion

1. Political neutrality is a sophisticated concept which developed in the 19th Century out of the social, economic and political circumstances of the British people. Can it be easily transplanted to other climes that do not have similar economic and social backgrounds?

2. Is the political neutrality of the British civil service not a fiction? If not, is the success of the principle not due to the fact that both the minister and the top civil servant belong to the same social class with similar education and economic backgrounds?

3. In the last twenty years, the relationship between ministers and top civil servants has been a recurring theme at seminars and workshops:

    a. What are the causes of the tension in the relationship?

    b. Is overemphasis on the differences between politics and administration possibly one of the causes?

    c. Is overprotection accorded by the magic words, *permanent and pensionable,* in the civil service rules, otherwise known as general orders, a contributory cause?

    d. Has the loyalty dichotomy created in the independence

constitutions by the establishment of independent public service commissions anything to do with it?

e. Is the inability of civil servants to share the enthusiasm and dynamism of politicians not a major cause?

(12)

The African Public Servant as a Public Policy-Maker ⬥

"Public policy-making denotes the whole process of articulating and defining problems, formulating possible solutions into political demands, channelling those demands into the political system, seeking sanctions, or the legitimation of the preferred course of action, implementation, monitoring and review (feedback). Who participates in what role in this process depends to a great extent on the structure of political decision-making."

Introduction

In many African countries, the term public servant is defined as *the holder of any office the emoluments attaching to which are paid out of the consolidated revenue fund or any other public fund.* Such a wide definition includes not only traditional civil servants but also holders of political and judicial offices, as well as holders of posts in public corporations and universities. For the purposes of this paper, however, the term will be used in its restricted sense of referring only to permanent and pensionable public officers, that is, civil servants.

Public policy may be defined as *a sanctioned course of action addressed to a particular problem or group of related problems that affect the society at large.* Public policy-making denotes the whole process of researching, articulating and defining problems, formulating possible solutions into political demands, channelling those demands into the political system, seeking sanctions, or the legitimation of the preferred course of action, implementation, monitoring and review (feedback). Who participates in what role

---

⬥   Paper presented to a roundtable conference on "African Public Services and Public Policy-Making in the 1980s", Mahe, Seychelles, September 22-29, 1980.

in this process depends to a great extent on the structure of political decision-making.

Viewed thus, the central argument of this paper is that the public servant as defined above is not and should not consider himself as a policy-maker. Admittedly, he has an important role to play in this process: he can collect, collate and analyse data, he can propose options or alternative courses of action, he can advise on possible consequences of the various options, but the question of choice of a course of action and the sanctioning of the same is political action which is the domain of politicians. Today in Britain, the ministers are determined to demonstrate that they, and not the civil servants, make policy.

Colonial & military aberrations

Civil servants, no matter how highly placed, should resist the temptation of arrogating to themselves a role that does not properly and legitimately belong to them. They must not allow the abnormal circumstances of colonialism and militarism to delude them into believing that they have a decisive role in policy-making. Nor should they be so naive as to interpret their important supportive role of assembling, collating and interpreting data and suggesting alternative policy implementation options as policy-making.

There is no doubt that during the colonial era, civil servants had very wide powers and appeared to be both initiators and executors of policy. To a casual observer, they played a double role of politicians and civil servants. A closer examination would, however, reveal that colonial civil servants from the governor to the district officer were merely executing the policies of the party in power, which were transmitted through the colonial office. No colonial governor would make any deviation from established policy without the sanction of his political master, the secretary of state for the colonies. He could, however, advice on policies he would like to be adopted but the final decision rested with the colonial secretary.

Top civil servants also had extensive powers during the early independence period and during the military regime. The first crop of politicians were the main freedom fighters. They concentrated on wresting power from the colonialists and had little time for articulating post-independence policies. The result was that on independence, they relied on civil servants to help them formulate government policies. In those days, it was very common for a minister to ask his permanent secretary to prepare a policy paper for the ministry. The paper did not, however, become government policy until the minister had taken it to the executive council and obtained the approval of his colleagues. As the ministers acquired administrative and political experience, they assumed their rightful roles as policy-makers. But no sooner were they able to do this than they were corrupted by power. This was the case in both Nigeria and Ghana. The result was military take-overs and the reversal of the trend towards the development of proper roles in the policy-making process. Young army officers were less educated and less politically experienced than the politicians they ousted. Civil servants were once again called upon to help formulate and execute policies. These roles, important as they were, should, however, be regarded as aberrations caused by the abnormal circumstances of colonialism and military intervention.

Role of civil servants in the context of recent developments

The question which this conference is called upon to answer is whether, in the circumstances of the eighties, the civil servant should continue to play this double and potentially precarious role. In answering this question, we must take note of two recent developments in the African political scene: the first is the move from the parliamentary to the presidential system of government. Today, there are very few parliamentary prime ministers in either Franco or Anglophone Africa. Most of the countries — Ivory Coast, Guinea, Senegal, Cameroon, Kenya, Sierra Leone, Tanzania and Zambia— have presidents whose powers are close to those of the American president. The argument is that the division of powers between the heads of states and heads of government is meaningless in the light of the many ugly experiences of that experiment in Africa. No African head of state has been content with the position of a mere figurehead. The experiences in Nigeria, Uganda, Lesotho and Swaziland are cases in point. In these countries, the system of sharing power has resulted in a clash of personalities and interests, a conflict of authority and an unnecessary complexity and uncertainty in government relations. The built-in conflicts make it difficult to determine ultimate responsibility for success or failure and, in crisis, who is to act.

The second political development is that of the one-party system, and the increasing popularity of the presidential system of government in Africa. Surprisingly, these developments, especially the increasing popularity of the presidential system, have not been accompanied by any changes in the parliamentary hierarchical structure of the civil service.

One of the greatest strains is the threat which the new political system poses to the integrity, authority and security of the Service. In almost every African State, the installation of a new president is accompanied by a series of premature retirements or termination of the appointments of top civil servants. In 1975, in Nigeria, over 1000 public servants lost their jobs when a new regime came to power. The harm done by the purge is still with the civil service. Outsiders and some relatively junior serving officers are usually appointed as replacements. Even when replacements come from within the Service, they are appointed without due regard to civil service norms and procedures. These actions are part of a determined attempt by politicians, particularly those operating the presidential system, to control top civil servants.

To an executive president, the hierarchical structure of the Service and the orientation of the incumbents of its top echelons, are not conducive to a programmed deliverance of his election promises. He requires not a hierarchy of generalist assistant secretaries, senior assistant secretaries, principal assistant secretaries, deputy secretaries, etc., but teams of action -oriented professional managers, engineers, architects, town planners, agronomists, veterinarians, teachers, lawyers, and doctors who are organised for the expeditious execution of specific projects.

As a politician and a man of action, he expects from civil servants not learned minutes in files but action on the ground.

These problems of structure, calibre and orientation of the civil service are not new. They have confronted older democracies and have been solved, at least in presidential systems, by the introduction of a structure that has a clear distinction between policy-makers and policy implementers, between politically-appointed officers and those appointed by an independent public service commission. The former are a cadre of elite specialists in various disciplines with sympathy for the success of the party in power. As specialists, they are able to martial all the necessary data and materials necessary for the formulation of party policies, and programmes. They occupy top and sensitive posts in ministries where some of them engage in policy formulation, and others in the supervision of their execution. It would be asking too much to expect a civil servant busily engaged with policy implementation and management of projects to find the time for policy deliberation. He could, however, make useful comments from his practical experience but he should *not* and must not be saddled with substantive policy-making.

A lot of the failure of government projects and programmes in the past could be traced to the amateurish use of busy civil servants in the formulation of government policies. Modern government is big business and if it is to succeed, it must adopt modern business methods. These include the use of consultants and experts in the formulation of policies. The success of the private sector largely depends on its proper use of human resources and modern tools of management. One of the ways of improving the management system of government would be to give some of its top officials, especially those in economic ministries, periods of secondment to industries. Such interchange would also help to improve the relationship between the two sectors.

It is interesting that even non presidential governments, like that of Britain, have realised the need for some top specialist appointments from outside the civil service in the fields of economics, science and technology. The new men come from industries and the universities to assist in policy matters. They were accepted by the Service because this recruitment does not affect the prospects of members of the career service. Besides the team of policy-makers, a presidential system has a cadre of career civil servants who form about 90% of the Service. The members consist of action-oriented professional men and women who get things done if they are to be done at all. They have the know-how and provide continuity and practical experience. They come under the public service commission which operates the merit system and provides protection against the pressures of politics. The execution of policies is as important, if not more important, than policy-making. Policies will remain dreams or blue-prints in file jackets unless they are implemented. This emphasises the importance of recruiting more professionals into the Service, and offering them attractive conditions in order to retain them. In the United States of America, three out of every five federal career civil servants are professionals.

The importance of a contented permanent civil service cannot be over-emphasised. They not only implement policies but also offer useful advice to policy-makers. More importantly, they provide continuity in government policies and, in times of great discontinuity, to the nation itself. Between 1947 and 1967, for instance, Italy had about thirty governments, some lasting only a matter of days. The nation, however, survived because it had an efficient permanent civil service. The same is also true of France which had in the past experienced frequent changes of government. During the heat of the Nigerian crisis in July 1966, it was the civil service that kept the country together.

If the civil service in the new African States is to survive, it has to adapt itself to the changes in the political structure. This adaptation will involve separating sensitive policy advising jobs from the normal civil service jobs and prescribing separate terms and conditions for each cadre. In practical terms, it would mean removing the posts of permanent secretary and heads of departments from the career cadre. Persons holding such posts will consequently lose their security of tenure and anonymity. They should formally retire from the Service and take up new appointments, preferably on contract. Contract appointments would enable the officer and the appointing administration to review further employment at regular intervals, and, in any case, at the end of each administration. Once the officers concerned have demonstrated intellectual competence and enthusiasm, the in-coming administration will want to retain their services. This has happened in Britain with the Rothchild group. They were brought in by the labour government to assist in policy matters (research and policy analysis) but due to their devotion and commitment, the succeeding conservative government retained them. In this manner, a third group of public officers are emerging — an elite group distinct from the straightforward political appointees (usually from outside the civil service) and professional civil servants. This group occupies the grey area between the two distinct cadres. They resemble what in America is known as *the in-and-outers*. These are men who come into government service for a limited number of years (three or four) and return to private life to be available at a future date for either further government or political appointment. There is a great need in African governments for such an elite professional group.

Conclusion

I have taken a rather negative view of the conference theme. This is largely because of my belief that policy-making is politics, and that it should not, in the generally improved educational circumstances of the eighties, be the responsibility of the traditional civil service. It should be the responsibility of politicians who are assisted by politically appointed experts who may be in the public service but outside the civil service. To saddle civil servants with policy-making will lead to the destruction of the attributes of the Service, namely, security, impartiality, anonymity, and pensionability. Civil servants should be eligible for appointment to political posts, but on such appointments, they should leave the civil service proper.

I am aware that such an ideal model of the relationship between politicians and civil servants in the process of policy-making can function satisfactorily where there is a big private sector with abundance of talent and expertise. African countries are bound to experience difficulties in the operations of this model in view of the real shortage of talent in both government and industry. But having opted for a presidential system of government, we should not drag our feet in fashioning out an appropriate civil service structure which is capable of servicing the political system.

13

Tenure of Office of Top Civil Servants ✦

"Changes are taking place all over Africa at such a pace that it is no longer prudent to look too far ahead into the future. There is always the danger of proposals and suggestions being overtaken by events. New ideas and social forces are bound to bring about new concepts."

Introduction

One of the traditions left behind by the British in their former African territories is that of a closed career civil service. This is a system by which a young man is recruited at an early age into the Service with an implied promise of a life-long career during which he works his way up the hierarchy of the Service. The promise of a career means an assurance of life-long employment which can be terminated only by mental or physical incapacity or the commission of a criminal offence. The system is a closed one because it has no adequate provision for the admission of outsiders (older, qualified and experienced persons) into the higher grades of the hierarchy. When such persons are employed, they are on contract and without the rights and privileges of the established and permanent staff.

Who are the top civil servants?

Before I consider the effects of the prevailing conditions on the tenure of office of top civil servants, we should first define the term. For the purposes of this paper, the term "top civil servants" will be used to describe the most senior officials in the civil service. They hold key positions which are normally graded super-scale. They work in close collaboration with ministers, advising them on policies, and implementing policy decisions. This group includes permanent secretaries, professional heads of departments, and their deputies. It excludes local government

---

✦ Paper presented at the Public Administration Seminar at Gaborone Botswana, 3rd-9th October, 1970.

employees and managers of public corporations and government companies, for we are here concerned with the traditional civil servants and not with the wider group of public servants. Numerically, this group represents less than one per cent of the total number of the staff in the civil service. The educational background of the members of this group is a mixed one. Majority are graduates, but there are still some who came up through the ranks with no more than secondary school education. This latter group may have considerable experience but they often lack the talent to deal with problems of development administration. In Ghana, at independence, the average age of men serving as permanent secretaries, and in equivalent posts, was thirty-eight. About half had entered the administrative service directly and had about ten years service in government. The others reached the top through the clerical service and had fifteen to twenty years service. In Kenya, the British permanent secretaries were replaced by Africans who were all graduates. Their average age was only thirty-three. Today, Kenya has twenty permanent secretaries, twelve of whom are graduates. The average age today is forty. In Uganda, six of twenty-one permanent secretaries have no academic qualifications, and the average age is forty-one.

Ecology of the top civil servants

Several developments have made it necessary to reappraise the suitability of the traditions of a career civil service particularly as they relate to the permanent and pensionable tenure of top civil servants:

Shift in the political power structure

First among these developments is the shift in the political power structure. Political power no longer has the demagogic agitational mass movement base it had in pre-independence days. It is acquiring a realistic and economic base. Political success and acceptability is no longer dependent on anti-imperialist slogans and promises of better days but on concrete achievements: the number of schools and hospitals built; the mileage of roads tarred; the improvement in the prices of primary products, and the general rise in the level of consumption. Political leaders are therefore realising that their continuance in power is dependent on their ability to bring about rapid social and economic changes in order to satisfy the aspirations and yearnings of their supporters. This is the reason for the various development plans and programmes that have become a common feature of every African government. A natural concomitant of this desire for change and progress is the desire to ensure that the civil service is responsive to political leadership. This means the control of top civil servants whose jobs have considerable political contents or extensive executive powers.

The argument of some politicians is that they do not see how they can discharge their ministerial responsibilities without controlling the civil servants who are responsible for the execution of their policies. How can they be held responsible for the official actions and conducts of civil servants if they have no part in their appointment, deployment and discipline? In support of this argument, they cite the case in the United Kingdom where the whole department is under the minister's control, including responsibility for every promotion within it.

I feel, however, that we must make a distinction between ministerial control of civil servants in Britain and the control demanded by ministers in new African States. In Britain, ministerial control is on the whole rather formal. Lesser appointments and promotions are conducted in the name of the minister by the senior officials of the ministry and the minister usually does not interfere. He may, however, take some interests in the appointment of some senior officials of the ministry such as assistant secretaries. In such cases, he will usually be content to accept the advice of his senior official advisers. Even in cases where his views are the deciding factor such as in the appointment of under-secretaries, he dares not depart from established conventions. If he makes prejudiced appointments, the staff would protest.

On the other hand, in Africa where traditions and conventions are not yet well-established, "ministerial control" would be interpreted as "absolute discretion". Africa has the further weakness of having an unenlightened public opinion which often enables many people to get away with irregularities, improprieties and even crimes. The more the people demanded progress, and the more development activities expanded, the more the politicians wanted to tighten their control of the top civil servants. The exercise of improper control has made the position of civil servants very sensitive and vulnerable. This has led to the great turnover of permanent secretaries, and to some resignations.

Decline in Status and Prestige

A second development which has made it necessary to reappraise the suitability of the tradition of a career civil service is the decline in the status and prestige of top civil servants. Civil service jobs no longer have the status and prestige they had during the colonial era or in the early years of independence when politicians were settling down to their jobs, powers and responsibilities. A great deal of the status and prestige belonging to the service has been lost to the politicians and to the managers of the expanding and influential private sector. In the 1960s, for example, a permanent secretary was among the top brass of the society, and his appointment usually appeared in the headlines of local newspapers. Today, such appointments receive only a minor mention, if at all.

The politician is not prepared to share his status and prestige with anybody, much less the civil servant. In fact, he seems jealous of whatever respect and confidence the public still has in the civil servant, and he does not lose any opportunity of putting him in his place, or of exposing his shortcomings and magnifying his mistakes—real and imaginary. The Hansard of some Parliaments contains several unwarranted and/or exaggerated attacks on the integrity and efficiency of civil servants. This lack of respect and regard has hurt the pride of ambitious civil servants who do not hesitate to recall that some of the politicians were in fact failures.

This unhealthy relationship has driven some top civil servants into politics and some into the private sector.

The attractions of the private sector have led, in some countries, to a definite brain drain from the Service. Other contributory factors for the brain drain from the civil service include:

1   *Professional frustration:* There are instances where professional officers have resigned because they were not allowed to practice their profession in accordance with generally accepted traditions and standards.

2   *The danger of narrow prospects in certain government departments, particularly in the scientific and technical fields:* In some departments, there is only one post and this will hardly attract or retain someone wishing to make a career in the Service. Even where there are several posts, the pyramid of senior appointments may have such a very narrow apex that it is frustrating to many officers struggling to climb the promotion ladder.

3   *Ethnicity:* Many African countries are yet to succeed in becoming Nation States. They are still a conglomeration of nationalities. It will take time to forge a national identity and a sense of common belonging among these entities. Unfortunately, many countries try to brush the matter aside as if it does not exist. It is no use doing so for the problem does exist, and people should come to terms with it. The solution requires a social revolution, and constant and conscious efforts to confront the problem. Some states have attempted to solve the problem by a policy of balancing the ethnic groups at the top. This is a process by which top jobs are distributed evenly among the different ethnic groups in the interest of peace and tranquillity. The result is that often junior and less competent officers are preferred to more senior and competent ones who may happen to belong to an ethnic group that is accused of having more than its "fair share of the national cake".

4   *Inefficiency:* Some top civil servants are incapable of

acquiring the skills currently demanded for the performance of development functions. They are, therefore, unable to play the role of entrepreneurs, catalysts and initiators of change and development.

5. The frustrations of post-independence expectations are often blamed on civil servants by impatient politicians, aggressive trade unionists, and an increasingly critical public.

Youthfulness of the Service

Another reason why it is necessary to rethink the idea of a career civil service in Africa is the youthfulness of the Service. Many African civil servants reach the top of their career at a very early age, sometimes in their early thirties. In East Africa, the average age at which officers become permanent secretaries is between thirty-three and thirty-five. With a retiring age of sixty, an officer will be in the same job for over twelve-years. It is well-known that once a person is at the top, there is only one way in which he can move, and that is downwards. Not only will efficiency deteriorate after about five to seven years in a top job, but, very often, the incumbent will be obstructing the advance of younger and more efficient officers. This will affect the morale and incentives of such officers, which will consequently affect the efficiency of the Service as a whole.

With the present regulations regarding retirement, a pensionable officer in Kenya wishing to leave the service before reaching the age of retirement, must resign and forego any claim to a retirement benefit. The harshness of the regulations was presented to the 1967 Kenya Salaries Commission in these words:

1. A number of officers have risen at a comparatively early age to posts from which they can expect no further promotion within the Service. If they are required to serve for another fifteen or twenty years before they can earn any retiring award, they will inevitably become stale, and their value as public servants will tend to diminish as the years go by.

2. Because so many of the senior posts in the Service are filled by comparatively young men, the promotion prospects of

other officers are severely limited. Because of this, they have insufficient incentive to give their best, and the standard of work throughout the Service is likely to fall.

3. Kenyanisation has proceeded more rapidly in the public sector than it has in the private sector. There is now pressure for more Kenyanisation at the upper levels in the private sector, and indeed the more progressive companies are anxious to appoint more Kenyans to their senior posts. The difficulty is that so many of the best men are already employed in the public sector, and yet if we are to take a broad view and look at the needs of the nation as a whole, it is clearly desirable that the best men should be more evenly spread between the two sectors. It is argued that it is in the best interest of the nation that there should be more flexibility in the system so that people may move freely from one sector to the other, as happens in other countries.

The commission thought the arguments cogent and recommended (for an experimental period of five years) that officers may be allowed to retire any time after completing ten years' service or attaining the age of forty-five, provided that the government and the officer mutually agree. The recommendation was accepted by the Kenya government in 1968, and since then not less than ten officers have retired under the rule.

The position in other countries

Before considering reforms in the tenure of top civil servants in emergent African countries, it would be helpful to examine the position in the developed countries for any valuable lessons. I will, here, limit myself only to a discussion of the systems in the United States and Britain.

The United States

In the United States, the civil service system is a mixture of the career and patronage systems. The top two per cent of the federal service is politically appointed and removed whilst the remaining ninety-eight per cent are under the merit system, managed and supervised by the Federal Public Service Commission or the agencies for which they work. The political appointees are heads of agencies, and occupy policy-making or confidential positions. In recent years, some of the political appointments were from career civil servants but the majority of them were persons who combined professional expertise with sympathy for the policies and programmes of the party in power. The argument has been that the career civil servant is by training, neutral and anonymous, and cannot, therefore, be expected to advocate or implement government policies with the same dynamism, devotion and commitment as a political appointee. Another argument is that the patronage system is necessary for the survival of political parties.

The remainder of the civil service comes under the open merit system. It is open because entry is possible at all levels. In fact, some of the top posts are filled by in-and-outers, men who come into government service for a limited number of years (three to four) and then return to private life to be available at a future date for either further government or political appointment. This group of in-and-outers is quite distinct from the straightforward political appointments. They are in a grey area between the political appointee and the professional civil servant.

The career system proper applies to the middle and lower grade civil servants. It is based on merit and fitness for appointment after a competitive examination. Although called a career system, it does not promise a life-long employment. A civil servant can, however, remain in office until the official retiring age of seventy, provided his services are required, and that he continues to meet the standards of conduct and performance required for his position.

The system is averse to any idea of' permanency with rights and privileges outside the common law, or which are not enjoyed by workers in other walks of life. The system developed out of the political philosophy of the country, and reflects the Americans' love of freedom and their constant desires to control the executive. The civil service is often looked upon as an extension of the executive and any idea of a permanent "administrative elite" is frowned upon as an extension of the power of the administration. In the context of the civil service in Africa, the American system raises the following questions which we shall consider in later paragraphs: What posts should properly constitute the area for political appointments? Should they include heads of professional departments? Where should the line be drawn between career administrators and political administrators? If a permanent secretary is politically appointed, should his deputy also be so appointed? How do you ensure that neither group transgresses into the field of competence of the other? How far can the system of in-and-outers succeed in a developing country with a limited private sector?

Britain

Top civil servants in Britain are covered by the career system under which they are recruited at an early age for life-long employment which ends with a pension calculated at about half the salary at retirement. Once recruited and confirmed, employees hardly leave the department and the Service. They soldier on slowly from grade to grade until the retiring age of sixty. The story of the rise from office boy to office manager is true of many British establishments. Incompetent officers and misfits are seldom dismissed; rather, they are found simpler jobs.

The higher civil servants in Britain belong mostly to the administrative class, but in recent years, a growing proportion is coming from the professions and the specialist groups. Unlike the United States where governmental employment has low prestige, because of the traditional idealisation of the businessman, the civil service in Britain is considered a worthy and honourable career and the higher civil servants have a high place and reputation among the professionals. There are several reasons for this: in the first place, Britain is a class society where the government is in the hands of a ruling class. This class structure enables the top strata of the society to obtain most of the best jobs, and makes it difficult for those from the lower strata to rise to real eminence in any field. This is reinforced by the educational system which provides the best opportunity in public schools that are the preserves of the privileged classes. The best institutions of higher learning (Oxford and Cambridge) are also weighted in favour of the same group. Because of this, most of the political leaders (particularly those from the Conservative Party) and leaders in the church, the army and the civil service, come from the same social and educational backgrounds. In the civil service, this group constitutes itself into an exclusive administrative elite, and considers its members to be endowed with superior wisdom and experience.

There is no doubt, however, that by their ability, discretion and undoubted integrity they have made themselves respected and indispensable to successive governments. Due to the expansion of governmental activities, the increasing technical and scientific nature of government duties, and the growing complexity of modern life, the top civil servant is becoming a real expert in many fields. This adds to his influence and prestige such that many politicians are beginning to consider ways and means of keeping some expertise in their own hands as a means of guarding against undue bureaucratic power. This may be one of the reasons why the labour government made several top specialist appointments from outside the civil service in the fields of economics, science and technology. The appointees came from the industries and universities, but were known to be sympathetic to labour ideals and aspirations. There were complaints that Britain was tending towards the spoils system but the labour government was at pains to explain that it had received the fullest co-operation from the civil service in making the appointments. The co-operation was understandable. The appointments were not administrative and no civil servant lost his job or was demoted. Also, the same civil servants as before remained at the head of the official hierarchy.

Possible reforms

It is argued in some quarters that the career system is unsuitable for the civil service of emergent African countries because ministers prefer, and, in fact, want to work with people who share their dynamism and emotional commitment to the success of their policies and programmes; that the system operates best where civil servants have a tradition of competence, impartiality and dedicated service to the nation — qualities which are, at present, rare in African countries. It is also argued that the system is expensive and should therefore not be introduced to the underdeveloped countries; that the system is bureaucratic, exclusive, stagnant and resistant to change whilst what African countries need is the constant introduction of new talents and men with ideas who will be agents and catalysts for change. Finally, it is widely believed that the system creates an administrative elite, which leads to the widening of the gap between the government and the governed.

In view of these criticisms, and given the current brain drain, what should be the ideal conditions for employing top civil servants in African countries?

Before attempting an answer, we must first draw a distinction between the merits of the career system *per se* and the wisdom of its application to the top layer of African civil services. We have no quarrel with its application to the great majority of civil servants, but we question its suitability for the top advisory posts in view of present evidence and experience.

The first suggestion for reform is that the civil service should cease to be a "closed shop" of career civil servants. It should be opened up for mature recruits from outside — from the universities, industries and the professions. Government business is becoming very technical and specialised and there is therefore the need to bring in specialists who are experienced and able to deal with the varied problems. It was in fact considerations like these that prompted the Fulton Committee into the British Civil Service to say:

> We are convinced that, both in the public interest and also for the health of the service itself, effective steps must be taken to ensure a very much larger and freer flow of men and women between the service and outside employment than there has been in the past. At middle and higher levels, there should also be more short-term

appointments for fixed periods; this would help to maintain regular movement in and out of the service. It would be particularly valuable in the case of those specialists, for example some engineers and scientists, whose special contribution would be up-to-date knowledge and practical experience of work outside government. It is also often the best way of using the talents of those, again mainly specialists, who are needed in an advisory capacity. For example, the present system by which professional economists come into the service from the universities for a few years and then return, perhaps to come back again for further spells later, has been of great value. We think that it should be adopted in other specialist fields. In the various administrative groups similar short-term appointments for those with relevant experience in industry, commerce or the Universities could also bring advantages.[1]

Unfortunately, career civil servants are not favourably disposed to such appointments. They argue that the recruits would block the promotion prospects of serving officers, and that they are likely to be people who failed in private life; that they would be either too old to be able to adjust to civil service methods or too young for high responsibility. My opinion is that these criticisms are not confirmed by the experience in developed countries where this lateral movement has been tried. A stronger argument, however, is that there is a real shortage of such talents and that both government and industries are in competition for personnel possessing the required specialised skills.

I feel that one of the ways of meeting the present difficulties of the career system would be the use of contract appointments, not only in cases of lateral movements but also for top civil servants whose jobs have a political content. It would not be a bad idea if the career service ended at the level of under-secretary or deputy permanent secretary. After that grade, officers could still continue to serve but the terms would be on a terminal basis to be mutually agreed between the government and the officer. This would enable either side to review further employment at regular intervals, and thereby prevent possibly embarrassing

---

situations. In recent years, several African governments have been faced with the problem of what to do with the obsolescent civil servant. He is in general an older officer who is unable to keep up with the pace of change. He has either run out of steam, or blunted his cutting edge. Terminal appointments would in such cases provide a convenient safety valve to either side.

The change-over from career to terminal service need not affect the pension and rights of the officer concerned. The period of contractual service could count for pension or the officer might elect to formally retire from the service, further employment being on normal contractual terms. What this suggestion means is that the implied guarantee of a continuous employment until retiring age should no longer be applicable to certain specified top posts. An officer aspiring to such posts does so with the knowledge that from then onwards, he serves on a basis of mutual agreement between himself and the government. This would result in increased efficiency, for the officer would know that his further employment depended on his performance and ability to meet adequately the demands and challenges of his position. It would also facilitate the introduction of fresh blood and talent into the service.

This brings us to the question of the appropriate age for retirement. We have noted earlier that the retiring age has been revised upwards by some countries since independence. This upward review has not been altogether satisfactory, as shown by the representation of Kenyan civil servants to the 1967 Salaries Review Commission. It is, however, too early to assess the effects of the temporary modification of the retiring age rule under which Kenyan civil servants could retire after ten years' service or after attaining the age of forty-five. The general tendency so far has been to look at the matter only from the point of view of the officer. Two considerations, however, arise from the point of view of the government. The first is that early retirements will put a heavy recurrent burden on government finances, which will be saddled with the payment of pensions for upwards of twenty-five years or more. This will actually require a review of the soundness of the pension funds. It must be certain that monthly contributions to the fund, plus interest on investments, are mathematically calculated to produce the average monthly pension without further demands on the budget. The funds should also be carefully safeguarded. Unless this is done, the government would default or be compelled to accumulate an unwieldy burden for future generations.

The second consideration is that forty-five years is the age at which most officers reach the peak of their performance. A study carried out in the United States by the Brooking Institution showed that most officers reach their top careers in their mid-forties, as illustrated by the following, table:

AGE AT WHICH HIGHEST GRADE WAS REACHED

Age Group	Per cent grade
Under 25	-
25-29	0.3
30-34	2.1
35-39	10.1
40-49	**23.2**
50-54	18.1
55-59	14.6
60-64	8.1
65-69	3.8
70 and above	0.9

Source: David T. Stanley, *The Higher Civil Service*, p.36.

Retirement at forty-five would, as the table above shows, rob the government of the dividends that should have accrued to it out of its investments in the education and training of the officer. The mid-forties is also the age at which most officers are anxious to leave for new opportunities, as illustrated by the following table:

AGE AT THE TIME OF RESIGNATION OR RETIREMENT

Age group	Per cent retrieved
Under 25	-
25-29	-
30-39	10.8
40-44	8.2
45-49	16.0
50-54	9.8
55-59	12.9
60-64	**19.1**
65-69	13.9
70 and above	6.2

Source: David T. Stanley *The Higher Civil Service.*
*Retirement was found to be the leading cause for departure in the 1960s.

A compromise solution might be to suspend the payment of pensions until the officer reached the normal retiring age. The pension could also be put into a lump sum payment which the officer would take on leaving the service. This would be less burdensome on government finances. A system which is widely in use in the industrialised countries is to make pension contributory and transferable so that officers, on leaving, could either take their contributions or transfer them to their next employer.

This will necessitate the abolition of the non-contributory pension scheme and the introduction of a national contributory scheme. Under such a scheme, both the employer and the employee will contribute to the retiring benefits fund. There is a qualifying period of service, normally five years, after which an employee is entitled to all the contributions plus the interests on them. If, however, he leaves his employer before the qualifying period, he takes only his contributions.

The Commission on the Structure and Remuneration of Ghana Public Services[2] recommended such a change in these words:

> 429: We have recommended that the non-contributory Civil
> Service Pension Scheme and it's equivalent in the teaching

be discontinued, and that in future, all public servants should come under the National Social Security Act, 1965. This should take effect from the date on which the new salaries are introduced, viz.: 1st July 1969.

432: We recommend that benefits under the National Social Security Act should become payable at the age of 50 years.

434: The conversion from the Civil Service Pension Scheme to the National Security Scheme will facilitate increased mobility of skills throughout the economy. We consider this to be a desirable end, but the Government as an employer should take steps to safeguard its staffing position — more particularly because it is institutionally difficult for it to react quickly to changes in the supply and demand positions. We recommend that under the new system, all public servants should be on a five- year renewable contract. Within this five years, an officer who voluntarily leaves the Public Service or who is dismissed for misconduct would forfeit the employers' contribution to the National Social Security Scheme. He would suffer no other penalty unless he was serving under a bond. At the end of the five-year contract, he would be free to leave the service without penalty and to enter into another five-year contract if this is offered following the assessment of his performance referred to above, and if his services continue to be required by his employer. In this way, we hope to provide misplaced civil servants with greater choice of occupation and employer while at the same time eliminating the timeserving attitude, which is often — we hope wrongly, attributed to pensionable civil servants.

436: The greater mobility of public officers provided under this scheme would render more importance than hitherto, to good personnel management. If the various public employing agencies wish to retain their good staff in competition with other agencies — and *with* the private sector, they will no longer be able to rely on the pull of the non-contributory Pension Scheme. It will be necessary to pursue positive personnel policies designed to maintain a working environment, which will induce good staff to stay. This we regard as a subsidiary but important benefit of the scheme we have proposed.

The Ghana government accepted recommendations regarding the abolition of the non-contributory pension scheme. It did not, however, accept the recommendation that all public servants should be on five-year renewable contracts, or that officers who resign or are dismissed should forfeit the employer's contribution to their pension scheme.

Conclusion

Let me underline that the solutions suggested above are only meant to be palliative measures for meeting current difficulties and problems. Changes are taking place all over Africa at such a pace that it is no longer prudent to look too far ahead into the future. There is always the danger of proposals and suggestions being overtaken by events. New ideas and social forces are bound to bring about new concepts. After about five to ten years, there will be the need for a review of the situation in the light of prevailing circumstances. In the United Kingdom, civil service conditions are reviewed every twenty to thirty years. In Africa, where both society and the civil service are yet to be stabilised, there is a need to keep the conditions under constant review. As in other countries, the solutions at every stage will have to reflect the economic, political and social conditions of the time.

(14)

The New Style Public Service ✚

"The new style public service is nothing but a result-oriented public service. It is a public service with a purpose, a Service that is out to achieve certain well-defined and well-articulated objectives; a Service whose performance can be measured and assessed."

Introduction

Thank you, Mr. Chairman, for your introduction. Thank you also for inviting me to speak on a non-controversial aspect of the Udoji Report. Our subject is *The New Style Public Service*. This is the most important of all the recommendations in the report. Unfortunately, it has become the most neglected and forgotten recommendation. In order to draw attention to its importance, my colleagues[1] and I placed this recommendation in the opening chapters of the report. We also proclaimed it as our main message.

You are all living witnesses of how this message was received. Today makes it one year and eighteen days since we handed in the report. Besides the acceptance of the new style public service and the white paper, I am not aware of any steps being taken towards its implementation. One is tempted to conclude that either the acceptance was half-hearted, or that there was not sufficient awareness among top civil servants of the need for change. This would be unfortunate, for Nigerian civil servants are well educated and well travelled, and should, therefore, be conversant with the modern methods of public management, which most progressive governments now use.

When we argue for change, we must be sure of what changes

✚ Speech presented at the Public Service Forum of the former Western State of Nigeria, October 13, 1975.

[1] The author was the chairman of the Public Service Review Commission. Other members of the commission were: Professor Akin Mabogunje, Dr. Robin Imishue, Dr. Mahmud Tukur, (all academics); Ahmed Talib, Abubakar Koko and Police Commissioner Ali Idowu (all from the public service). From the private sector came Gamaliel Onosode who was then the chairman of a multinational company.

we are talking about. I am told that since the change in political leadership[2], civil servants now go to work on time, that they now treat the public with civility, and that they no longer use office hours to do private business. These are welcome changes but they have very little to do with the new style public service that we are advocating. Punctuality and civility are gimmicks. At best they have only cosmetic effects.

The change we are advocating for must be real, substantial, holistic and demonstrative. It must be seen, not in the office, but on the ground. It must be seen in concrete results — in more food production, more and better-maintained roads, efficient utilities and communication networks, taps that carry water, telephones that carry messages, and in wires that carry current. It must also be reflected in better and cheaper housing, health and educational services.

The new style public service

The new style public service is nothing but a result-oriented public service. It is a public service with a purpose, a Service that is out to achieve certain well-defined and well-articulated objectives; a Service whose performance can be measured and assessed. It is a Service that is run by specialists and professionals and not by amateurs; a Service that welcomes experts in every field and at all levels of its hierarchy; a Service where concrete performance in the achievement of predetermined departmental or organisational goals and targets is the main criterion for advancement and not the ethnic group, language, or sex of the officer concerned. The new style public service is a Service where remuneration and other compensations depend not only on paper qualifications and seniority but on performance or proven ability to meet the demands of the job; a Service where advancement to the very top is open to all officers, their particular disciplines notwithstanding. It is a Service that takes pride in excellence and

---

[2]   Meaning the toppling of the Gowon regime on 29 July 1975, and the coming into power of the Murtala Mohammed regime.

jobs well-done; a Service that constantly updates itself and keeps abreast of the latest technique's in public management; a Service where professionalism is extolled and amateurism discouraged; a Service which is modest enough to recognise that modern government is big business and therefore requires the use of experts both in the formulation of policies and in their implementations. It is a Service that does not ask for conditions that are not applicable in other walks of life; a Service that does not surround itself with protective regulations and orders against easy removal for incompetence, obsolescence, or any other cause; a Service where permanency of tenure depends on efficient performance and continued ability to meet the demands of one's position. In short, the new style public service is one that adopts modern methods of management in three key areas: in the definition of its objectives and programmes, recruitment and development of staff to carry them out, and the execution of projects that constitute the programmes.

A result-oriented public service

Having enumerated some of the distinguishing attributes of the new style public service, I intend to devote the rest of our time to examining two of them in greater detail. The first is the attribute of being result-oriented. We have already indicated that a result-oriented public service is a public service with a purpose, a service that has well-defined objectives which have to be achieved within certain time targets. The questions that easily come to mind are, what are the objectives and purposes of the public service, and where can they be found? Gentlemen, such objectives are not shrouded in mystery nor are they contained in abstract philosophies of academic administration pundits. They are contained in the national development plans and in the annual budgets. These two documents constitute the law, and the "bible" for every public officer. Unfortunately, it is often alleged that some senior officers, including some heads of ministries. are not conversant with the contents of the development plans. This would be an unpardonable offence. If the allegation is true, one may wonder what such officers are doing in their posts. Obviously, they must be timeservers, that is, workers who believe that they have done a good day's job by pushing files from the in-tray to the out-tray without minding what actually happens on the ground. Such officers should not only be removed but should be charged with receiving their salaries under false pretence! I need not, however, add that such removals must be in accordance with the rules.

Result-oriented and achievement-motivated public servants, on the other hand, are conversant, not only with the contents of the entire development plan, but also of the role and contribution of their ministries or corporation in the achievement of the objectives of these plans. They ensure that the sector plan of their ministries or corporations is broken up into specific programmes and activities, and that each senior officer knows what is expected of him or her at any given period of time. In the execution of the projects under their care, they apply modern methods of management such as project management, critical path analysis, cost- benefits analysis, etc.

Tenure depends on performance

The second attribute of the new style public servant is lack of undue concern over their tenure of office. We have already noted that they are specialists in particular fields (agriculture, engineering, education, economics, finance, law, management, etc.). They keep themselves abreast of the advances in their fields of specialisation. They are constantly learning, and are aware, that in a technological age one must run fast in order to keep pace. Such officers depend, therefore, on their speciality and expertise for survival. They do not, therefore, dance around politicians and commissioners nor do they carry tales to them in order to get on. They are, in short, no-nonsense people on their jobs. That is, they will discharge their duties in accordance with the dictates of their consciences and the ethics of their professions. Such public servants can therefore resist improper influences from any quarters. They do not worry unduly about their tenure of office since they know that their abilities and expertise will take good care of that.

There is another reason why the new style public service should not be a career Service particularly for those on top. By a *career service*, I mean a Service with a promise of a life-long employment, which can be terminated only by mental or physical incapacity, or the commission of a criminal offence. Once recruited, an officer soldiers on from grade to grade until retirement with pension on account of age. This system is one of the service traditions which we inherited from Britain where the role of a top civil servant is different from what it is in Nigeria. In Britain, the job of a top civil servant does not have the overwhelming development orientation and content it has in Nigeria. There, development is mostly in the hands of the private sector and the job of a top civil servant is mostly to help his minister in the control of this sector through appropriate legislation. There, the civil servant is not necessarily more knowledgeable than his minister, and does not, therefore, initiate policy. His job is to assist his minister in carrying out decided policies, which are already formulated by party stalwarts. The Nigerian civil servant, on the other hand, is a development administrator and a catalyst for change. Being among the best educated in the community, he is expected to initiate and manage change. In the field of development, he is an entrepreneur and a partner in progress. Hence, in countries like Zambia, Tanzania and Kenya[3] he is expected to join the political party and help in the formulation of party policies. In these circumstances the role of an African top civil servant is indistinguishably tied up with that of his minister or commissioner. It is only fair that civil service traditions and terms of service should reflect such a role. But this is not the case, and as a result, the typical top African civil servant lacks an identity, and is groping for one. He does not know where he belongs. Is he politically appointed or is he a career officer? Is he under the merit system or the patronage system? There are

---

[3] These three countries, which were one-party states at the time the speech was made, have since become multiparty states.

no easy answers to these questions. But these questions need to be confronted, and civil servants should, in their own interests, initiate action in this regard. Among the matters to be investigated are the following:

☐ Who are the top civil servants and what is the nature of their duties?

☐ Where the duties and responsibilities of public officers involve the formulation of policies, to what extent should the terms and conditions of such officers differ from those of politicians? Should such conditions include permanent and pensionable terms?

☐ Where should the line be drawn between officers holding ordinary civil service jobs and those in sensitive political posts?

☐ If such public officers are appointed from within the Service, should they retire from the career service before accepting such positions or should their service in the new post count for pension?

☐ How can we ensure that appointment to such posts (if they are not permanent and pensionable) does not rob the career service of leaders in different professional cadres?

☐ How far can the system of political appointment and removal of heads of ministries and departments be applicable in an economy where the government is still the largest employer of labour?

I would suggest that until rigorous researches are conducted into the above questions, the career service should end at the level of deputy permanent secretary and deputy head of department. Any appointment above these levels should be on contract, which is renewable only by mutual agreement. This would provide the opportunity for both sides to keep the appointment under constant review, and to make changes when necessary without any loss of face. Also, as an interim measure, service after the termination of the contract period should count for pension, provided that there is no break in service continuity.

Let me conclude by saying that the introduction of the new

style public service in all its facets will not only enable the service to redeem its tarnished image but will lead to the establishment of a tradition of honest, dedicated, efficient and effective public service.

Implications of the Public Service Review Commission's Report for Management Education and Training✦

> *"Available evidence is that the general philosophy of management, which is currently being practised in the civil service and public corporations, is inadequate to meet the needs of the country. The system of management now in use was largely designed for running a stable country, whereas Nigeria needs a system which can respond to the demands of a rapidly changing society."*

Introduction

Mr. Chairman, Ladies and Gentlemen. You have asked me to speak on the *Implications of the Review Commission's Report for Management Education and Training in Nigeria.* To do justice to your request would mean more than speaking on the chapter on training in the report. It would actually mean speaking about the whole report, because throughout its seven volumes, constant references were made to the need for equipping public officers with the requisite skills that would enable them to function effectively in the achievement of developmental goals. The one theme that ran consistently through the report is that if the development goals of the nation are to be achieved, there must be a profound change in the way public services are managed, in the way they undertake their tasks, and in their internal social attitudes and behaviour. The need for change constitutes the main message of the report. It is the basis on which other recommendations were made.

Achievement of national goals and objectives will largely depend on the effectiveness of the civil services, the parastatals, universities and, of course, the private sector. In turn, the

---

✦ Address presented to the National Conference of Management Educators, Benin, May 15, 1975.

effectiveness of these organisations will largely depend on the capabilities and motivations of the men who lead them. A substantial part of the commission's enquiry was, therefore, concerned with what must be done to ensure high level capability, and a high level of motivation for those who hold senior posts.

Available evidence is that the general philosophy of management, which is currently being practised in the civil service and public corporations, is inadequate to meet the needs of the country. The system of management now in use was largely designed for running a stable country, whereas Nigeria needs a system which can respond to the demands of a rapidly changing society. Today, the public services of Nigeria (meaning the federal and the state public services) are involved in affairs which were beyond the imagination of their predecessors fifteen years ago. They are now selling insurance and minting coins, they are refining oil, sailing ships and assembling cars; they are distilling gin and brewing beer, tomorrow they may be forging steel or sending people to the outer space.

With these new and important socio-economic objectives, the management of the public sector must be deliberately directed towards the realisation of these goals. This calls for a shift from management by administrative controls to result-oriented management and a shift from management by crisis to management by planned objectives. This requires a total re-focusing of all public service organisations, including federal and state civil services, public enterprises and universities.

Result-oriented management is the effective mobilisation of resources to attain clearly defined objectives. It requires a complete process of restructuring systems, whether human or material, for doing work. It also requires restructuring attitudes and the level of knowledge of workers. It requires that leaders define clearly where the organisation is going, how to get there, and an insistence that the route is followed. Above all, result-oriented management enables workers to synchronise their individual aims and aspirations with those of their organisations, thereby ensuring identification and commitment.

To translate this concept into practice requires a well-organised training programme which is structured to cater for the various cadres of the public service — permanent secretaries and chief executives of corporations, supervisors, and various categories of skilled specialists. I will, below, discuss briefly different areas of training which the report identified.

General management training

This is one of the most critical areas where training is needed, and is mostly required by permanent secretaries and corporations' executives. Without an effective training programme for these leaders, the public service will not be able to respond to the demands of a development-oriented society. This group must learn to be proficient in the latest techniques of management, and must suitably adapt them to the Nigerian situation. In particular, they have to be up-to-date with the latest techniques on how to establish goals and objectives, how to measure achievements, how to plan and budget for results, how to organise projects and create multidisciplinary and multiministry task forces, how to lead and motivate staff, and the like. In short, they must know how to organise both men and technology for the purpose of attaining desired results in the most effective manner.

Supervisory training

This is the next in importance to training in general management. The present standard of supervisory skills in the public service is poor. Yet supervisors are the key men in any organisation, for they instruct, advise and direct the workers; they see that the aims and objectives of management are met. Supervisory functions run from the simple tasks of the charge hand for a labour gang, up to the more complex tasks of the senior sub-manager responsible for many highly skilled people. Among the areas supervisors should have adequate training and skills in are:

1. work planning;
2. work organisation and control;
3. human relations;

4. communications;
5. general administrative principles.

Skilled manpower training

These are the men who will implement the many specialist technologies recommended by the report of the commission. The most significant functions identified as needing such training include: financial management, information management , personnel management, materials management, and management services. Permit me to briefly elaborate on these:

a. *Financial management:* We found that the financial control system in the public services needs a complete overhaul. It must be changed from a book-keeping and control-oriented system into one in which financial management is one of the subordinate management systems whose responsibility is to ensure the most effective use of financial resources. This group requires expertise in:

1. programme budgeting;
2. cashflow projections;
3. advanced payroll methods;
4. project and cost accounting;
5. financial reporting.

(All the above are, however, in addition to, not in lieu of, the regulatory and control aspects of financial management, which must continue. Thus, the more traditional aspects of training book-keepers, accountants and auditors will continue but will be modified as necessary to equip these officers with the skills which are demanded by the new financial systems and methods).

b. *Information management:* This group is responsible for managing the information resources of the government, not its public relations. The enquiry revealed that Nigeria is seriously handicapped by the lack of current and adequate information data and statistics. An information management group would do much to alleviate this problem. The group requires expertise in:

1. information systems design;
2. information handling technology (including data processing);
3. information storage techniques;
4. information retrieval and presentation techniques.

c. *Personnel management:* The commission noted that personnel management has not yet become a speciality in Nigeria. Many failures in the personnel management system can be attributed to this lack of specialised expertise. An underlying principle throughout the report is the need to utilise specialist skills to do specialist jobs. This requires personnel managers who know how to get and develop such skills. There is an urgent need for training in the following functional areas:

1. personnel policy development and administration;
2. manpower planning;
3. recruitment;
4. job analysis, description and specification writing;
5. job evaluation, using standard techniques;
6. auditing and evaluation of results;
7. internal and external pay research methods;
8. wage and salary administration techniques;
9. training;
10. performance appraisal;
11. labour relations.

d. *Materials management:* The public service seems to view this aspect of management as merely store-keeping, a custodial and clerical function. This is akin to viewing financial management as mere book-keeping. Materials management is a sophisticated function that is rapidly gaining importance as the public service invests more and more in capital improvements, both construction and maintenance. Urgent areas of training here include:

1. procurement — tendering and purchasing;
2. inventory management;
3. warehouse and transportation management;
4. stock control and stores reporting;
5. disposal of materials and control of wastage.

e. *Management service:* Existing O & M[1] units are seriously understaffed and, for the most part, the staff they have, possess neither the skills nor experience for effective performance. Management service people require skills in all of the management functions listed above. They should spend at least 25% of their time on training and development, since they are change agents that get things done through others.

Training the trainers

The training of trainers is a key responsibility for all who are to participate in this training activity, especially non-Nigerians. The training consultant should ensure that his client is able to replicate the work he does. This requires selecting the superior trainees from the various programmes, and giving them competence in training others so that the Nigerian government becomes independent of outside assistance in this area as early as possible.

Tentative forecast of training needs

The public services of today are characterised by too few senior managers who have far too much to do. At the middle level, the pattern is pretty much the same. Managers are tied to their desks with details that they are unable to leave their offices to ensure that the public is being served properly. The permanent secretary Federal Ministry of Establishments, has estimated that the most senior managers (levels 14-17) constitute less than 0.3% of the federal public service, and that the next line of managers (levels 11-13) constitute slightly more than 2%. It follows that the entire management comprises less than 3% of the Service . The permanent secretary believes that at least a five-fold increase is

---

[1] Organisation and Management

necessary if the public sector is to achieve the results forecast in the national plan. With a base population of 700,000, this group would number a little over 100,000, i.e., 15%. With this group of newcomers you must add the present 3%, or 20,000 incumbents, who are also in need of one form of training or another. This, gentlemen, is a rough idea of the number of managers, supervisors and specialists who require training.

The role of training institutions

Having outlined areas of training and training needs, I will spend a few minutes on the role of training institutions. All management training institutions should be brought actively into helping to close this yawning managerial capability gap. The following institutions must bear the brunt of this massive training task: the Centre for Management Development; the Nigerian Institute of Management; the Institutes of Administration at Ife and Zaria, the Institute of Management and Technology, Enugu; the Administrative Staff College of Nigeria; as well as universities and polytechnics. In addition, the existing training schools that are principally designed to serve other needs should also be utilised. Our estimated need for training some 100,000 people in nine distinct areas would exhaust the entire physical capacity of existing institutions, as well as their staff. This would therefore make them unable to meet their current commitments. Also, many of the commission's recommendations will entail new systems, new methods and technologies, which at present are beyond the training capacities of Nigeria. In such cases, there should be no objection to the selective use of appropriate overseas training institutions.

Another area which training institutions should develop is consultancy training. This is best suited for the development of new techniques as well as for the training of senior executives. The consultant works with managers and supervisors at their workplace and thereby brings the training resource to the particular situation of the organisation. By participating in the analysis and solution of problems, the consultant helps to develop the skills and capacities of the staff of the organisation. Already, some training institutions like the Nigerian Institute of Management are providing such services to the private sector. The practice should be extended to the public sector.

The magnitude of the tasks

The magnitude of the tasks requires an urgent need for co-ordination among training institutions. The possibility of waste, duplication of effort, and irrelevant training, must be avoided if the government is to receive reasonable return on its total investment on training. The co-ordination efforts should certainly touch on such matters as how the various training institutes that conduct management training relate to the Nigerian Council for Management Education and Training. There is also a need to define the relationship between the Council and the Standing Committee on Staff Development since a major part of staff development should be concerned with management training.

Another compelling reason for co-ordination among training institutions is the shortage of indigenous management educators. For management education to succeed in Nigeria, we must be able to develop a relevant body of knowledge as well as the men with the ability to expand and impart it. At present, we are short of both. The relevant body of knowledge must be developed by men whose approach is basically intellectual but who have a problem-solving approach derived from industrial experience. The urgent need, therefore, is to increase both the number and calibre of our management trainers and to produce a hardcore of specialists with the intellectual capacity to develop a corpus of knowledge and material which is of international standard, but based on national experience, situations, and needs.

The universities must help in the development of Nigerian management educators. They have in the past tended to concentrate mostly on public administration because of the demands of Nigerianisation. Though many of them are now turning to management education, they have shown certain traits that are ill-suited to management development. They are not always practical-oriented, and their preoccupations both with academic standards and the pressure of undergraduate courses, have tended to distract their interest from postgraduate or non-degree programmes. Furthermore, many of the academic staff have not always exhibited the quality or experience which would capture the confidence of business management and encourage their use in consultancy services which would help to acquaint them with the realities of the commercial world.

Universities should, therefore, adopt flexible and imaginative staffing arrangements in order to help solve the problem. They should recruit qualified retired managers from the industrial, commercial and public service worlds to their teaching staff. Serving managers can be used for short, *ad hoc* assignments. Academic staff should also be encouraged to undertake consultancy assignments wherever possible, or to help with in-house training schemes with organisations. Interchange between the world of education and practice needs promotion at every opportunity.

Mr. Chairman, before I take my seat, I would like to leave two thoughts with the conference. The first is that if our management education and training courses are to attract or cater for top executives—permanent secretaries and general managers— they must be of very high standard and conducted by experts in various aspects of management. The experts need not be on the staff of the institutions. They could be drawn from the industries, universities, consultancy firms and international organisations. Related to this is the status of the heads of the management institutions. You do not, for example, expect a lieutenant colonel to attend courses run by a second lieutenant. Here, we can borrow a leaf from the practice in the armed forces.

The second thought is that in implementing the recommendations of the commission, we must avoid the mistakes of the recent past. Some of you will agree with me that one of the main reasons for the flood of protests that attended the grading and salary award was partly due to lack of adequate information. People will react better if they know when a change is to occur, the reason for it, and what there is in it for them.

Finally, let me suggest that before embarking on management training, before pouring the petro-naira out on new buildings, equipment and staff, there should be an appraisal of the performance of existing institutions. It is only as a result of such appraisal that effective ones should be encouraged, while the indifferent ones should either be scrapped or revitalised. If institutions are to teach result-oriented management through regular appraisal of results, they should start with themselves by first putting their houses in order.

(16)

Social and Economic Effects of Udoji ✦

"We have been witnesses of a new phenomenon — the emergence of worker-power. I hope that the Nigerian worker will use his new found power wisely and for the common good."

Introduction

Thank you, Mr. Chairman, for your introduction. Thank you also for a most enjoyable meal, which has demonstrated that if Udoji has had any effect on your monthly luncheons, it has been for the better!

You requested me to speak on the *Social and Economic Effects of Udoji*. But you did not indicate which Udoji you had in mind. Is it the Udoji of the Public Service Review Commission recommendations or is it the Udoji of the government white paper? Those of you who have read the report will not fail to discover that in many respects, particularly as regards wages and salaries, the Udoji of the report is very different from the Udoji of the white paper.

For our purpose this afternoon, I think it would help us to get our parameters right by starting with a brief account of the Public Service Review Commission and its recommendations — at least for the benefit of those who have not read the report. One thing which the critics of the report and the white paper have failed to do, is to give credit to the government for its wisdom, and shall I add, its modesty, in setting up the commission. To appreciate these qualities one has to look at the commission's terms of reference. It is an admission of certain inadequacies, and represents a genuine desire on the part of the government to remodel the inherited structures and management practices so

✦ Address presented to the Ibadan Chamber of Commerce, May 9, 1975.

that they could be more efficient and effective instruments of development.

It was in this very spirit of ensuring the achievement of development goals that the commission approached its tasks. On the very first meeting of the commission, the members agreed that the best interpretation of the terms of reference was to imagine that the government was waving before us the development plan, and asking us to enquire whether with it's existing structures, attitudes, practices and procedures it could achieve the targets set out in the plan. This was why, early in the report, we declared that our main message was the introduction of a new style public service. This we explained as a result-minded public service, a Service where ministries take the achievements of their sector plans as the frame of reference for all their activities and accordingly organise that individual officers work towards the achievement of definite assignments in the plan, within definite time targets. It is a Service where accountability on the basis of individual assessment of performance of agreed quantifiable jobs would replace the present anonymity and subjective appraisal of ill-defined and unquantifiable workloads.

Under such a system, the government will know at a glance what precisely it is doing, the departments and persons responsible for specific programmes and projects, as well as the time for their completion. The citizen, on the other hand, will be able to discover what government has in store for him under specific programmes, like port facilities and telecommunications. Under such a style of management, it would be uncharitable to blame a whole government for the congestion at the ports, the congestion on the roads, or the inadequacy of telephone and mail services. If the ports were congested, the nation would be able to know whether it was the Ministry of Planning that failed to take necessary expansion into account in its national macro planning and, if not, whether it was the Ministry of Transport that failed to quantify what expansion in terms of berths, cranes and warehouses it expected the Ports Authority, as its agent, to execute during a specified period. It might, however, be discovered that both the Ministries of Planning and Transport were not at fault but that it was the general manager of the Ports Authority who was sitting on the project because of inadequacy and inability to manage a project of such magnitude. The facts would speak for themselves, and in such situations there would be no difficulty in discovering bottlenecks, applying remedial measures and, in appropriate cases, sanctions.

Mr. Chairman, we did not merely advocate a result-oriented management. We actually prescribed how it could be achieved through the installation, with the aid of consultants, of a new system of management which allows the use of modern management tools such as: programmed budgeting, management by objectives, project management and open assessment of performance based on previously agreed workloads. We particularly stressed the abolition of civil service classes and recommended a unified structure where all officers — professionals and administrators — would consider themselves as entrepreneurs engaged in a single enterprise for the common good. In a nutshell, our recommendations were aimed at orienting the Nigerian bureaucracy to think in modern management terms if it were to meet the development goals of the nation.

Besides remodelling the structure and management of the public service to make them efficient and relevant to the country's needs, our other preoccupation was to bridge the gap in pay and rewards between the public service and the private sector. I know that it is difficult for any casual observer to comprehend the recent salary and wage increases. Everyone agrees that there should be wage and salary increase for workers but not everyone agrees that there should be arrears of nine to twelve months! As this part of the report has led to a lot of misunderstanding, I think it would be appropriate for me to explain what the commission actually recommended and why.

The commission's recommendations on wage increases

Our mandate was to harmonise wages and salaries in the two sectors. To achieve this, we had to conduct an extensive survey into wages and salaries in the private sector. This was done by a massive survey of 250 firms and over 160,000 private sector jobs. We surveyed all companies outside Lagos that were employing 100 persons and over. In Lagos, we surveyed companies employing 200 and over. These were companies that have rational organisational policies and personnel comparable to those in the public sector. Our finding was that at the bottom level, the level of cleaners, porters and messengers, the private sector was paying very lowly. In fact about 40% of all private sector employees were receiving less than ₦400 a year. Surely, this is not a living wage in Nigeria of today. At the middle level, the level of professionals, secretaries, accountants and engineers, there was very little to choose between the sectors. At top level, however, the private sector was paying much higher than the public sector. Although government was paying better than the private sector at bottom level, its wages, considering the rise in national productivity and the cost of living, was not good enough. Here we deliberately applied a social equity factor to raise the wages to ₦720 per annum. And I believe that anyone with a social conscience will agree that this is justified and equitable.

At the middle level, we hardly recommended any increases because of the comparability of the prevailing salaries at that level. At top level, however, we recommended increases which would bring top public sector executives nearer but not at par with their counterparts in the private sector. Here, our aim was harmonisation and comparability, and not parity. The increases at this level have been criticised in certain quarters, but to us, they are justified in view of the increased responsibilities imposed on top executives by the new style of management. If you want a first class service, you must provide first class conditions.

I must emphasise that we did not make the salary recommendations blindly or in vacuum. We made them in the context of the country's productivity and cost of living. We also took into account the inflationary effects of any increases, and made anti-inflationary recommendations accordingly. Because of your particular interest in the matter, I have sent the commission's consideration of the economic consequences of the salary award, and our recommendations to counter inflation, to your chairman for distribution before this meeting. The counter inflationary recommendations were aimed at stimulating supply on the one hand and controlling demand on the other. Those regarding supply stimulation include:

a. That increased supply of consumer goods, foodstuffs and building materials should be encouraged through the reduction of duties on those goods, and abolition, altogether, of duties on such basic foods as milk, flour and sugar.

b. That temporary importation of executive and professional skills that are in short domestic supply should be encouraged in the private sector in order to meet the long-term needs of the indigenisation policy as well as the short-term requirements of the expanding economy.

c. That massive food production should be encouraged through the following assistance to farmers:
   — Provision of fertilisers at greatly subsidised prices.
   — High-yielding seed multiplication and distribution at greatly subsidised prices.
   — Provision of fishing boats, nets and other equipment at greatly subsidised prices.
   — Large-scale expansion of agricultural extension services
   — Massive irrigation of drought affected areas.
   — Improved transportation facilities of farm to market roads.
   — Introduction of intermediate technology in agriculture in order to maximise the result of these subsidies.

d. On demand control we recommended:
   — no arrears of salaries and wages; and
   — that the new salary scales should be implemented in two phases: 60% of the increase in one phase and the remaining 40% a year after.

Mr. Chairman, Ladies and Gentlemen, these are our recommendations. I leave it to you to assess their economic and social effects.

A reply to some of the criticisms of the report

Before I take my seat, I would, however, like to take a few minutes to answer some of the criticisms levelled at the commission's report. There are those who said that instead of recommending increases in wages and salaries, the commission should have recommended the provision of welfare services, such as free health and education services. My answer to them is that no matter how attractive or desirable that might be, it was not our mandate. It is, however, interesting that these critics were among the first to collect their awards and to complain of their inadequacy. If they are honest in their criticism they should have handed their increases to the social welfare department.

The loudest criticism, however, is that the increases are the cause of shortage and high prices otherwise known as inflation. Every housewife knows that there had been shortages, and that prices had been soaring even before the award. In fact, the award was designed to bring wages in line with the cost of living. Every student of the Nigerian economy knows that inflation in Nigeria has three principal causes: the first is large-scale government spending particularly in non-productive projects, the second is imported inflation which comes into the country with the high prices of imports. Again, it is the resulting inflation that made the awards necessary. In this regard, I am grateful to one Mr. Stanley Joseph for pointing out to the critics in his article in the March issue of *Afriscope* their error in mistaking effects for causes, and for confusing symptoms with the disease.

The third major cause of inflation in Nigeria is the low productivity of the Nigerian worker. The Nigerian farmer must produce more and the office and factory worker must work harder so that we can match consumption with production. As long as there is a gap between the two, and as long as government continues to pump large sums of money into unproductive projects, so long will a lot of money continue to chase few goods.

Another major criticism of the report is that the increased wages will cause unemployment. This is taking a negative view of the situation. If workers give an honest day's work for an honest day's pay, if they match increased pay with increased production, then instead of redundancy there will be expansion. Furthermore, increase in wages hardly result in increase in personal savings. They generally lead to increased domestic demand for consumer goods, which in turn should lead to more investment in the expansion of local manufacturing industries and, therefore, more employment.

Related to this unemployment scare is the complaint in the private sector circles that the commission did not appear to take into account the probable effects of its recommendations on private sector wages bearing in mind what happened after the Adebo report. My answer to this criticism is that the private sector's interest in the commission was rather belated. I publicly appealed to them to present their case to the commission during the inquiry but no one came forward. From private discussions, however, I gathered the impression that the commission did not really concern them and that what interested them was that government should lift the ban on wage increases so that they could implement the wage increase which they had negotiated with their workers. In the circumstances, all that the commission did on completing its work was to advise government to lift the ban. Unfortunately, it did not, because it feared that it might make public officers more dissatisfied and thereby create an unfavourable atmosphere for the release of government's white paper.

Finally, let me touch briefly on a matter which the critics appeared to ignore. It is management/labour relations. I think that management/labour relations in this country have undergone a great change in the last four months. We have been witnesses of a new phenomenon — the emergence of worker-power. I hope that the Nigerian worker will use his new found power wisely and for the common good. In this regard, employers must show more interest in the education of their workers. So far, employers have shown interest only in the training of workers, and left their education to outsiders who may be ignorant and often downright irresponsible. It is not enough for a company to train its workers in the mechanical processes of the production line. It must educate them to understand what the company stands for, its aims and objectives, its slogans, programmes and philosophies. It is only on the basis, of knowledge and understanding that workers could be expected to identify themselves with the objectives of their company, and to appreciate that their future is inextricably bound with that of the company. Only then will they see and seek their advancement with the company, in the company and through the company. This is what I call commitment and pride of belonging. I am told that this is one of the things that made Japan great.

Another management/labour phenomenon is the position of the window-dressing manager in some of the expatriate controlled firms. This era has certainly come to an end. With the new wage bill, no firm can any longer afford the luxury of having glorified clerks masquerading as managers behind big desks. The companies will be forced to demand commensurate results from anyone who goes under the designation of manager. He must henceforth manage and not be managed. In the same manner, the public has the duty and responsibility to demand better and effective service from public officers. This the public can do first by reading the report — at least the chapter on implementation — and secondly by insisting that the accepted recommendations for a new management system be installed so that the public will get the result from which they are paying some money. The report is unequivocal on the matter. It says:

> These salaries are inextricably and firmly linked with the reformed public service we have recommended. Any attempt to implement one independent of the other will be serious both for the economy and the public service itself. On the present salary recommendations, the economy cannot afford to carry any 'passengers'. The Public Service Commissions should therefore be vigilant and not hesitate to remove any officer who is unable to meet the demands of his job. To fail to do so would amount to cheating the public. We believe that the economy can support these higher salary levels if, but only if, productivity is increased and inefficient practices and inefficient personnel do not constitute an unnecessary burden.

Mr. Chairman, let me conclude by saying that whatever some people may say of our salary recommendations, I know many admit that it was a redistribution of income which benefited not only the wage earners but also farmers and landlords. The recommendations are equally a means of raising the dignity and status of the Nigerian worker from his erstwhile starvation level. In fact, some regard it as the *Workers' Charter*. You are free to reach your own conclusions.

(17)

Udoji and Inflationary Pressures in the Economy ✦

"The recommended salary increases were... designed to correct the disparity between wages and the cost of living. This is the practice the world over. To blame inflation on such salary awards is to mistake effects for causes and to confuse symptoms with the disease."

Introduction

Thank you, Mr. Chairman, for your introduction. Thank you also for asking me to open your annual conference. I must say that I accepted your invitation with great trepidation because as a layman to your profession, and a poor mathematician at that, I feel most unqualified to address such a galaxy of eminent accountants, economists and mathematicians. I was, however, assured that my invitation was motivated by a desire for an outsider's viewpoint on both the institute and the theme of its conference.

May I first of all congratulate the institute for attaining the age of ten. This is an important milestone not only in the lives of new nations but also in the lives of organisations and associations operating within their boundaries. Such a landmark provides an opportunity for stocktaking, reviewing past achievements and charting out strategies and programmes of action for the future. I do not propose to recount your achievements during the past decade. I will leave that to those better qualified to do so. Any attempt on my part will involve probing into your past, and since many of you are now engaged in probing the activities of certain individuals and organisations, I think I should spare you the embarrassment. I will therefore restrict my observations to the institute alone.

✦ Address presented to the Nigerian Institute of Chartered Accountants during a conference on "Inflation", which was organised to mark the tenth anniversary of the institute.

I believe that at our present stage of development, the institute can play a very important developmental role. We have just embarked on transforming the country from subsistence to an industrial and commercial economy. This transformation is creating problems of adjustment. Some of these manifest themselves in the lack of business ethics, honesty, reliability, and respect for time and numbers. No other profession than the institute is in a better and privileged position to inculcate these qualities in our entrepreneurs and businessmen. Again, recent disclosures of mismanagement of public funds indicate that all is not well with our system of public accounting. I believe that as a public professional body established by an Act of Parliament, the institute has a duty to air its views on the present state of public finances. Such views should be constructive in that they should contain advice on how, in the opinion of the institute, the nation's financial resources should be managed and accounted for.

I also advocate that the time has come, indeed it is overdue, when accountants should come out of their traditional book-keeping shells to play the modern role of managers and financial controllers. I therefore look forward to seeing more and more accountants being appointed general managers of their organisations. I am, no doubt, aware that this suggestion requires an attitudinal adjustment on the part of accountants. It will require the adoption of a new concept, a concept which perceives accounting as a decision-making process with regards to future actions rather than as a post mortem exercise of past events. I hope I have not given the impression that keeping of books and records are not important. In fact, I consider that record keeping is a matter about which the institute should undertake to educate the public. The average Nigerian does not appreciate the value of keeping records, data and statistics. He may be a good shopkeeper but he is certainly not a good record keeper. He tends to treat numbers with the same disrespect and careless abandon as he treats time, and I have heard it said that the easiest way to lose a Nigerian friend is to ask him to render an account.

During our recent enquiry into the operations of government departments, I was consistently frustrated by the absence of up-to-date data, reports and statistical records. These are essential tools of management; without them an executive finds himself without systematic information as to what is going on in his organisation, and he can neither plan properly nor make corrections for errors of omission or commission. The institute will, therefore, be rendering an important service to the public if it draws the attention of not only its clients but also the general public to the importance of keeping records. This service could be rendered through, for example, the publication of simple pamphlets which are designed for the education of the Nigerian entrepreneur as well as for the layman who wants to know more about the companies in which he owns shares, or is considering becoming a stockholder. They should avoid the use of specialised vocabularies and be as practical as possible. I am sure that articles like: how to read a balance sheet; how to set about producing a financial plan; how to avoid cashflow problems; and how to estimate future earnings correctly; will not only be of great interest to Nigerian investors and entrepreneurs, but will boost the role of the institute and its members in the eyes of both the public and the management of public companies.

I will conclude this part of my address by referring to the most important service of all, the training of more accountants. I understand that at the moment, there are only 1,000 chartered accountants in the country. On the basis of an estimated population of 80,000,000[1], we have only one accountant for every 80,000 of the population. The need is obviously colossal, and even with a tenfold increase it will still be inadequate. Something, therefore, must be done, and quickly, to remedy the acute situation. I urge the institute to look into how, without necessarily lowering standards, more and more accountants could be produced quickly. One of such ways would be for all Nigerian bodies engaged in the training of accountants, the institute, universities and polytechnics to co-ordinate their efforts and pull their resources together. In this regard, it might be necessary to

---

[1] Nigeria's population is currently estimated at over 100 million.

have a look at the syllabuses covered by universities and polytechnics in the training of accountants to see how they could be made more practical and relevant with a view to reducing the period necessary for the training of postgraduate accountants. At the moment, it takes a graduate a total of eight years to qualify as a chartered accountant after school certificate compared with the five years it takes an articled clerk. I would like to believe that accountancy is not among the professions that are accused of creating artificial scarcities through the prescription of over-stringent pre-registration qualifications.

In my view, the greatest bottleneck in the training of accountants is the narrow base upon which their training takes place. This narrow base is the office of the professional accountant. Since we have very few of them, and since the number that each can admit at a time is limited, it follows that only a very limited number can be produced every year. The answer, therefore, lies in widening the base, and one of the ways of doing this would be the use of institutions of higher learning. I see no reason why universities and professional offices should not co-operate in producing qualified chartered accountants in say four sessions of nine months each, cycled in such a way that the office complements the courses at the university.

The final thought I would like to leave with you regarding the profession is the need for specialisation in the various fields. I am thinking of areas like oil accounting, banking accounting, construction accounting, management accounting, etc.

The 'Udoji Award' and the recent inflationary pressures

I will now say a few words on the subject-matter of your conference — inflation. This is a word which some people have used as if it is interchangeable and synonymous with the name Udoji. This association is the result of failure on the part of the mass media and other commentators including university men and intellectuals, to distinguish, for the benefit of the general public, the difference between the recommendations of the review commission and what was accepted and implemented by government. This failure is, to say the least, unfair to both the commission and myself.

It is painful to note that when people discuss inflation in relation to the salary increases, they do so as if the commission never addressed its mind to the problem, that is, the possible inflationary effects of any increases. We devoted a whole section to discussing the matter and we made definite recommendations that would minimise any inflationary effects. None of the commentators have had the courtesy to refer to those recommendations or the courage to put the blame where it rightly belongs. The impression has, therefore, been created as if the salary recommendations were made blindly and without regard to their possible economic consequences. In this regard, I would like to refer the conference to paragraphs 712 to 723 of the main report, where we discussed the economic impact of the salary increases and ended with several deflationary recommendations. Some of these recommendations were not only disregarded but inflationary awards not recommended by the commission were implemented. It is, therefore, wrong to attribute the cause of inflation in the country to the salary increases recommended by the commission.

It is a well-known fact that by the time the commission submitted its report, inflation was already running at a very high rate and prices were approximately double what they used to be a few years before. The principal causes of this were the quantum of public spending, some of which are essential in a developing economy, the low productivity of the non-oil sector of the Nigerian economy, and the increasingly high cost of imported consumer and capital goods. The recommended salary increases were, therefore, designed to correct the disparity between wages and the cost of living. This is the practice the world over. To blame inflation on such salary awards is to mistake effects for causes and to confuse symptoms with the disease.

In order, however, to prevent any fresh price increases which would result in workers' real income being less than anticipated, the commission made several recommendations which were aimed at stimulating supply on the one hand and controlling demand and prices on the other. On the supply side, we made four major recommendations. The first is that massive food production should be encouraged through the following assistance to farmers:

❑ Provision and distribution of fertilisers at greatly subsidised price.

❑ High-yielding seed multiplication and distribution at greatly subsidised prices.

❑ Provision of fishing boats, nets and other equipment at greatly subsidised prices.

❑ Large scale expansion of agricultural extension services.

❑ Massive irrigation of drought affected areas.

❑ Improved transportation facilities from farm to market roads.

❑ Introduction of intermediate technology in agriculture, in order to maximise the results of these subsidies.

The second recommendation is that increased supply of consumer goods, foodstuff and building materials should be encouraged through the reduction of duties on those goods and the abolition altogether of duties on such basic foods as milk, sugar, and flour. The third is that temporary importation of executive and professional skills that are in short domestic supply should be encouraged in the private sector in order to meet the long-term needs of the indigenisation policy as well as the short-term requirements of the expanding economy.

Our fourth recommendation is that public officers must be made to be more productive through the introduction of structural and management reforms contained in the report. We warned against taking the new salaries without implementing the management reforms in these words.

> These salaries are inextricably and firmly linked with the reformed Public Service we have recommended. Any attempt to implement one independent of the other will be serious both for the economy and the public service itself. On the present salary recommendations, the economy cannot afford to carry any 'passengers'. The Public Service Commission should therefore be

vigilant and not hesitate to remove any officer who is unable to meet the demands of his job. To fail to do so would amount to cheating the public. We believe that the economy can support these higher salary levels if, but only if, productivity is increased and inefficient practices and inefficient personnel do not constitute an unnecessary burden.

On demand control, we did not only recommend that there should be no arrears of salaries and wages, but also we went further to say that the new salary scales should be implemented over a two-year period in order to give the economy some chance of adjusting to the changes in demand, and to enable importation and food production programmes to be fully operational. We reckoned that by the time Phase II was implemented, the economy could be more capable of absorbing further increases in demand, and the public and private sectors would have had an opportunity to evaluate the effects of the earlier increases.

On price control, we recognised the difficulty, if not the impossibility, of operating a general price control system, and recommended that the following steps be taken in that direction:

i. The Price Control Board should be retained to perform a monitoring and controlling role in such areas of the market as can be regulated without requiring an unmanageable bureaucracy. An area in which it might be expected to be effective would be in prices of commodities coming from countries with currencies depreciating markedly against the naira.

ii. The Nigeria National Supply Company should be given the task of detecting impending scarcities and procuring goods from abroad to smoothen out the flow to the market.

iii. The Ministry of Trade should establish a unit for identifying and recommending action against monopolistic practices.

iv. Public corporations and government -owned companies which sell goods or services to the public should be required to show what steps they have taken to improve efficiency and productivity before government action is taken on approval of proposed price increases.

I have deliberately gone to this length to show that the commission was fully aware of the possible inflationary effects of any salary increases, and that we provided appropriate counter measures to guard against such a possibility. Whether the counter measures were accepted and implemented is a different matter. If they were, we would accept any blame arising from their implementation, but if, as is the case, these recommendations were not accepted and implemented, then the blame should be laid where it properly belongs.

Recent events have now, to some extent, overtaken the recommendations of the Public Service Review Commission, but I would commend government to again study the recommendations and determine which of them can be relevant in transforming our country into a developed economy.

(18)

Public Enterprises and Privatisation ✢

"Fortunately or unfortunately, Nigeria now has her economic back to the wall and is prepared to try any option. With her cashflow problems and subsequent cuts in credit lines by both the London and Paris clubs of creditors, she has no option but to look for alternative sources of finance."

Introduction

There is a growing concern in Nigeria and other developing countries about the use of public enterprises as instruments for bringing about rapid economic and social development. This concern is not new but it is becoming loud and urgent. Accusing fingers are pointing at public enterprises from all directions. Our economists, bankers and money market operators, our external creditors — the London and Paris clubs — our overseas visitors, experts from the World Bank and the International Monetary Fund as well as representatives of our joint venture partners, all are disenchanted with the performance of our public enterprises. In this paper, I shall attempt a review of the objectives and rationale for establishing public enterprises, examine whether the objectives are being achieved, and if not, what attempts are being made to improve their performance, and why privatisation is now a viable option.

The case for public enterprises

On the achievement of independence in the sixties, African politicians discovered to their dismay that what they got was the shell without the substance of independence. It was independence in an empty stomach. The wealth of the country was in the hands of foreigners who controlled both the commercial and industrial sectors of the economy. The situation was unhealthy economically

---

✢   Paper presented at the "Public Service Forum" of Cross River State, Calabar, October 27, 1988. Cross River State has since been split into two states.

and politically. Unless they acted quickly to control the economy, the tide of rising expectations in their followers would change to a tide of rising frustrations. And having promised life more abundant, they realised that they could remain in power only as long as they were able to improve the standards of living of the people. For them, therefore, it was politically risky, if not suicidal, to leave the control of the economy in the hands of foreign entrepreneurs. Without this control, they could not plan economic growth, nor bring about indigenous participation in business nor solve the problem of unemployment.

Many politicians had also come to the conclusion that the urgent problems of development could not be solved by private enterprises alone, and that governments must get away from their traditional caretaker and regulatory functions and move into active participation in the productive sector. There were areas like infrastructure where private enterprises were hesitant to venture into either because of the huge capital investments involved or because of the low rates of return. Most people, therefore, bought the idea of public corporations and supported government intervention as the appropriate and quickest route for achieving rapid economic growth. The belief was that State enterprises would generate resources for further investment, and would act as a catalyst for expanded industrialisation and rural development. One of the results of this was the domination of the economic scene by State-owned commercial and industrial enterprises so much so that they now constitute a threat to private enterprise and initiative. In some developing countries, only farming, small-scale manufacturing and personal services are left to the private sector.

Today, the Federal Government of Nigeria has over 300 enterprises[1] in agriculture, mining, petroleum refining, rolling mills, breweries, paper, hotels, banking and insurance. State governments have joined in the race. Most of them have breweries, hotels, banks and insurance companies. Some have gone further

---

[1] Since the 1980s, many of these enterprises have been either wholly or partially privatised.

to engage in such small-scale enterprises like laundry and supermarkets. As long as the oil money was flowing, and as long as the economy was buoyant, no questions were asked and the public sector continued to grow until it became an octopus and a colossus bestriding the entire economy.

Are the objectives being achieved?

The failure or inability of most public enterprises to achieve the objectives for which they were created is no longer in doubt. As far back as 1966, the head of the Federal Military Government was quoted as saying:

> The present state of State-owned companies have given the Federal Military Government some cause for anxiety. Sufficient time has elapsed to enable an objective judgement to be passed on whether or not these enterprises have creditably satisfied their objectives. The spate of public opinion in the last five years and more provide available evidence that these enterprises have failed to fulfil expectations.

The series of public enquiries into their operations reflect public dissatisfaction with their performance. At least fifty per cent of public enterprises in Nigeria have had public enquires conducted into their operations. Between 1960 and 1966, for example, the Nigerian Railway Corporation alone had thirteen enquires into its activities. In 1965, it had a deficit of 35 million naira and the World Bank described its finances as "disastrous". A recent report revealed that Nigeria's investment in its 300 enterprises was 23 billion naira made up of 11.4 million naira in equity, 10.2 billion naira in loans and 1.4 billion naira in loan guarantees. The dividends received from this investment for the period 1980-85 was 933.7 million naira. This, in real terms, is not more than two per cent and is below the cost of capital even for concessional loans. Such an investment in the private sector could have yielded between ten and fifteen per cent, i.e., between 2.3 and 3.4 billion naira.

The situation in other African countries is no better. In Ghana, for instance, an inquiry into the affairs of the Timber Marketing

Board found that the Board failed to render adequate services to the timber industry, and that it was "a mere collecting agency and dispenser of funds."[2] A 1982 report on Kenya public enterprises noted that "Government involvement in commercial ventures has tended to tarnish the image of Government because the parastatals and other ventures which were expected to be viable have not been profitable."[3] In Tanzania, President Nyerere[4] commenting on the "disastrous results" of the nationalised sisal plantation which have "turned into wildlife sanctuaries" said, "I must admit that we failed to manage these estates."[5]

Reasons for the failure of public enterprises

There are several reasons for the failure of public enterprises to achieve their objectives. The first is that the objectives of each enterprise are never clearly defined. For example, the law establishing some of the development corporations says that the objectives of the corporation shall be to "facilitate and promote economic development." This is a very wide and vague objective. With such an objective, the corporation can do anything from running a private school to building roads, for both will facilitate and promote economic development. This actually happened with the Nigerian Railway Corporation which, in spite of the unsatisfactory state of its finances described above, proceeded to build a medical centre at a cost of 2.7milion naira. Governments do not appear to know what exactly they want the enterprises to do. The objectives may be stated in the enabling Act or company law in general terms but these should be translated into particular and quantifiable targets by the responsible ministry over definite planning periods. For example, the Ministry of Agriculture should

---

2   See the report of the commission into Ghana Timber Marketing Board and Ghana Co-operative Union , 1967.

3   See the report and recommendations of the Working Party on Government Expenditures, Nairobi, 1982.

4   Nyerere was one of the few independence leaders in Africa who did not seek to perpetuate himself in power. He voluntarily gave up the presidency of his country.

5   Quoted in the *Daily Nation*, May 6, 1985.

be able to tell an agricultural enterprise that in the next four years it has to increase the acreage under maize cultivation by 750,000 hectares, or to tell the Tourist Corporation that it has, in the plan period (i.e.,four years), to increase the number of tourists visiting the country by 200,000. When the objectives are vague, the tendency is for governments to exercise rigid control in its anxiety to ensure that the enterprise does not go astray.

Another reason for the poor performance of public enterprises is fundamental non-viability of some projects. Often, the failure of a public enterprise is due to lack of competent and detailed pre-investment survey and market research. Sometimes the only survey is that by an interested European machine peddler whose main interest is to sell machinery and not the success of the enterprise. To sell, he has to put up such rosy prospects which deliberately ignore some vital considerations. This was, for example, the case with the unsuccessful rolling mill, ceramic and glass factories in the former Eastern Region of Nigeria. The losses incurred by Western Nigeria's canning factory were due largely to inadequate survey. After the factory had been established, and a full complement of European managers and technicians had been assembled, it was discovered that there was not enough grapefruit in the Ibadan area to feed the factory.

An equally important reason for the failure of public enterprises is political patronage in the appointment of board members and staff. In Nigeria, politicians see hope for success in life by becoming active and vocal members of a political party that has a reasonable chance of coming to power. If the party wins, they expect their reward in some paid employment. Because of the rigid traditions and procedures of the civil service, the politicians are unable to tamper with the Service but they find no such restrictions in the service of public enterprises. Appointments based on patronage were so prevalent in Nigeria that board membership was openly shared between the two political parties that controlled the government of the First Republic. Little or no regard was paid to qualifications and experience. Such appointments had disastrous effects on the objectives and operations of the enterprise. They became instruments of political rather than economic policy. One of the commissions that inquired into the Nigerian Railway Corporation quoted a witness who said that a one-time chairman of the board of directors was so politically motivated that "he did not know the difference between the office of the corporation and that of his political party".

Other managerial and financial reasons which contributed to the failure of public corporations include:

i.   Lack of managerial and financial autonomy. Many enterprises are not allowed access to the open market for the hire of expert staff or for the procurement of necessary capital. They are also not free to determine their pricing policies or investment priorities.

ii.   Lack of financial responsibility and accountability. This is the result of over-protection and over-dependence on government for loans and/or subventions. There are examples of enterprises that have not produced annual audited accounts for more than five consecutive years.

iii. Absence of competition and other commercial pressures that are responsible for managerial efficiency ,cost consciousness, innovations and success. Because government is the owner, there is very little pressure to earn surpluses and declare dividends.

iv.   Bureaucratic interference and red tape. Very often, the management of public enterprises spends a lot of time dealing with bureaucracy rather than with productive efficiency. Enterprise managers often complain that they have too many masters — top civil servants, ministers, top military officers and members of Parliament, where they exist.

Attempted reforms

Over the years, several attempts have been made to grapple with the complex problems of public enterprises. The first attempt was the exercise of rigid control over their operations. This had disastrous consequences as it emasculated management initiative.

The second move was the injection of civil servants into the boards of the enterprises. This, in turn, has several disadvantages. Among these disadvantages are:

i. Civil servants are normally appointed by virtue of their offices, and because of the great turnover in staff, they are never on the board long enough to develop a sense of identification with an enterprise. By the time they get acquainted with the problems of a particular enterprise, they are moved to other jobs.

ii. Civil servants are, by training, service-oriented rather than profit-oriented. They are cautious and averse to taking the kind of risks necessary for the success of commercial enterprises.

iii. There is also a tendency on the part of civil servants to act as watchdogs rather than as planners. They also tend to apply civil service forms and procedures which have the effect of dampening entrepreneurship.

iv. Civil servants also are inclined to equate their remuneration and conditions of service with those of public enterprises with the result that public enterprises are often unable to attract or compete with private enterprises in the recruitment and retention of scarce manpower.

Other measures tried include the establishment of a statutory corporation service commission to be responsible for appointment, promotion and dismissal of the staff of public corporations and State enterprises.

Another reform was the establishment of standing tenders boards for the award of contracts. These attempts were later scrapped because they worsened the situation by further restricting the autonomy of enterprises. Recently, two other experiments were tried. The first was an attempt to compel the enterprises to operate on commercial principles, that is, to charge customers the cost of services rendered. This was done by reducing their subventions to 50% of the 1985 level. This sudden change was introduced in the 1986 budget , and it sent shock waves to the management of the enterprises. The second experiment was the appointment of task forces over and above the boards of public enterprises. Furthermore, the task forces are expensive and are likely to increase the indebtedness of public enterprises or increase the quantum of public funds channelled into them as subsidies.[6] The question now being asked is whether public enterprises are beyond redemption, and whether there are any other options?

The option of privatisation

I will like to argue that one reason for the failure of the several measures tried so far is that they were implemented half-heartedly. This was due to the overpowering influence of politics and bureaucracy. Over the years, public enterprises had become an instrument of personal power for those in power including the bureaucratic elite. Fortunately or unfortunately, Nigeria now has her economic back to the wall and is prepared to try any option. With her cashflow problems, and subsequent cuts in credit lines by both the London and Paris clubs of creditors, she has no option but to look for alternative sources of finance. She turned to the World Bank and the International Monetary Fund. These organisations were willing to provide funds but insisted on our putting our house in order — massive cuts in public expenditures and privatisation of public enterprises, which gulped funds that could otherwise have gone to such essential sectors as health and education.

This is how privatisation came into the language and dictionary of the Nigerian government. This is why it became one of the key policy measures of the Structural Adjustment Programme (SAP) introduced by the Babangida administration in July 1986. The other key elements of the programme are: the Second-Tier Foreign Exchange Market (SFEM), which in July 1987 metamorphosed into the Foreign Exchange Market (FEM); debt rescheduling, which has been progressing fairly well; and the

---

[6]   See, for example, *The Guardian* of April 23, 1988 (p.11), where the finance commissioner of Gongola State was reported as saying that the state spent ₦ 5.8 million between January and April 1988 on "the development of task forces".

new tariff structure which was introduced in the 1988 budget and designed to last for another seven years. So far, the only major SAP measures on which very little has been done is privatisation.

Reasons for the slow progress in privatisation and the conditions for a successful privatisation

There are several reasons why Nigeria is slow to privatise. In the first place, privatisation is not an easy exercise. It is a difficult process which requires careful planning and considerable skill, if it is to succeed. The preparations relate to the enterprises, relevant interest groups, and the general public. It is not enough for the government to want to dispose off an enterprise. Someone else must want to buy it. To attract buyers, the enterprises must be worth buying. It must also be dressed up for the market. Preparation for the market might involve a programme of reform such as restructuring the capital base of the enterprise and converting it into a public limited liability company. These processes are both expensive and time-consuming. In some countries, a sale is not contemplated until the enterprise has become viable, and a going concern. This is important for, in the absence of viability, it will be difficult to put a price on the enterprise, and pricing is an important element of the privatisation process.

The orthodox bases of price fixing are assets and projected earnings of the company. Where, as it is likely the case with many public enterprises, there are valuable assets as well as losses in the operations of the enterprises, pricing becomes much more difficult. In such cases, the vendor will tend to look at the assets and the purchaser on the losses and what it would take him to refurbish the enterprise in order to bring it back to viability. A good example is the case of hotels. Some of them are on good sites but require a lot of money for renovation, re-equipment and re-training of staff. A further difficulty in pricing will arise where enterprises have not had audited accounts for years. Where these difficulties cannot be overcome, other forms of sale will have to be considered other than a public offer through the stock exchange which is the most politically acceptable method of sale. Other forms of sale are sales to the employees of the enterprise or sale by private placing. Whatever method is used, all relevant particulars and circumstances of the enterprise have got to be disclosed and put right before sale. There is the story of a government hotel that was recently up for sale but just before the sale was concluded, it was discovered that the vendor had no Certificate of Occupancy to the property.

Next to preparing the enterprise for the market is the need to identify, at an early stage, relevant interest groups and satisfy them. These include workers, management staff, prospective investors, commentators and opponents of privatisation. Workers' support could be enlisted by the offer of some free shares. Management, on the other hand, should be involved to the greatest extent possible in order to neutralise possible opposition. In this regard, the temptation to suspend some of their existing privileges should be resisted. The support of the general public, including the opponents of privatisation, could be secured through a programme of public information during which the case for privatisation should be argued effectively and enthusiastically. The ordinary citizen must know the overall economic reasons for privatisation. He should also know what, as a citizen, he stands to gain by the purchase of shares. A projection of profitability in terms of dividends and future capital gains should form part of the information package.

Public information should also be directed at dispelling ignorance and misconceptions that surround privatisation. Many Nigerians are not aware that privatisation is not really new to the country. It was first practised in eastern Nigeria in the early sixties when the government of that region sold its shares in the Nkalagu Cement Company to the public. It has in recent years been practised by the Cross River State Government when it sold its shares in the Cross River Breweries, and by the Imo State Government that sold its shares in Golden Guinea. Both sales were to the public through the Stock Exchange.

A common misconception is that privatisation will make the rich richer, for they will use their connections to acquire enterprises at give-away prices. Those who hold this view are probably not aware of the Securities and Exchange Commission whose responsibility is to determine the prices of shares and supervise their allocation. There is also an allocation committee comprising of the Security and Exchange Commission, the Nigeria Stock Exchange and the Nigerian Enterprises Promotion Board. One of the guidelines of this committee is to ensure that priority is given to small investors, and in a case of over-subscription, their demands should be met in full. This was the practice during the indigenisation exercise.

Other misconceptions relate to possible high costs of services and reduction in staff when an enterprise comes under the management of the private sector. This is a short-term view. In the long run and when the enterprise succeeds and expands, more staff are bound to be employed. The question of cost of goods and services is determined by market forces. After all, the essence of privatisation is the transfer of management from the bureaucratic regulations of the public sector to the competition of the marketplace, the forces which ensure that consumers get the best price, as no producer wants to price himself out of the market. There is no doubt, however, that in the short run, when the problem is that of survival, the one solution open to a new owner is to improve the quality of goods and services, bring down costs, reduce staff, and ensure that the performance of those that remain go up.

The political opposition of those who fear that certain ethnic groups might buy up most of the shares and thereby consolidate their control of the economy should not be ignored. The fear, real or imaginary, has, however, been taken care of by Section 7 of the Privatisation Decree which provides that shares shall be reserved for associations and interest groups including the staff of the company before allotment to the general public.

The propaganda that privatisation is a neo-colonialist ploy for the control of the economies of former dependent territories by their former colonial masters must be refuted. I believe that the propaganda must have arisen through suggestions by some World Bank economists that privatisation is an opportunity for debt conversion.[7] My view is that the two programmes should be tackled separately. There will be no need for outside shareholders in the privatisation exercise, as there will be adequate local demand. Those in charge of privatisation will find it difficult to satisfy the demand. Foreign shareholders will only be necessary in cases where local management expertise is not available.

Second, debt-equity swap should be used to attract new foreign capital. In Argentina, the condition for debt conversion is that investors must bring at least one new dollar for every dollar that is converted. That aside, those in charge of privatisation should collect and disseminate information about what is happening in other countries, developed and developing. The fact is that since the downturn of the world economy, privatisation has been embraced world-wide — in Europe, Asia and America. Even socialist countries have not escaped the wind of change. In China, it is called *individualisation*. In Russia, it is *perestroica* (meaning reform). It is, however, more evident in France and Britain. In Britain, 25 billion pounds worth of shares have been sold by the British government, and 600,000 workers have moved to the private sector. One in five of the adult population in Britain is now a shareholder. There, the performances of privatised companies have also improved. The profits of some have trebled, and some have gone up sevenfold.[8]

Everything possible should, therefore, be done to give privatisation widespread popular appeal. In some countries, small shareholders are offered bonus shares if they are able to purchase a minimum number of shares, and retain them for a specified period. In others, easy terms of purchase are provided. An important strategy is to start with enterprises that are likely to appeal to buyers. It would be unwise to start with the big money losers. Companies that easily come to mind here are Unipetrol, African Petroleum, hotels, breweries and insurance companies.

[7]   See, for instance, "Debt-Equity Conversion and Privatisation" by Nair and Mark Frazier in *Economic Impact*, No. 60, p. 14.

[8]   From a paper on privatisation which was delivered by Gerry Grimstone at a seminar organised by the Templeton College of Oxford University.

quoted on the Stock Exchange. Those responsible for privatisation must realise that privatisation is not just a sale. The companies, which are created must be successful, for the success of privatised companies is the best advocate for further privatisation. In this connection, I shall refer to what is described by some as the *CORE Theory*, and by others as the *Golden Share*. This is the concept of ensuring that in each privatised enterprise, there is a hard-core of shareholders with sufficient stake in the company. The result can be terrific if the hard-core is also in possession of relevant expertise. This group has a dual function: to guide management and to protect the interests of the generality of shareholders, for sometimes management tends to believe that what is good for management is also good for the shareholders. A further advantage of an indigenous hard-core is that it can prevent foreign predators and unhealthy take-over bids.

The Privatisation Decree

Having discussed what I consider the pre-conditions for a successful implementation of privatisation, I shall proceed to make one or two comments on the Privatisation Decree. Section 2 of the Decree provides that "the control, management and composition of the Board of Directors of privatised enterprises shall, as from the date of privatisation, reflect the ownership structure of the enterprise." It is not clear whether control and management envisaged refers to the enterprise as a whole or only to the board of directors. One of the administrative guidelines of the Enterprises Promotion Board is that the composition of the board of indigenised companies should reflect the ownership structure of the company as between foreign and indigenous shareholders. Section 2 of the Privatisation Decree has gone furthermore than that to include control and management. Already this provision has been interpreted by Union Bank to mean that "Owners of the privatised enterprises will now be able to have their own representatives at the general management level of privatised companies in proportion to their level of equity

---

9   See the *Economic Newsletter* of the Union Bank, No. 33, p. 13.

shareholding."[9]

Such a situation will certainly create problems in the control and management of the company, as it would be difficult, if not impossible, to reconcile the different interest groups. To give effects to this provision in cases of partial privatisation is to restore political interference and other influences which have been the bane of public enterprises. The main purpose of privatisation is to increase the economic efficiency of the affected enterprises. To achieve this, enterprise managers must be free to make investment and personnel decisions without considerations of group interests. In other words, in the management of men, money and materials for the achievement of productive and allocative efficiency, the competitive forces of the marketplace must guide them. Furthermore, the management of a company must identify itself, not with individual interests but with the corporate interest and objectives of the company. Shareholders, no matter the size of their shareholding, must seek their interest through, with, and in the company as a whole. In the same manner, the board of directors, no matter how constituted, must act as trustees of the entire corpus of shareholders.

Another observation on Section 2 is the importance of drawing a distinction between ownership and management. Ownership is one thing, management is another. Owner-managers can be successful in small scale businesses but once a business has grown and the span of control is up to the five fingers of one hand, management has got to be professionalised, i.e., management must then be separated from ownership. To fail to do so will be to prevent the enterprise from developing expertise in the different fields of management — finance, production, marketing and personnel, etc.

The next provision of the Privatisation Decree that needs examination is Section 7, which provides for the wide spread of shares. This is politically desirable but, if care is not taken, a situation might arise where the shares are so thinly spread that the monitoring of management becomes difficult. Government could do such monitoring with its controlling share (golden share) but the problem is that government monitoring often degenerates into political control and interference with management. An alternative might be to allot a sizeable shareholding — ten to twenty per cent — to a core-group comprising preferably of persons in the line of business so that with their expertise they can monitor management. It is a different story when you have three or four groups of sizeable shareholders without the relevant expertise. It must, however, be emphasised that monitoring is different from management envisaged in Section 2 of the Decree. Monitoring connotes warning, checking and guidance provided by a third party whilst management is an action by an insider, a line manager. It is hoped that Section 2 applies only to the board of directors and does not, as the Union Bank newsletter believes, apply to the management level.

Parts I and II of Schedule I of the Decree list enterprises which are to be partially and fully privatised. It is difficult to discover the criteria for the classification. One guess is that the government wants to retain ownership and control of viable enterprises like banks and strategic industries like steel. One can understand the reasons for the government wanting to retain control of strategic companies like the Steel Rolling Mills, the Federal Radio Corporation of Nigeria, the Nigerian Security Printing and Minting Company Limited. Government should also control industries and companies that have a supportive role in facilitating economic development. Examples are the River Basin Development Authority, the Nigerian Industrial Development Bank, the Federal Mortgage Bank of Nigeria, agricultural banks, and the Nigerian Bank for Commerce and Industry. Because of their developmental roles, they should, where necessary, be subsidised, and should not be privatised either fully or partially.

On the other hand, viable companies like commercial banks, oil marketing companies, or companies that have potential for profitability if efficiently managed, such as the Nigeria Airways the Nigeria National Shipping Line , paper mills, sugar companies, cement companies, motor vehicles and truck assembly companies, etc., should be fully privatised. Government might, if it so desires, retain a token equity in them. But the percentage of the equity which the government has decreed to retain in the companies which are slated for partial privatisation is too high for comfort. If government's intention in retaining a sizeable amount of equity is financial, then it should have no hesitation in reducing its holding in order to allow the private sector to have control and management, for I would rather have five or ten per cent equity in a well-managed and profitable company than forty per cent in an inefficiently managed and unprofitable company.

If government, however, insists on retaining controlling interest, it means that it wants, in the light of Section 2 of the Decree, to continue to control and manage the companies. Where then is the need for privatisation or attraction for private investors? It is worth repeating that the essence of privatisation is deregulation and de-bureaucratisation, that is, substitution of government control with marketplace competitive forces, which will ensure better economic efficiency. If government has been managing these enterprises for the past two decades without success, why does it want to continue to do so under partial privatisation? If privatisation is going to be a viable alternative, government must be prepared to give up control and management for, in business, government's hand is a dead hand.

I would like to end with the following extract from an article by Alan Rufus Waters, professor of international business at California State University:

> Is privatisation a viable policy? This question is being asked now in many nations, developed and developing. The answer lies in the response to another question: What are the goals of those controlling the governments of those nations? If their goals include achieving a rising level of national prosperity , greater national economic power, and an open competitive society, privatisation will be regarded as attractive. On the other hand, if what they seek is personal gain for themselves, personal power, and a controlled society, privatisation will be anathema to them.

(19)

The Civil Service in the Year 2000 and Beyond ⬧

"... not even a prophet can, in the present unstable and unpredictable Nigerian situation, foretell what would happen in the next few months, let alone years and decades."

Introduction

For sometime now, I have decided to refrain from public engagements. The reason is that I believe the time has come, indeed it is overdue, when my generation should not only step aside, but completely vacate the stage for the younger generation. As long as we are here, even in a corner, our shadows are bound to obstruct the views and perceptions of the up and coming generation. Why then, you will ask, have I made an exception today? The simple answer is that I am concerned about the conflicting danger signals coming out of Abuja in recent months. The signals indicate that the civil service is on a collision course with future politicians. In the event of that collision, the civil service cannot win, but will come out bruised and humiliated. I have, therefore, decided to take advantage of this invitation to sound the alarm for those who care to listen. The details of the danger will unfold themselves as we go along.

Your invitation is that I address you on the subject of "The Civil Service in the Year 2000 and Beyond." This is a difficult task, for not even a prophet can, in the present unstable and unpredictable Nigerian situation, foretell what would happen in the next few months, let alone years and decades. Furthermore, the civil service structure and functions in any country depend on that country's political system of government. After all, the job of a civil servant is to carry out

---

⬧ An address delivered to the Delta State Public Service Forum, Asaba, April 26, 1995.

173

the legitimate wishes of his political master. How he carries
them out depends not only on the country's political system but
also on the tenure of government as well as on whether the
executive power of government is single or collegiate, that is to
say, whether executive powers are vested in one person as in
the presidential system, or on a group of persons as in the
parliamentary system.

It would have been presumptuous of us to discuss the role
and function of the civil service when the form of government is
yet to be determined. We are, however, encouraged to do so
because of the conflicting signals referred to above. The signals
are political on the one hand, and bureaucratic or civil service
on the order. The political signal coming from the constitutional
conference[1] is pointing to a presidential system of government
whilst the bureaucratic /civil service signal coming from the
office of the secretary to the military government is pointing to a
parliamentary type civil service.

Let me say straight away that you cannot service a
presidential system of government with a parliamentary civil
service. It will not work, and will lead to friction between the
president and top civil servants. Let me then describe the two
systems for us to see if they can go together. The two systems
are often referred to as the White House and Whitehall systems
of government. White House is the official Washington residence
of the United States president whilst Whitehall is the name of
the London Street where the main British government offices
are, including the Houses of Parliament and the residence of the
British prime minister.

Briefly, and for the benefit of the younger members of the
audience, the American system is a form of government where
all the executive powers of government are vested, for a
definite period, in one man known as the president. He is the

---

[1] A Conference inaugurated by the Abacha regime to prepare the draft of a constitution
that would usher in the Third Republic.

person who went round the country and got the mandate to rule. Once elected, he is free to appoint any person or persons considered capable of helping him to deliver his mandate. Those appointed may be politicians or professional civil servants. He puts them in charge of ministries, departments, bureaux, corporations, foreign missions or as advisers. One thing that is common to all the appointees is that they are professionals in their own fields, and share, or at least have sympathy for, the political philosophy of the president. Should any of the appointed officers be found wanting, the president will have no scruples in relieving the officer of his responsibilities. Whenever the president leaves office, he leaves with his men. An in-coming administration may or may not retain them. When a civil servant is appointed to a policy position he loses his tenure, neutrality and anonymity whilst in the post. At the end of the administration, he may revert to his civil service post or retire if he is not assigned to a new job. The American argument in support of political appointments, whether from the civil service or outside, is that a career civil servant is, by training, neutral and anonymous, and cannot, therefore, be expected to advocate or implement government policies with the same dynamism, devotion and commitment as a political appointee.

In general, the civil service in a presidential system is a mixture of the career and patronage systems, that is to say, a mixture of those appointed politically and those appointed on merit. Only less than two per cent of the American civil service is politically appointed whilst the remaining ninety-eight per cent are appointed on merit, and are supervised by the federal public service commission or by the agencies for which they work.

The merit or career system proper applies to the middle and lower grade civil servants. It is based on merit and fitness for appointment after a competitive examination. Although called a career system, it does not, like the British career system, promise a life-long employment. The American officer can, however, remain in office until the official retiring age of seventy provided he continues to meet the standards of conduct and performance required for his position. The system is averse to any idea of permanency with rights and privileges that are not enjoyed by workers in other walks of life. The American system has also a small third group of officers who are in-between political appointees and the professional civil servants. They are known as the *in-and-outers*. These are professionals who come into government service for a limited number of years (three or four) and then return to private life to be available at a future date for either future government or political appointment. In this way, they are quite distinct from the straightforward political appointees. They are in the grey area between the political appointees and professional civil servants.

The parliamentary system, on the other hand, is a collegiate and participatory system where the supreme executive and legislative authorities rest with the Parliament. The leader of the majority party in Parliament becomes the prime minister. He selects his cabinet from the members of the House and they have collective responsibility for government. In Britain as well as in the countries of Western Europe, development is mainly in the hands of the private sector and the main job of Parliament is to make laws for the control of that sector. The laws are not executed by Parliament or the staff of Whitehall but are passed down to local governments and other statutory bodies for implementation.

The main job of the British permanent secretary is to assist his minister in getting legislation through the Parliament. He also advises on policy and deals, with difficulties which may arise in carrying out existing policies and forecasts the possible effects of new measures and regulations. As we have seen, he does not implement parliamentary legislation but passes it on to local governments and statutory bodies. At best his job is that of a monitor.

The difference between top civil servants of both systems is not only in their tenures and methods of appointment, but also in their qualifications and functions. The American, unlike the British, is appointed on the basis of his own professional expertise, and is assigned to a department, or bureau, where his job is to get things done, that is, to achieve certain results within the specific period of the administration. He is a manager rather than an administrator, a professional rather than a generalist. His British counterpart is a permanent officer whose job is mainly advisory and as such he is politically neutral and does not take blame for policy failures. I am sure some of you have seen the comedy or read the book *'Yes Minister'*.

One observation that must be made is that there is hardly any difference in the functions of the middle and lower civil service of both systems. They are both engaged in the day-to-day conduct of government business, such as the collection of taxes, accounts and audit. Our concern, therefore, is with top civil servants.

Now that we have described the operation of the two civil services, the question that arises is that of choice. Which of the two systems should Nigeria adopt. The simple answer will seem to be that our Service should be tailored to our system of government, that if our government is presidential, we should adopt the presidential type of civil service but if it is parliamentary, we should adopt the parliamentary type of civil service. This simple answer, however, is not enough. It does not take into account the fact that both the type of government and its attendant civil service grew out of the special circumstances of the country as well as its level of economic and social development. Consequently, they are not for wholesale export or transplant. So far we have tried both systems without success.

Let us, therefore, consider one system after the other, beginning with the parliamentary or Whitehall type which we seem to be hankering after. The first problem that comes to mind is the problem of the differences in the level of development. The parliamentary system operates in a developed economy and as such both the government and its civil service are not saddled with the problem of bringing about economic development. Their main job is to control and monitor the private sector, unlike the job of the government and civil service of a developing economy which are expected to bring about social and economic development. Because of this expectation, the success and acceptability of any government in the developing countries depend on concrete achievements, for example, on the mileage of roads tarred and maintained, the number of schools and hospitals built, the improvement in the prices of primary products, and in the rise in general living standards. Political leaders are, therefore, aware that their continuance in power depends on their ability to bring about rapid social and economic changes in order to satisfy the aspirations and yearnings of their people. This is the main reason for the various development plans and programmes that have become a common feature of most developing countries. The concomitant of this clamour for progress and change is the desire of politicians to ensure that the civil service is responsive to political leadership. Responsiveness is here interpreted to mean control of those civil servants whose jobs have considerable political content or extensive executive powers.

In support of control, politicians often argue that they do not see how they can discharge their responsibilities without controlling the civil servants who are responsible for the execution of their policies. And the control demanded is with regards to their appointment, deployment, assignment and discipline. The more people demand progress the more the politicians want to tighten their hold and control of top civil servants, i.e., permanent secretaries.

We know that under the parliamentary system a permanent secretary has security of tenure, he is politically neutral and anonymous. The question is, how far can a Nigerian permanent secretary, or any officer at that level, be really apolitical and anonymous bearing in mind that both his appointment and functions are extremely political? I submit that in the present circumstances, it is unrealistic and a fiction to expect security and political neutrality from officers at that level. If the politics is only with regards to his appointment, as in Britain, the problem would not be very difficult to contain but the real issue is with regards to his responsibilities as a catalyst for change, an officer saddled with bringing about physical change. The final question is, can the present Nigerian career generalist, apolitical and anonymous permanent secretary satisfy the present requirements of the job as well as bear the pressures of his political master? Does his job profile not call for new men with new ideas, professionals with appropriate management expertise? Let us now also examine the application of the presidential civil service. Responsibility wise, the job of the presidential top civil servant is akin to what is expected from the Nigerian permanent secretary for both are expected to see to the execution of a definite programme of work. But the Nigerian permanent secretary resembles the British permanent secretary in that he is a generalist and does not have the American expertise necessary for accomplishing tasks. Again, even if he has the expertise, he will not like to leave office with Mr. President because the Nigerian economy is not yet capable of absorbing his expertise.

Another problem in applying the presidential system is the difficulty of the various cadres of officers being able to work harmoniously and appropriately in their different roles in a ministry or department. We have yet to learn how to work together as a team, at different levels, towards a common purpose and without being bossy and overbearing.

Conclusion

I do not want to sound as a prophet of doom but I honestly believe that the presidential system of government and its civil service has little chances of success in Nigeria at its present stage of development. For one reason, we have not developed to the stage in which we can confidently surrender the powers of governance to one man. We are not yet a nation-state, and we have to achieve national integration and loyalty. This is precisely why the constitutional conference is discussing rotational presidency. In my opinion, what we need for the time being is participatory government, that is, a government in which the powers of government are shared between a president and a prime minister. The president should be elected on a non-partisan basis from one zone but the prime minister should be elected on party basis and should run the government with ministers drawn from the Parliament. In this way, the prime minister will be controlled by the House. Some important subjects should, however, be reserved for the president, such as defence, foreign affairs, census, elections, and citizenship. To enlist the confidence of the whole country, the president should be assisted in the discharge of his service by a presidential council elected from each of the states on a non-party basis. Under such a structure, every state will have a voice in the presidential council as well as in Parliament where the prime minister and his ministers are accountable to all the members elected by the parties under universal adult suffrage.[2]

Since the unmodified presidential system is what the constitutional conference appears to be inclined towards, we have to adapt our civil service to serve that system. The adaptation should not be a wholesale adoption of the parliamentary system of civil service as is being mooted. Such an adoption will, I submit, not succeed. It can succeed with the military but not with a civilian government that will be geared to achieving quick and visible results because of its time frame. The possible conflict situation will not, I submit, favour the civil service. I recommend the following adaptations:

a.   First, there must be a clear distinction between the conditions of service of politically appointed civil servants and the conditions of service of those appointed and controlled by the public service commission under the career system.

b.   Second, the career service should end at the level of professional head of department. That should be the highest expectation of any civil servant, as well as the end of the pensionable service. This will ensure that any appointments above that level will not entail loss of career prospects.

c.   Third, in view of the development needs of the country, the Service, particularly its upper echelons, should be manned by professionals rather than generalists, and by

---

[2] For this novel system, the author made no specific recommendations regarding its civil service, since the system was not under consideration by the constitutional conference.

managers rather than administrators.

d. Fourth, any civil servant appointed to a political post should retire with his earned pension and be on contract for the duration of the administration that appointed him. With his pension and professional expertise he can be comfortably available for future services if, and when required. In this way, we can begin to develop our own core of professional in-and-outers.

Section 2: The Private Sector

The time has come when government's role in development should be de-emphasised in favour of more responsibility to the private sector.

— From report of interview with *Business Contact* Magazine, July and August 1991.

It is an indisputable fact that in democratic economies no amount of government action or even subsidies will make a nation great. Rather, the greatness of a nation depends on the efforts and enterpreneurship of its people.

—From a paper on *Entrepreneurship in Africa* presented at AAPAM Conference in Mahe, Seychelles, November 27 – December 1, 1989.

(20)

Productivity and the Rewards of Labour✦

"Productivity is very important because that is what determines the size of the output to be shared... When you add what each person produces, no matter the type of work, you get what economists call Gross National Product (GNP) which is the nearest to what many politicians call the 'national cake'. If the GNP or 'national cake' does not grow while the population is growing, everybody is worse off."

Introduction

Mr. Chairman, the Principal and Staff, Graduands, Distinguished Guests, Ladies and Gentlemen. It gives me pleasure to be here today to bring this message to our youths who are now ready to join their colleagues in the task of building Nigeria into a developed and self-reliant nation. As you leave the walls of this college, you will naturally worry about jobs — whether you are going to be employed at all, and whether the employment will be in the public or private sector. You will also certainly worry about how much you are going to be paid if you get a job, and whether your pay will be commensurate with your skills, and comparable with what your colleagues in other employments get. These worries are quite natural since schooling is not an end in itself. Most of us who are older were once in the same worrying position. But let me tell you right away, that you are very lucky. You are lucky in the sense that you are growing up when the economy is expanding fast, and this expansion provides lots of job opportunities. Let me explain.

The governments of this country, I mean the federal and state governments, are investing a lot of money in establishing industries, building roads and highways, building dams, expanding telecommunications, building steel mills, etc. Also, individuals and private companies are investing more in

---

✦ Speech presented in the mid 70s to the graduands of Yaba College of Technlogy, Lagos.

industries which produce various consumer goods such as cigarettes, shoes, batteries, textiles, etc. This means that both the government and the private sector are creating jobs through these investments. In other words, investments create jobs. When a person decides to invest his money in producing consumer goods on a large scale, he builds a factory, buys machines, raw materials, vehicles, etc. Now, it is evident that one person cannot do everything. He needs engineers, technicians, artisans, and other skilled workmen to run the factory and maintain the machines. This means jobs. He needs salesmen, drivers, packers, clerks, accountants, managers, etc. This means even more jobs!

Labour

When he brings together men, machines, and materials, he then manages them in such a way that the goods he wants to produce are produced. All the men and women he brings to his factory will have different skills and knowledge to contribute. This contribution by the workers is called *Labour*. On his part, the owner provides employment, machines and materials. But neither machines nor materials, nor skill alone can create a product. All must work together in a complementary manner to produce goods.

Productivity

This brings me to the first part of the message I was asked to bring to you — productivity. But what is productivity? There are several ways of looking at it. Let us suppose that a factory is built to produce a certain quantity of products, e.g., one million packets of cigarette a month, if all is right. This is called *installed capacity*. But it may happen that due to cuts in electricity supply, late arrival of raw materials, the breakdown of machinery, lack of the necessary skills, lateness or absenteeism, the factory produces only 400,000 packets of cigarette a month. In this case, we can say that productivity is low, and that the factory is not producing at full capacity. The owner of the factory will not be happy because he is not getting the full benefits from men, machines and raw materials.

Men, machines and materials can be made to produce more within the same time frame, if labour (that is, skill and knowledge) can be improved and made to become more dedicated to the job. If this happens, the factory may increase its productivity to say 600,000 or 800,000 packets a month. In this case, we can say that there is increased productivity. This is of course still below the installed capacity. There will be full efficiency and productivity only when the factory produces one million packets, which is its installed capacity.

Let us look at productivity from another angle and with a different example. Those who make glass bottles make them from a mixture of sand and a kind of clay called dolomite. A factory might use two tons of sand and half a ton of dolomite to make 1,000 bottles, whereas another factory of the same size can use the same quantity of sand and dolomite to produce 1500 bottles. In this case, if both factories employ the same number of men and machines, the second factory is definitely more productive than the first where it would seem that a lot of materials is being wasted. Productivity is thus a measure of efficiency in the use of the factors of production, namely, men, money and materials, including machinery.

Rewards of labour

Now, let us look at the other half of what I have to say this morning — the rewards of labour. Some two hundred years ago, people, especially economists, thought that everything of value was the result of a man's sweat or labour. That meant labour was understood as the only factor of production. In those days, there was a feeling that all the rewards arising out of production should go to labour in the form of wages and other perquisites known as fringe benefits. Later, economists began recognising other factors of production that needed also to be rewarded. These are land, capital and entrepreneurship.

There is a risk in putting out one's money to start a business, there is a risk in building a factory which may take as long as two years to complete. There is also risk in hiring people and paying them even before they produce anything. Economists believe that the man who does all these — the entrepreneur — should also be rewarded. What he gets as his reward is called profit. If he makes a lot of profit, his business grows, i.e., he ploughs back part of the profit into expansion, thus creating more jobs. In this scheme of rewards, the reward for labour is wages and salaries.

Connection between productivity and wages/salaries

What is the connection between productivity on the one hand, and wages and salaries on the other? Naturally, every worker, whether he is a brain worker or a manual worker, is interested in his wages or salaries increasing from time to time, just as the entrepreneur is also interested in his profits increasing from time to time. For this to happen, therefore, the entrepreneur and his workers must work to ensure that productivity is always increasing. To go back to our earlier examples: if our cigarette factory was barely able to pay a wage bill of ₦400 when it was producing 400,000 packets of cigarette a month, there is no way it can increase that wage bill to say ₦600 without sustaining a loss or cutting profits — assuming that other factor costs remain constant. But if our entrepreneur can get more out of a given set of factors of production, then he can afford to increase wages. If, for example, he is confronted with a higher wage bill, to the extent that paying it means no profits (i.e., losses), he may do so, only if he hopes that in the longer term, productivity will increase to absorb the extra wage. But if he continually makes losses or makes no profits, i.e., his own reward for bearing the risk of starting the business, he will close down and everybody will lose his or her job.

Therefore, in any production system, be it a farm, workshop, factory, or the economy as a whole, productivity is very important because that is what determines the size of the output to be shared. One of the problems Nigerian manufacturers have is that the productivity of the average Nigerian worker is very low while the wage is relatively very high. To illustrate, if one divides the total number of cars produced in one year in a country by the total number of persons employed in the car industry in that year, one gets the productivity of the car industry in man per year, given a steady state of technology. With this kind of index, it is said that the productivity of a Japanese car industry worker is about nineteen cars a year, Germany 7.4, France 6.5, and U.K. 2.4. I think if we do the same for Nigeria where we merely assemble components manufactured elsewhere, we would find it to be below the productivity level in most parts of the world.

Reasons for the relatively low productivity of the Nigerian worker

There are many reasons why the productivity of an average Nigerian worker is low. Among these are:

1. He is generally not backed by modern tools. Sometimes even when he has them, he doesn't know how to use them properly, and cannot maintain them regularly, resulting in frequent breakdowns.
2. In the case of industrial work, there is a certain rhythm and discipline required of workers in the factory which the Nigerian worker is yet to learn. Many of us are products of simple rural farming communities. The cycle of life in a farming community is more leisurely than that of a factory. This affects the workers' attitude to work.
3. Talking about attitudes, many Nigerian workers just like to receive their wages, but do not like to work for them. How often do we see people who are supposed to be working chatting and telling stories, or simply loitering where they ought not to be. Once they leave their places of work the organisations employing them lose something in the way of productivity.
4. Often, the condition of the workplace is such that the employee is not motivated to put in his best.

I feel that when you put all the above together, they can explain why national productivity is relatively low. When you add what each person produces, no matter the type of work, you get what economists call Gross National Product which is nearest to what many politicians call the *national cake*. If the GNP or national cake does not grow while the population is growing, everybody is worse off. Since most factors of production can only increase so much, and some, like land, cannot increase at all, the only way to increase the GNP is to increase the productivity of the other factors of production, especially men and machines. This is what technology is all about.

So, Graduands, as you leave this College of Technology, I want you to have it as your objective that you will always do your very best on the job that is given to you. You happen to be in the area where we in the Nigerian industry need many more to be trained. The only way we can catch up with other countries is for you to aspire to be as good as, if not better than, your counterparts in other parts of the world. That way, your productivity will definitely earn a handsome reward for your labour.

Thank You.

21

Entrepreneurship in Africa's Private Sector✢

"The generally accepted argument among development economists is that even where physical, human and financial capital are not really lacking, the absence of a binding force to combine them for output generation could well explain the difference between growth and stagnation; hence, in the search for an explanation for the slow pace of development in Africa, entrepreneurship has often been identified as the one critical scarce input."

Introduction

Africa is the least developed of the continents. According to a 1982 World Bank world development report, nineteen of the thirty-three poorest countries in the world are in Africa. For most African countries, the record of economic development is grim and it is no exaggeration to talk of crisis. All the indicators of economic trouble are evident — slow overall economic growth, sluggish agricultural performance, rapid population growth, and balance of payments and fiscal crises. Whichever socio-economic indicator one looks at, whether per capita income, school enrolment, ratio of doctors to population, share of manufacturing in gross domestic products, access to safe water and life expectancy, African countries are at the bottom of the scale. This has become a source of concern for many African countries, and since the last two decades, several futile attempts have been made to remedy the situation.

In 1978, the Fourth Conference of African Ministers of Industry stressed the need to examine existing policies and strategies with a view to restructuring them to speed up the industrialisation of Africa. The conference requested the

✢ Paper presented at the African Association for Public Administration and Management (AAPAM) conference at Mahe, Seychelles, November 27-December 1, 1989

secretaries of OAU, ECA and UNIDO¹ to organise a symposium on industrial policies and strategies. This was eventually held in Nairobi in 1979. The Fifth Conference of African Ministers of Industry after reviewing the recommendations of the symposium again requested the three secretaries to take appropriate action to have the period 1980 –1990 declared the Industrial Development Decade for Africa(IDDA). Almost simultaneously, the OAU heads of state meeting in Monrovia in 1979 also viewed with seriousness the critical and bleak economic conditions facing each of their countries. That meeting adopted what has come to be called the Monrovia Strategy for the Development of Africa. Other recommendations of the meeting included that the period 1980-1990 be declared as Africa's Industrial Development Decade "for the purposes of focusing greater attention and evoking greater political commitment and financial and technical support at the national, regional and international levels for the industrialisation of Africa". At an ordinary meeting of the OAU heads of state in Lagos, April 1980, a plan of action for the implementation of the Monrovia Strategy for the Economic Development of Africa was adopted, and became known as the Lagos Plan of Action.

At the same time, UNIDO and ECA took the matter up to the UN General Assembly, which adopted resolution 35/66B proclaiming the 1980s as the Industrial Development Decade for Africa. UNIDO, ECA and OAU were asked to formulate proposals to implement the programme as contained in the Lagos Plan of Action. By 1981, a programme for the IDDA had been worked out based on the twin principles of self-reliance and self-sufficiency as embodied in the Lagos Plan of Action. It will be recalled that the two topmost priorities in the Lagos Plan of Action were self-sufficiency in food production and self-sustaining industrialisation, as necessary conditions for the economic freedom of Africa from the shackles of poverty, disease and dearth

---

¹ Organisation for African Unity, Economic Commision for Africa and United Nations Industrial Development Organisation.

of the necessities of life.

Many African countries lagged behind on the programme of IDDA. In 1985, worried about the slow pace of action at the national and sub-regional levels, the OAU heads of state reviewed the progress made thus far, and then adopted the Africa's Priority Programme for Economic Recovery 1986-1990 (OAU, Addis Ababa). In it, the OAU noted the progress made in the implementation of the programme from the IDDA, and in addition, recommended the following specific short-term measures in the industrial field:

i.   A critical assessment should be made of major industrial enterprises in order to rationalise them.
ii.   Urgent measures should be taken to identify industrial skills and technical capabilities required for the implementation of industrial programmes and projects.
iii. A national programme for industrial maintenance should be developed.
iv.   Measures should be taken to promote standardisation and quality control of industrial production. For the medium and long terms, it provided that "existing national mechanisms should be strengthened to mobilise the entire national capabilities for the identification, preparation, evaluation, negotiation and implementation of projects especially the strategic core industries identified in the programme for IDDA."

The reason for this historical account is to show that there has not been any lack of awareness regarding the depressing economic conditions in Africa.

The missing link

All the foregoing attempts by national governments, regional bodies and international organisations like UNIDO, OAU, and ECA have one common element: all of them concentrated on what governments should do to speed up economic development. In all their declarations and programmes of action, no role was assigned to the private sector. Even the development programmes of individual countries have the same defect. They were very often a shopping list of government investments in prestige projects with little or no participation by the private sector. But it is an indisputable fact that in democratic economies no amount of government action or even subsidies will make a nation great. The greatness of a nation will depend on the efforts that individual citizens make by themselves to better their life prospects.

No doubt, governments have a role in development, as we shall see later. But at this stage of our discussion, I make bold to say that Africa's underdevelopment, its present economic debt crisis, and alarming levels of unemployment, are intricately connected with its low level of entrepreneurship, as well as the low or no priority accorded to private initiatives. Governments do not seem to recognise this connection, and, where they do, there has not been commensurate action in support of those initiatives. The establishment of public enterprises in areas normally considered the domain of the private sector is an evidence of this lack of recognition of the role of private entrepreneurship in economic development. In some countries, government has even gone into competition with its citizens in fields like retail trading (supermarkets), road transport, hotels and dry cleaning.

Entrepreneurship

Experts at Harvard Business School have defined entrepreneurship as an attempt to create value, "through recognition of significant business opportunities, or through the drive to manage 'risk taking' appropriate to business, or through the exercise of management skills necessary to mobilise rapidly the human, material and financial resources that will bring a project to function." There are two aspects to this definition: the first relates to what can be called *routine entrepreneurship*, which is concerned purely with management functions. This deals with the co-ordination and control of a well-established, on-going business concern. The second aspect of the definition entails creation of an enterprise that involves not only the identification or conception of ideas but also translating them into concrete functioning projects. This is entrepreneurship par excellence. Invariably, entrepreneurship is innovative, and one may therefore say that where management is innovative, it is also entrepreneurial, hence the term "routine entrepreneurship". In this sense, the distinction between management and entrepreneurship becomes blurred.

Viewed from this broad spectrum, entrepreneurship is certainly not a homogeneous function. In his book, *Entrepreneurship and Economic Development* (1971), Peter Kilby listed thirteen aspects of the tasks of the entrepreneur. Four of them deal with technical innovation in production. Three are concerned with purchasing and marketing. Another three deal with personnel, financial and production management. The rest relate to perceiving opportunities, obtaining resources, and the capacity to successfully deal with the political arena in which the entrepreneur is to operate in order to translate those opportunities into fruitful results. It is in this sense that an entrepreneur is seen as the prime mover in the development process. The generally accepted argument among development economists is that even where physical, human and financial capital are not really lacking, the absence of a binding force to combine them for output generation could well explain the difference between growth and stagnation; hence, in the search for an explanation for the slow pace of development in Africa, entrepreneurship has often been identified as the one critical scarce input.

Entrepreneurship in Africa's private sector

Traditional African societies had their entrepreneurs. The successful farmer, the wood worker, the carver, the weaver, the sculptor, and the blacksmith were innovative in their particular trades. Although those entrepreneurs had both economic and non-economic motivations, they were, however, entrepreneurs because of their innovative skills. Had traditional subsistence societies the advantage of a money economy there would have been no hesitation in grouping them with modern entrepreneurs. We are, however, concerned, in this discussion, with entrepreneurs in the modern organised private sector.

The subject of African entrepreneurship has been a topic of discussion by many writers. Much of what has been written or discussed have tended to be gloomy. In almost all the writings, Africans have been portrayed as inexperienced, incompetent and lacking in the various aspects of entrepreneurship functions in which the success of a business organisation depends. Here is an often quoted passage from a 1965 study by Harris and Rowe on 269 leading industries in Nigeria, which they regard as a typical representation of indigenous African entrepreneurship:

> Generally, the level of efficiency within the firms was very low. Substantial increases in output could be achieved without additional investment. Closer supervision, better organisation, improved layout, and quality control are desperately needed on the production side. Low levels of capacity utilisation are largely a result of management deficiency.
>
> The general standard of financial management is also very low. Although 249 of the firms had some kind of accounting systems, they were not systematically used as management tools. The larger firms had annual statements prepared by outside auditors for the purpose of establishing tax liability (thus avoiding arbitrary assessment), but for most part these documents were lying on the shelf gathering dust. Surprisingly, records of asset values were more available than records of output and sales.
>
> This widespread lack of financial control was reflected in the fact that barely more than half of the entrepreneurs had an adequate understanding of depreciation, and only one-half of them could make a reasonable estimate of the minimum production per day needed to break even. Only 31 of them had any organised system of cost accounting, and separation of business and personal accounts was rare.
>
> Most of the firms were one-man operations. When the business expands beyond the point that the owner can control everything himself, serious problems are encountered. The ability to delegate responsibility and authority, while still keeping control, is generally lacking. Admittedly, it is difficult to find capable subordinates and managers in Nigeria, but little has been done by these entrepreneurs to train and develop such personnel. Several cases were encountered of successful small firms foundering badly after major expansion. Experience of the entrepreneurs with hired expatriate managers has been largely unhappy.

While I agree that it may not be difficult to point to a few large businesses that have suffered, or been run badly by some inexperienced African managers, I will argue that there is an element of over-dramatisation and generalisation in the above quotations. In the restrictive environment of the colonial and immediate post-independence years, the situation painted by Harris and Rowe could have been a common experience. But today one can certainly say that such a situation is no longer a universally shared view. No doubt such conclusions still have validity today if one considers the dismal performance of state-owned enterprises. But the situation in the private sector is definitely different. This view is shared by P.T. Bauer who had this to say in the *West African Trade* (Cambridge Press) as early as 1954:

> The general impression I formed was always the same: exceptional effort, foresight, resourcefulness, thrift and ability to perceive economic opportunities.

Again, S.P. Schartz , in his *Nigerian Capitalism* (1977) agreed with Bauer. He said of Nigerians that they:

> ...are responsive to the possibility of gain, and ready to pursue economic advantage vigorously and strenuously; they are flexible and venturesome, willing to seek far and wide and to take risks in quest of profit.

The conclusions of some of these writers with a positive view of entrepreneurship in West Africa have been repeated in the writings of other writers about other African countries. For example, in a study of *Entrepreneurship and Development in Kenya* (1971), P. Harris and A. Somerset came to the conclusion that there was no lack of entrepreneurship in that country.

Need to encourage indigenous private entrepreneurship

The case for the encouragement of indigenous private entrepreneurship is so evident that one wonders why African governments are so tardy in formulating strategies in that regard. This is in spite of the fact that on the achievement of independence, African governments discovered to their dismay that the commercial and industrial sectors of the economy were largely under the control of foreigners. For instance, a survey in Uganda made shortly before the mass exodus of expatriate businesses revealed that 4,000 non-Africans controlled 70% of the distributive trade whilst 16,000 Africans were responsible for only 30% of the trade. The situation in the industrial sector was even worse. Foreigners controlled it almost entirely. In Kenya, it was revealed that in 1955 alone, 246 new companies owned by Europeans with a nominal capital of 8.9 million pounds sterling, and 99 companies owned by Asians with a nominal capital of 3.6 million pounds, were registered, while only one company with a nominal capital of 250 pounds was registered by an African. Such a situation is unhealthy both economically and politically. Although no country in the modern world can be an economic island, it is however a fact that political independence will be meaningless without a good measure of economic independence, hence, the major concern of every African country is to bring about rapid economic growth. This can only materialise when all the natural resources of the country are harnessed in such a manner as to give maximum benefits to the citizens of that country. Such a desirable objective cannot be achieved if the exploitation of the resources is left to foreign predators and compradors. Furthermore, foreign investment is selective and will only venture into areas of maximum profit, usually on the basis of between 20 and 25% return on capital. There is also the disadvantage of foreign investment being capital intensive and unable to absorb Africa's rising population of job seekers. One should here draw attention to the fact that State-owned enterprises have the same disadvantages as foreign investments in that they are also selective and capital intensive.

Indigenous private entrepreneurs, on the other hand, are usually in the area of small scale and medium sized industries which are labour intensive. Unlike enterprises by multinationals, they spring up all over the country and provide growth centres for development. In Uganda, small-scale industries are estimated to contribute 70% of industrial output and most of the employment opportunities (FES, 1988). Their development and dispersal also help to stem the drift from rural to urban areas. In the absence of adequate African private entrepreneurial resources, the necessary structural transformation of the continent's development will be unattainable. It will mean that Africa cannot initiate, undertake and sustain activities in the vast range of production management or research and development, marketing and other innovative competence on which sustained industrial development hinges. No matter what people say about transfer of technology, it is something that those who need must effect by themselves, but only if they have the entrepreneurial talent.

The strongest argument, however, for the development of private entrepreneurship is the growing concern about the use of State-owned enterprises as instruments for bringing about rapid social and economic development. This concern is not new but it is growing loud and urgent with accusing fingers pointing at SOEs[2] from all directions. Economists, bankers, money market operators, external creditors (the London & Paris clubs), overseas representatives of joint venture partners, and experts from such international organisations as the World Bank and the International Monetary Fund, are all disenchanted with the performance of State-owned enterprises. Rather than generate resources for further investment, and act as catalysts for expanded industrialisation and rural development, they have become liabilities with the accumulation of large debts and complete reliance on the treasury for their existence, and this, for purposes that are sometimes more personal than public.

Is privatisation an alternative to the development of private entrepreneurship?

This is a convenient place to discuss the present pressure by international donor agencies (World Bank and IMF) on several African countries to privatise their public enterprises. Due to such external pressures, more attention is being devoted to

---

[2] State-Owned Enterprises?

privatisation than to the promotion of indigenous entrepreneurship. Below is the data on privatisation in Africa as of 1987. The source is World Bank Discussion Paper No.11 by Elliot Berg and Mary Shirley on Divestiture in Developing Countries.

Country (1)	Total number (2)	Liquidations and closures (3)	Targeted sales (4)	Actual sales (5)	Leases and management contracts (6)
Cameroon	80	5	12		6-10
Ghana	130				
Guinea	65	16	43		1
Ivory Coast	113	10	20	4	3
Kenya	180	5			
Liberia	23		7		
Madagascar	130	5	15		5
Mali	54	9	11	2	1
Mauritania	108	4	10		
Niger	54	3	24	1	
Senegal	104	25	10	5	
Sierra Leone	26	1	10		4
Somalia			3		
Sudan	136	10	na	7	
Togo	73	9	40		
Uganda	130		67		
Zaire	138	3	37	11	3

The column on actual sales (5) indicates that many countries are pursuing privatisation half-heartedly. Unfortunately, the reservations are not in favour of developing private entrepreneurship but are due to governments' unwillingness to divest themselves completely of their holdings in viable commercial ventures like banks and trading companies. The point, however, is that the percentages of equity retained in some of the privatised companies are too high for effective participation of the private sector. In some cases, government retains between 40 and 51%. Such percentages are too high for comfort.

Major constraints to the development of private entrepreneurship in Africa

The factors that combine to militate against African entrepreneurs are as extensive as they are frustrating, and cannot all be outlined in a paper of this scope. Attempts will, however, be made to summarise the major constraints under the following categories:

1. Socio-cultural constraints
2. Economic constraints
3. Infrastructural constraints
4. Governmental constraints

Socio-cultural constraints

These have traditional, religious and colonial connotations. Until recently, the traditional occupation of every African country was subsistence farming on communal family land. This communal ownership of the means of production must have been responsible for the development of the extended family system by which a successful member is expected to assist not only his immediate family but also other members of the extended family/clan that might be in need. In such a society, the accumulation of capital for investment becomes impossible. Another restrictive custom in traditional societies is the discrimination against women in matters of real property ownership and inheritance. This has adverse effects on enterprising women found in parts of West and East Africa. These traditional constraints are now on the decline as a result of rapid urbanisation and the emergence of the modern sector. Unfortunately, this decline is being superseded by the resurgence of several religious sects, some of whose beliefs have a tendency towards fatalism, and a feeling that a person cannot influence his future or change the circumstances of his life. Begging by able-bodied persons is a manifestation of this attitude of mind.

Another cultural constraint is that arising from our colonial past. This is often referred to as colonial mentality. It is a culture that extols obedience and strict observance of rules, regulations and precedents even when they are outdated. It is a tradition that discourages and often punishes initiative and innovation. No wonder the reluctance of several public officers to venture into entrepreneurial activities on leaving office even at an early age. It is also unfortunate that some African professionals prefer to make a life career in the public service instead of venturing into the private sector as entrepreneurs. Those of them who have the courage to leave, do so for other paid employment. This trait might be explained by the absence of investment culture and extreme risk aversion in some Africans. They place a premium on quick-return investments.

An ill-effect of the colonial heritage is the lack of loyalty, dedication and commitment to an employer by workers. A wrong notion of paid employment was developed because colonial service was regarded either as white man's job or no man's job. This led to malingering, perfunctory performance of duties, corruption, and low productivity generally. An African industrialist once said that his reason for employing expatriates was that no matter how well he paid a fellow African, he would always prefer what he got by cheating him. He cited the case of a quantity surveyor he attracted by doubling his civil service pay, in addition to a free car and house which he never had in government, yet he was not loyal to him.

Economic constraints

One of the most critical constraints to the development of indigenous entrepreneurship is lack of capital, which has its origin in the general low level of per capita income of the people. We have seen that this is accentuated by the extended family system which militates against the accumulation of capital for investment. Many commercially viable projects initiated by far-sighted individuals are often not realised because the prospective investors are unable to generate the necessary finance.

Under normal circumstances, this would not have posed an insurmountable problem were the banking institutions willing to readily make credit available to prospective industrial investors. But by their nature of operations, commercial banks are conservative in advancing loans for long-term projects, preferring always quick-pay-back projects. Applications for loans for trading and real estates developments naturally get preference. On the other hand, industrial projects with their long-term gestation nature receive no attention except for working capital, and for that against stringent collateral requirements. The practice of merchant banks has not been much better. To succeed, prospective investors must produce feasibility studies establishing the viability of their projects. The cost of such studies are often beyond the reach of small enterprise investors.

In recognition of these difficulties, most African governments have established development banks and other investment finance corporations. But the big snag in these development banks is their weak capital base. This has naturally reduced their level of impact. Varying degrees of default in loan repayments has also compounded their problems. Furthermore, their contribution to stimulating the growth of entrepreneurship appears to be in grave danger because of the external pressure on government to commercialise their operations. This will mean the reversal of the original philosophy behind the setting up of the banks, i.e., provision of loans at concessionary rates. This is already having adverse effects on small-scale and medium-scale industries, many of which have sprung up in recent years. Owing to government prodding, many indigenous entrepreneurs in trade and commerce diversified into investments in small-scale industrial projects, though with weak capital bases. The new measures, together with the various policies introduced under the structural adjustment programme, including interest rate deregulation and massive depreciation in the value of local currencies, have served to exacerbate their financial problems. The result is that most of the up-coming first generation indigenous industrial entrepreneurs have gone under; some have either shut down or gone into receivership.

Infrastructural constraints

By far, the most critical constraint is the lack of basic social and physical infrastructural facilities. In many African countries such basic infrastructures as roads, water, power and communications as well as education and health, are not only inadequate but are inefficiently operated. Many entrepreneurs have to resort to creating their own make-shift solutions — standby generating sets, bore-holes, roads, radio-link and security. All these add to costs, making the cost of production quite high. This is further exacerbated by the shortage of foreign exchange. In these circumstances, there is underutilisation of installed capacity and the local entrepreneur cannot compete on equal terms with an overseas manufacturer of the same product. Unfortunately, the local population who often complain about the high cost of locally made products do not seem to appreciate that the local manufacturer, unlike his overseas counterpart, operates under a high cost environment.

Education and knowledge are basic and indispensable infrastructures for both the entrepreneur and his workers. On the part of the entrepreneur, this requirement is referred to as technical know-how. Many Africans have ideas but are unable to transfer them on to a drawing board, and from there to the ground. In this regard, technical skill is more important than capital. Skills result in greater productivity and the accumulation of capital. Without skill, the entrepreneur cannot perform the functions of owner and supervisor. There is also inadequate institutional infrastructure for skill development. The educational system has been grossly deficient in the area of technical and vocational training. The polytechnics and institutes of technology in several African countries have not been able to supply the needs of the industrial sector. This is hardly surprising, as most of the institutes have been engaged in duplicative efforts, working at cross-purposes instead of being complementary. This should, however, be expected considering that, over the years, there was no clearly defined focus of activities for such institutes.

Research endeavours have tended not to be problem-solving oriented. It is, therefore, not surprising that Africa has a great shortage of industrial manpower. Entrepreneurs are thus obliged to either enter into joint venture partnership with expatriates or to hire them at great costs in terms of salaries, housing and other fringe benefits.

Constraints arising out of government policies
There is no doubt that government has a major role to play in the development of African entrepreneurship. Entrepreneurial activities do not operate in a vacuum but in a political environment created by the government. This environment can be either favourable or unfavourable, depending on government's policies towards entrepreneurs, and the way and manner the policies are interpreted and administered by government bureaucrats. In the first place, mention should be made of the inconsistency in government policies. Frequent changes in policy direction render business calculations and planning virtually impossible. An entrepreneur requires a reasonable degree of certainty to minimise the risks that long-term investments normally entail. He would at least expect the conditions prevailing when the investment decision was made to continue for a reasonable time. For example, the sudden ban on wheat importation by the Nigerian government almost ruined the private sector flour mills installed at great cost a few years before the ban.

Over the years, African entrepreneurs have witnessed a high degree of instability in government policies, as reflected in stop-and-go measures. Policies of import restrictions and austerities have alternated with some liberalisation in sympathy with the country's external fortunes. The result has been too many changes in policies which tend to occur annually with each budget speech. Such frequent changes in the rules of the game create a high degree of uncertainty, and this has kept investors, foreign and local, at bay.

The inconsistency in government policies is mostly a result of the absence of a well-articulated industrial policy and strategy. The first attempts at industrial planning by African governments were contained in the development plans of the early and mid sixties. Those plans extolled the policy of import substitution, which provided incentives to European trading companies to enable them embark on the local manufacture of what they have been previously importing. In later years, the import substitution policy with its low percentage of local value-added was found to be detrimental to the development of local raw materials as well as a drain on the foreign exchange reserves of the countries. Most of the previous incentives were abrogated but steps had yet to be taken to produce either a comprehensive industrial policy or an investment code.

Not only is there an absence of a comprehensive industrial policy, but what policies there are, are inefficiently, indifferently and tardily administered by public officers. The procedures for the granting of various licenses, permits and incentives are bewildering, cumbersome and frustrating to investors. A prospective investor has to deal with as many as seven different government agencies in order to obtain one kind of permit or another. What is more, each agency takes its time to deal with the application with the result that periods of six to twelve months often elapse before approvals are granted or refused. The Third National Development Plan of Nigeria 1975-1980 acknowledged this situation in the following words:

> Unecessary restrictions and administrative bottlenecks have frustrated a number of worthy projects; in particular the multiplicity of authority from whom various permits, licenses, etc, have to be assembled, and the lack of streamlined procedure for getting them, combine to confuse the intending entrepreneur and to create the possibility of abuse. Lack of clarity of government policy on the payment of royalties, license fees, technical and managerial fees, etc, have added to the difficulties associated with the transfer of technology.

It went further to say:

> The existing situation whereby intending investors have to call on many agencies of government for various permits, licenses and approvals often delay the implementation of worthy industrial projects.

The challenges for Africa's entrepreneurial development in the 1990s

The first step in the direction of developing Africa's private entrepreneurship is to accept the philosophy of greater role to the private sector in the whole development process. Given this, the next necessary steps will be to create the environment that is necessary to sustain the growth and expansion of private entrepreneurial activities. All these will require substantial changes in policy regime so as to remove restrictions on the private sector. This places a special premium on removing the entire bottleneck to indigenous entrepreneurial growth highlighted in this paper.

First, the problem of finance should be addressed squarely as this represents a major deterrent to entrepreneurship. It is a matter of interest that in virtually all countries, much effort has gone into the establishment of development and other credit institutions with a view to providing loans at concessionary rates. The intention is that in the process, the barrier posed by high interest rates and stringent collateral requirements would be reduced. But in what looks like a twist of fate, the IMF/World Bank's doctrine of commercialisation of public enterprises being almost indiscriminately foisted on the debt-ridden countries of the Third World is whittling away this incentive. On sober reflection, one finds it somewhat difficult to reconcile this position with the other alluring religion of across-the-board divestment of governments' holdings in all economic enterprises equally espoused by the two organisations. What is a bit disconcerting is that such espousal is in total disregard of the varying peculiarities and levels of development of various countries. The regression this is bound to impose on progress persuades one into believing in a need for a fundamental rethinking of the whole thesis. For Africa, this is particularly necessary if her efforts at stimulating the emergence of indigenous entrepreneurship are not to be stultified. By all means, African governments should be persuaded to privatise or commercialise their industrial and commercial activities. They should, however, retain those industries and companies that have a supportive role in facilitating economic development. Agricultural and industrial development banks are in this exception category.

Another, and by far a more critical area that should receive priority attention, is the provision of a full complement of efficiently functioning infrastructural support to services, including estates/layouts. With respect to industrial estates/layouts their establishment and locations should be guided by well laid out system of land use planning and population distribution. One cannot overemphasise the importance of excellent power facilities, water supplies, communications and adequate transportation facilities, without which business activities can hardly flourish. The creation of proper infrastructure should also include the establishment of an organisational arrangement that facilitates land acquisition for business ventures. This needs mention because experiences in many countries have shown that many worthwhile projects have often foundered on the alter of tedious laws and procedures with in-built delays for land acquisition.

In order not to discourage the expansion of industrial and other business activities in the continent, African countries should pay particular attention to their array of industrial and other macro-economic policies to ensure that they produce the most favourable effects. The general experience has been that such policies have tended to be excessively restrictive. Most of the policies emphasise revenue collection at the expense of development promotion. In order not to stifle the emergence and sustenance of Africa's entrepreneurship, rationalisation, consistency, stability and efficiency of their administration should be the watchword of policy formulation and implementation. The overall regulatory environment, as represented by necessary permits and laws for the setting up of business, should be simplified and relieved of the maze of documentation that is characteristic of such laws in many countries.

Monetary and fiscal policies should be fashioned with an eye to providing a climate that spurs rather than discourage industrial growth. A package of fiscal incentives that incorporate substantial measures of tax relief, and in some cases investment subsides, should be provided. In the area of monetary policy, deliberate efforts should be made to avoid high interest rates which act as effective deterrent to investment. In fact, for the small scale and medium enterprises (SSMEs) in the Africa-type economies, concessionary credit and other financial facilities still represent very much-needed incentive instruments. No matter what both the IMF and the World Bank may say about such schemes, I strongly believe that they still constitute a potent force for the growth of SSMEs' entrepreneurs in the Third World, if not in the advanced ones. For optimal results, however, they should be rationally and effectively applied.

Again, African countries should give more serious attention to technological/technical education in the overall direction of their educational policy. This forms the basis for increasing the technological capabilities of their citizenry. An aspect of this process includes giving more attention to improving the ability of indigenous entrepreneurs to make good technological choices in their investment decisions. By so doing, a significant step will be taken, or at least be seen to be taken, towards eliminating the most fatal deficiency of SSMEs, i.e., technological inexperience that reflects most adversely on their production management.

Also, institutional arrangements should be established to provide training to both the entrepreneurs and their workers in various managerial and administrative skills such as marketing, accounting and finance, labour management, etc. Such institutions should also provide services in the area of preparing feasibility studies and securing easier access to credit and other production inputs.

Finally, I would like to draw attention to what in the final analysis will spell success or failure of the development of private entrepreneurship in Africa. It is fostering and maintaining proper relationship between government and the private sector. At the moment, such relationship is anything but cordial. It is characterised by mistrust and suspicion on either side. On the one hand, government, especially in socialist-oriented African countries,[3] look at entrepreneurs as "exploiters" and "suckers" whose only motivation is relentless pursuit of profit without any obligations and contributions to the community or economy. Because of this, these governments believe that their activities are to be strictly controlled and restricted in the overall interest of the citizenry. Such view, however, fails to appreciate the contributions of the private sector in the areas of employment generation, economic recovery and diversification.

Entrepreneurs on the other hand are not always aware of the constraints under which African governments operate, and that sometimes their policies are as a result of internal and external pressures. Entrepreneurs also tend to think that their requirements are the only considerations in the formulation of economic policies. They often fail to appreciate that government has to balance their demands along with those of other sectors of the community. What is required, therefore, is constant consultation so that both sides will learn and appreciate each other. In particular, government will take advantage of the detailed practical knowledge and experience of the operators of the economy, in particular, during the formative stages of an economic policy. I understand that the economic success of Japan is partly due to their policy of government-private sector relationship in which both sectors co-operate to shape and guide the economy.

For the 1990s, the choice for Africa is clear. The sleeping giant will wake from his slumber through the combined efforts of African governments and their indigenous entrepreneurs.

---

[3]   Since the end of the cold war in the late eighties and early nineties, almost all countries in the world now openly embrace market economies. "Socialism" is seen as being outdated.

22

Private Sector, and not the Government, should be the Engine of Development✦

"I hold the view that the time has come when government's role in development should be de-emphasised in favour of more responsibilities to the private sector. Our rate of development will be quickened the sooner we get away from the socialist belief that government is the best and only engine of development."

Childhood days

Contact: Chief (Dr) Jerome Udoji is our special guest and cover personality for the month. While welcoming you to our special guest/cover personality column, we would like to acknowledge your giant stride in both the public and private sectors of the Nigerian economy. Taking you back a bit, Sir, what was your childhood like, and has it affected your disposition to life?

Udoji: My childhood was one of anxiety. After my birth, my mother was very ill and unable to breast-feed me. Somehow the European missionaries resident in the village got to know of my predicament and regularly brought tinned milk for my feeding. They showed my mother how to use it. As my father was not sure of the nutritional value of the white man's food, he also arranged for me to be breast-fed by the wife of his cousin who two weeks before my birth had delivered her first child. No one believed that I could survive, so when it came to giving me a name, my father reflected and gave me the name Oputa, meaning "a surprise he is alive today". In appreciation of the kindness of the missionaries, I was sent to school at a very tender age. No school fees were paid. The missionaries attracted the children by occasionally giving them groundnuts during recreation time. Ready-made dresses were also distributed at Christmas. The mission compound was a place of great activity.

✦ An interview published in the July/August 1991 edition of *Business Contact* magazine.

We returned there after classes to play football.

The school curriculum was very simple: reading, writing, arithmetic, religious knowledge, grammar, hygiene, singing and plant life. It was not until I got to St Charles Teachers' Training College, Onitsha, that subjects like history and geography came into the syllabus. St Charles was a post-primary school where bright young school leavers were prepared for the teaching profession. It was there that I came in contact with a teacher who made the greatest impression on me. He was Rev Father Macloskey, a Briton, from Northern Ireland. He was our English teacher. He was so versatile that he used his period to teach us everything under the sun — government, politics, law, religion, science, history, geography, you name it. He not only gave us a broad-based education but also planted in us the seeds of enterprise and ambition. My colleagues in his class included Raymond Njoku who later became a federal minister, Moses Balonwu who later became a chief justice, and Peter Chukwura who was a proprietor of schools and a member of the Eastern House of Assembly. The religious and moral education of my early years have certainly influenced my outlook in life.

Hobbies

Contact: What do you do in your spare-time? Do you belong to any social or business clubs?

Udoji: When I have time to spare, I either read or work in the garden. When I was resident in Lagos, I belonged to the Metropolitan Club. Now that I live in my village, I belong to a newly formed club called Country Club. I am also a life member of both the Manufacturers Association of Nigeria and the Nigeria Stock Exchange.

Secrets of good health

Contact: For a man of your age, you are still very agile and active. What will you say is the secret of your longevity and good health?

Udoji: I am sure that this is a question only my creator and my doctor can answer. However, as a lay mortal, I believe that longevity and good health largely depend on one's constitution and lifestyle. Barring accidents, a person that lives a moderate and disciplined life has a better chance of living longer than his neighbour who indulges in excesses. In addition to moderation are the healthy and psychic effects of a life full of interests. Don't forget that I told you earlier on that a man ceases to live when he ceases to take interest in what is happening around him.

Happiness in a life of moderation

Conctact: Bearing in mind your monumental achievements, Sir, we will like to ask what has been the moving spirit behind your achievements?

Udoji: Your question is capable of two interpretations. If you mean what is responsible for whatever success you think I have achieved, I believe it must be due to several factors—my family background, my Christian upbringing, the discipline of the legal education and the attention to details and take-nothing-for granted training in administration and management. If, on the other hand, you mean what has sustained me all these years, it is a life of moderation and interest in whichever environment I find myself, be it the home, garden, farm, office, factory, church, or community. To me, a man ceases to live when he ceases to take interest in his surroundings or in what is happening around him.

Contact: If there is any Nigerian who can be said to have lived a successful life, you are indeed one of them. What can we say are the secrets behind your success?

Udoji: There are no secrets to success. If there are any, they are hardwork, aspiration for excellence and self-discipline. Hardwork has magic power, and discipline ensures peace of mind. Last, but not the least, is what some people refer to as luck and others as the hand of providence.

Advice to the youth

Contact: Bearing in mind your achievements, what word of advice would you offer the young generation of Nigerians as a way of bettering their living conditions and living a more worthy life?

Udoji: My advice to young men of the present generation is that they should make haste slowly, that they will reach their goals in life if only they would be of good behaviour, disciplined, industrious and aspire to excel in whatever they do. They should also adopt a moderate lifestyle with the correct moral and social values. This will make them realise that money is a good servant but a bad master that must not be worshipped.

Contact: One notices the increase in vices in our society. I mean such vices as drug abuse, the get-rich-quick syndrome, and lack of patriotic flavour among our youths.

a. What do you think are the consequences of such behaviour on our social life, and how can they be curbed?
b. What advice do you have for them?

Udoji: The consequences of delinquent and deviant behaviour among the youth are too obvious for enumeration. Some of them are premature death, imprisonment, broken homes, wasted working life, unhappy old age and disgrace to parents and relatives. Some of the ways to curb delinquency are: home training, especially by example; religious and civic education in schools; vocationalisation of all levels of education; and enhancement of employment opportunities in the private sector.

Adjusting to life in the private sector

Contact: You were in public service for several years, and now, you are in the private sector of the economy. How, Sir, were you able to adjust from the bureaucratic bottleneck of the civil service to the more dynamic private sector?

Udoji: I required very little adjustment for I come from an enterprise-oriented family. My father was a successful farmer, my mother a fish and kolanut trader, and my maternal uncles were among the early traders of the famous Onitsha market. As a child I accompanied my mother in some of her journeys to buy and sell kolanuts, and often spent my holidays helping in the general merchandise shops of my uncles. Whilst in the civil service, and especially as head of the service, I regularly updated general orders in line with current needs and changes in the service. I was more interested in results than in the rules. As

long as the desired results were achieved economically, honestly
and expeditiously, it did not matter if the rules were breached.
That would be a good case for amending the rules which were
made for the Service and not vice versa. I must, however, add
that my course at the Economic Development Institute of the
World Bank, and my four years service with the Ford Foundation
of America increased my apathy towards bureaucracy and my
predilection for the private sector.

Contact: What will you say are:

a. the differences between the civil service of your days and
    what obtains today?
b. Do you share in the notion that the civil service of today has
    lost its prestige?
c. If so, how do you think the situation could be remedied?

Udoji: There is a world of difference between the Service I knew
and the Service of today. The circumstances, orientations and
motivations are different. For example, the Service of my time
had the traditions of a selfless service, a career system, and
political neutrality. Selfless service meant that civil servants of
all grades should display transparent honesty and integrity in
the discharge of their duties. In particular, they should not use
their public powers to enhance their private personal interests.
Specific provisions in the civil service rules prohibited corruption,.
abuse of office and engaging in businesses which might conflict
with official duties. Selflessness, disinterestedness, impartiality,
objectivity, fairness, openness, devotion, courtesy and humility
were among the qualities demanded of the Service by the public.
A number of commentators believe that these qualities can now
be found only among a few civil servants.

The career system was a system by which a young man was
recruited at an early age into the Service with an implied promise
of a life career during which he worked his way up the hierarchy
of the Service. His service could only be terminated by mental
or physical incapacity or the commission of a criminal offence.
There were series of protective regulations against dismissal or
termination of appointment. Today, the civil service has lost its

claim to permanency and security of tenure.

Political neutrality means that a civil servant must give loyal service and support to the government of the day, irrespective of that government's political colour. He must also refrain from participating in political activities and controversies. This requirement is the natural consequence and *quid-pro-quo* of the advantages of the career system. Without a career system, political neutrality will have no base. The present civil service reform has removed the veil of political neutrality, at least from top civil servants.

With the destruction of these three traditions, the Service lost its identity, prestige and credibility. It is, however, difficult to apportion blame for the present situation. In my opinion, the civil war and the oil boom were equally contributory factors. Also, the traditions of a presidential system of government are different from those of the parliamentary system of my time. The solution, in my opinion, lies in the development of a professional, responsive and result-oriented public service that readily adapts itself to political developments. The reforms of the present administration are welcome but there are areas which need further examination and clarification. For example, there is need for further delineation of the functions, terms and conditions of permanent civil servants (career service), and those of director-generals who are politically appointed. Also the status and relationship between ministers and director-generals need further examination. One would like to know whether the relationship is collegiate or subordinate.

From boom to recession

Contact: You witnessed the boom period of the Nigerian economy. Now, we are in a period of recession. Sir, from your experience what will you say really went wrong with our economy?

Udoji: A lot went wrong with our economy. In the first place, we were extravagant with the oil wealth. Instead of using it to lay the foundations of development by investing it in such basic infrastructure like water, electricity, roads and communication for every community and saving something for the rainy day, we spent the wealth in unproductive prestige projects (FESTAC, All Africa Games, etc.) and in the massive importation of consumer goods. We also pursued wrong economic policies like import substitution and the neglect of agriculture.

The Udoji Award

Contact: A lot of people easily trace Nigeria's present buying habit and dependence on foreign goods to the Udoji Award[1] which suddenly put more money into the hands of Nigerians.

a.   Sir, how far is this assertion correct?

b.   What were the aims of the Udoji Award?

c.   Do you think that these aims were largely achieved?

Udoji: You are right. The 1974 salary award increased the purchasing power of workers. The short-term aim of the award was to bring wages in line with the cost of living, to motivate workers and make them more productive. The expected motivation and productivity was not achieved because of the manner in which the recommendations were implemented. Instead of phasing the increases as recommended in order to avoid inflation, they were awarded in one fell swoop and with arrears that were not recommended. Again, the salary increase which was tied and made subject to the implementation of management and productivity recommendations was implemented as a separate package. The warning that any attempt to implement one independent of the other will be serious both for the economy and the public service itself was ignored. The long-term objective of the recommendations was to establish equitable, competitive, acceptable and self-maintaining salary structure. To ensure self-maintenance, the commission recommended the establishment of a permanent Pay Research Unit which would, on a continuing basis, adjust salaries in line with changes in the cost of living,

---

[1]   J.O. Udoji was the chairman of the Public Service Review Commission (September 1972 September 1974). The commission is often called the "Udoji Commission", and the salary awards which the Gowon's regime awarded civil servants in the name of the commission was subsequently called the "Udoji Award". For further details read section 2.

productivity and other economic data. The purpose was to obviate the necessity of periodic massive surveys and the consequences of announcement and expectation. This recommendation has apparently not been implemented.

The lost opportunity under Gowon's regime

Contact: Critics trace our present economic woes to failures on the part of the Gowon administration to lay a solid foundation for the diversification of the Nigerian economy from its oil base. As a key player in that regime, what do you say to this?

Udoji: Your observation is correct. The Gowon administration should have used the oil wealth in laying the foundation for economic growth. Had the money been spent in providing such basic infrastructure as water, electricity, roads and communication for every community, Nigeria by now would have been on the road to an economic take-off. I would, however, like to believe that the misallocation of resources at the time was a mistake of the head and not of the heart. The euphoria of wealth after the privations and austerity of the civil war was too much a temptation for a young country of fourteen years. No wonder the wealth was spent on prestigious projects and in conspicuous consumption of imported consumer goods. We have, however, learnt from the costly experience.

Babangida's economic policies

Contact: How will you rate the economic policies of the present regime especially the Structural Adjustment Programme, Foreign Exchange Market (FEM), and other related policies and their effects on industries?

Udoji: I compliment the Babangida administration for its boldness in imposing the Structural Adjustment Programme (SAP) on the country. It was inevitable, having regards to the economic circumstances of the mid-80s. Due to the policies of past regimes, the country was economically unable to stand erect on its feet: domestic production was below domestic consumption, scarcities forced prices up and there was a drop in the price of oil resulting in insufficient foreign exchange to pay for mounting imports.

The country ran out of cash and credit and creditors were knocking at the door. Government was, therefore, compelled to introduce a package of reforms to remedy the crisis situation. These reforms have since been christened SAP. The components of the package are: devaluation of the naira; raising productivity in agriculture and industries; diversification of our exports away from oil; deregulation, including an end to import licensing; the establishment of a foreign exchange market; privatisation and ending subsidies to ailing parastatals. Last, but not the least, living within our means.

In spite of the hardships that SAP has brought on individuals, e.g., retrenchment and unemployment, it has on the whole been beneficial to the economy. In the first place, it has deflated the ego of those Nigerians who parade themselves in the streets of London, Paris and New York as citizens of a rich oil country. Secondly, by making imports very expensive, it has forced Nigerians to patronise home-made goods and to develop a maintenance culture. Thirdly, it has encouraged agricultural production by putting more money in the pockets of rural producers of primary products. Fourthly, the establishment of a foreign exchange market has enabled manufacturers to obtain foreign exchange for essential raw materials and machinery. Industries have also been more enterprising in the sourcing of local raw materials. Finally, the setting up of the Directorate of Food, Roads and Rural Infrastructure is laying the foundations for the balanced development of the countryside.

Import substitution and backward integration

Contact: As a giant of commerce and industry, what will you say is the position of the organised private sector on import substitution and inward sourcing of raw materials?

Udoji: Import substitution was an industrial policy adopted by the national government immediately after independence. It was a policy of importing everything—machinery, raw materials and expert staff—for the local production of imported consumer goods. The policy was predicated by a desire to control the economy, which was completely in the hands of expatriates.

Another motivation was to provide employment. There was no visible and better method of achieving these objectives than to adopt the import substitution practices of the multinationals. The policy was extolled in the first and second development plans. It was not until the economic problems of the early eighties that Nigeria was able to discover how costly the policy was in terms of foreign exchange. Furthermore, the economic advantages of local raw materials, backward integration, and industrial linkages were recognised. I recall that it was the Manufacturers Association of Nigeria that took the initiative and organised, in July 1983, a workshop on the development of local raw materials in partnership with NISER[2] and the Ministry of Commerce. Again, in November 1984, the matter was the subject of discussion at a quarterly luncheon between the organised private sector and government. One of the recommendations of the workshop was the establishment of a council on raw materials development at which government, industries and universities would be members. Since then, many industries have gone a long way to source available raw materials locally. There are, however, areas where industries cannot make progress until the petrochemical, machine tools and steel plants are fully operational. Petrochemicals form at least 40% of the raw materials at present imported by industries. Machine tools, on the other hand, will produce some of the spare parts now imported from abroad. It is encouraging to learn that the present administration is pursuing the petrochemical project vigorously.

The private sector is the real engine of development

Contact: In what areas of development would you advise the present government to concentrate on as a means of realising our economic potentials?

Udoji: I hope your question does not imply expansion of government responsibility for development because I hold the view that the time has come when government's role in development should be de-emphasised in favour of more

---

[2] National Institute for Social and Economic Research.

responsibilities to the private sector. Our rate of development will be quickened the sooner we get away from the socialist belief that government is the best and only engine of development. Such beliefs give rise to over-regulation and economic over-government.

Government, however, still has a role in the development process. This role is in the areas of maintenance of peace and security, the provision of basic infrastructure—water, roads, power and communication. In a developing country, however, government should also provide core industries—iron and steel, petrochemicals and machine tools. Above all, it is also government's responsibility to provide an attractive environment for private investment.

It is commendable that the present administration is taking steps through its privatisation programme to reduce the dominance of the public sector. Its present policy of encouraging Nigerians to venture into all sectors of the economy is also commendable.

The Block-Farm Model as a Strategy for Increasing the Income of Peasant Farmers ♦

"This block-farm is NTC's modest attempt at solving some of the well-known problems besetting the Nigerian peasant farmer. These problems include scattered and fragmented holdings, use of antiquated and unproductive implements such as hoes and machetes, lack of access to improved varieties of seeds, absence of on-the-spot help, and guidance on a continuing basis, etc.

Introduction

Your Excellency, Your Highnesses, Ladies and Gentlemen. I have a great pleasure in welcoming you all to this opening ceremony of the Nigerian Tobacco Company's block-farm at Ekwotso. This block farm is NTC's modest attempt at solving some of the well-known problems besetting the Nigerian peasant farmer. These problems include scattered and fragmented holdings, use of antiquated and unproductive implements such as hoes and machetes, lack of access to improved varieties of seeds, absence of on-the-spot help, and absence of guidance on a continuing basis, etc.

Our first step was to acquire a tract of land where about forty farmers could each cultivate two hectares. The next step was to clear, plough and ridge the farm with the use of bulldozers and tractors. As you can see, the two crops grown by the farmers are tobacco and cassava — one a cash crop and the other a food crop. The proposal is that half the land will be under tobacco and the other under food crop cultivation. Because of this, it was decided that half the land will be under tobacco, and the other half under cassava cultivation on a rotational basis. The farmer is entirely responsible for cultivating the crops on his individual

♦ Speech presented as chairman of the Nigerian Tobacco Company (NTC) Limited on the occasion of the opening of the NTC's block-farm at Ekwotso, Agenebode, by the then military governor of the then Bendel State, Commodore Husaini Abdullahi, on June 21, 1978.

holding. What we have done is to provide him with the best tobacco seeds and a high-yielding cassava obtained through the good offices of Shell BP Community Development Project at Warri and the National Root Crop Research Institute at Umudike in Umuahia. I understand that this high-yielding cassava was developed by the International Institute for Tropical Agriculture at Ibadan, and that it has a yield of between 25 and 30 tons per acre as against 7 tons per acre of the old variety. We have also provided the farmers with fertilisers and finance. Above all, our field staff are available all the time to help solve any problems that might arise.

Projected incomes for the farmers

Our estimate is that the incomes from 40 hectares of cassava will be between ₦60, 000 and ₦80,000 per annum, and tobacco about ₦52,000. This will give each of the forty farmers an annual income of about ₦3,000. This is a modest estimate, for already six of our old farmers exceeded an income of ₦3,000 last year from tobacco farming alone. With the combination of tobacco and cassava farming, the return could even reach up to ₦5, 000 per annum.

It is our hope to introduce this system of block-farm to other areas of Bendel State[1] as well as to other states of the federation. I would like to emphasise that this project is a joint effort of the NTC and the Ekwotso community under the wise leadership of the Oba of Agenebode, Chief Amo II. The farmers of Ekwotso are particularly industrious and this, more than anything else, has ensured the success of the project. I must also mention the tremendous help given to the Ekwotso community by the Bendel Food Corporation, as well as by Tiffanny Limited. Without these helps, we could not have gotten the project off the ground in so short a time.

Your Excellency, may I say how very pleased we are that you are able, in spite of your other engagements, to find time to be

---

[1] This has since been split into more states.

with us. It demonstrates the importance which this administration, and your government in particular, attaches to modern agricultural production. May I, therefore, on behalf of Ekwotso community and the Nigerian Tobacco Company, invite you to formally open our block-farm.

24

Effects of the Unstable Crude Oil Price on the Nigerian Economy✢

"Almost all our industries are of the import substitution type, which depend heavily on imported inputs. Thus, our industrialisation started with a structural disadvantage. Instead of starting from our strengths, they started from our weaknesses. Instead of starting with what we had in abundance, they started with what we had very little of."

Introduction

Thank you for inviting me to address the Onitsha Branch of the Nigerian Society of Engineers. You asked me to speak on the *Effects of the Unstable Crude Oil Price on the Nigerian Economy.* You also requested that I touch on the *Second-Tier Foreign Exchange Market.* I congratulate you on your choice of topic. It shows your breadth of outlook, and your concern about the economy on which the general well-being and future of the country depends. How I wish that other professionals — architects, surveyors, lawyers and doctors will borrow a leaf from you and show more interest in the problems of the world around them.

It is a matter for regret that many of our professionals are "learned" but not "educated". This is especially true of those who, like myself, have the 'misfortune' of an English-type university education. We are "uneducated" in the sense that our education though in-depth, is narrow and not broad-based; we are like professors who wear blinkers. One of the consequences of such an education is a lack of adequate interest in matters outside one's particular area of specialisation. Is there, therefore, any wonder that in spite of the level of higher education and literacy in Nigeria, we still have an unenlightened public opinion where people are able to get away with a lot of wrong doing,

---

✢ Address presented to the Nigerian Society of Engineers, Onitsha Branch, November 12, 1986.

even murder! I recommend that whatever our profession, and whatever our specialisation, we should continue to learn and broaden our education, for when a man ceases to learn he ceases to live.

Scope of the subject

To speak about the effects of the unstable crude oil price is to speak about the Nigerian nation particularly in the last ten to twelve years. That will take more than a lecture because the repercussions have affected not only our economy, but also our politics. You will recall that the tottering economy was one of the reasons for the overthrow of both the Shagari and Buhari regimes. As one involved mostly with the economy and not politics, I will deal with the economic effects and leave politics for those who are better qualified than myself. I propose, therefore, to deal with the subject under the following four headings:

1.   The oil boom and its effects on the economy
2.   Causes and effects of the fall in oil prices
3.   The structural adjustment programme and the SFEM
4.   Advantages of the oil glut and the challenge to engineers

The oil boom and its effects

The greatest effect of the oil boom period (1973 – 1981), was that it produced adverse structural changes in the Nigerian economy. It transformed a peasant-based agricultural economy that was thriving with exports of cocoa, rubber, groundnuts and palm produce into an oil economy that is subject to the vagaries of an unpredictable market. The economy became dependent on one export crop — oil, which accounted for about 80% of the total government revenue and some 90% of the total export earnings. Agriculture, which before had accounted for about 40% of our gross domestic product and was our major foreign exchange earner, became relegated to the background. Its contribution to the GDP went down from about 40% in the seventies to about 20% in the eighties. The dominance of oil in the economy between 1970 and 1980 is illustrated in the following table:

	1970	1980
GDP	10%	22%
Government revenue	26.3%	81%
Export earnings	57.6%	96%

The huge revenue from oil brought about the expansion and dominance of the public sector. Government invested over ₦11 billion in several prestige projects, the economies of which were of doubtful viability. In all, the federal government had about 180 parastatals, 70 non-commercial and 110 commercial projects. At the state level, the story is the same. This is an unproductive situation, because a naira in the hands of the private sector is often much more productive than a naira in the hands of the government. Although many of the government projects were losing money, they succeeded in attracting people from rural to urban area.

The availability of foreign exchange, coupled with an overvalued naira encouraged the importation of goods rather than their local production. Because of their relative cheapness, Nigerians developed a penchant for imported goods, including imported foods. Our importation of cereals, for example, grew six folds between 1974 and 1983. Until recently, we were spending over one million naira a day in the importation of wheat for flour milling. Almost all our industries are of the import substitution type, which depend heavily on imported inputs. Thus, our industrialisation started with a structural disadvantage. Instead of starting from our strengths, they started from our weaknesses. Instead of starting with what we had in abundance, they started with what we had very little of. And as long as foreign exchange was flowing from oil nobody bothered. In fact, the early development plans extolled the import substitution policy.

Causes and effects of the fall in oil prices

The first indication of crisis in the economy was in 1977/78 when a slump in the prices of oil in the world market reared its head. The experience was, however, short-lived. In the second half of 1981, however, there was a more devastating crisis, the effects of which have continued till today. For instance, from 39.75 US dollars a barrel in January 1981, the price fell to 36.04 US dollars in October of the same year. From then, the trend has been one of continuous decline. This year the price fell from 30 dollars in January to below 10 in April. The fall in the price of oil is due to several causes. The first is the global economic recession which made supply to exceed demands. Second, is the influence of OPEC, an oil cartel, in pushing up oil prices in the seventies. This angered the oil-consuming countries, and they vowed to call off the bluff of OPEC. This they did by searching for alternative sources of energy including solar energy. Third, the oil-consuming countries embarked on conservation policies which include stock piling and the design of automobiles that consume less fuel. Fourth, was the emergence of the North Sea oil and the refusal of non OPEC producers like Britain, Norway, Mexico, Argentina, Malaysia and Oman to co-operate with OPEC in stabilising prices. For example, in January this year, Britain reduced the price of her crude from $30.10 a barrel to $26.50 against OPEC's price of $28. Even OPEC members have difficulty in observing agreements about production quotas and prices. Some resort to barter deals to increase their production and some adopt various discount devices in order to beat agreed prices. The political differences among OPEC members do not help the matter. With the absence of the stabilising influence of Sheik Yamani, the Saudi oil minister, it is doubtful if OPEC will be able to resolve the political and economic differences among its members. At the moment, they are still arguing on a set of criteria for the allocation of permanent quotas. In the circumstances, there is little hope of the price returning to its 1979/1980 level in the foreseeable future.

The 1986 fall in price from $30 in January to below $10 in

August threatened Babangida's budget which every one described as the most comprehensive ever put together by any government. Some called it a mini-development plan whose implementation would see Nigeria out of the economic woods. The budget expected a revenue of ₦15 billion; 1 billion from 30% import levy would be used for export promotion; 900 million from the reduction of petroleum subsidy would be used for developing 60,000 km of rural feeder roads; and 500 million from the economic recovery fund would be channelled to the revival of health and education sectors. The budget also promised to increase the manufacturing sector to 55% of installed capacity. All these sound proposals could not be implemented for lack of funds, despite the assurances of Mr. Kuye, the director of budget, that the budget has a self-adjusting mechanism! Nigeria, which a few years ago was considered under-borrowed, has become Africa's largest debtor with total outstanding loans exceeding US $21 billion. Forty-four per cent of Nigeria's foreign exchange earnings go to service this debt. Payments due in 1985 amount to $4.4 billion and will rise to $4.8 billion in 1986. When uninsured trade debts are included, Nigeria's service obligations will peak at over US $7 billion in 1987.

We are now almost like Mexico that uses all her foreign exchange earnings to service her debts. It is this situation, and our refusal to seek accommodation with the IMF, that made our creditors, the Paris and London clubs, refuse to grant us any further credits. We had then our backs to the wall with no room for manoeuvre. No imports were coming in and our industries had to shut down and retrench workers. This is the background to the structural adjustment programme and the SFEM.

The Structural Adjustment Programme (SAP)

I have attempted to sketch the main problems which Nigeria faces as a result of the misuse of her oil wealth. They include:

- ⊃ A mainly public sector economy which is overregulated and heavily subsidised.
- ⊃ An economy with a crippling debt burden and an acute shortage of foreign exchange.

➲ An economy with a weak industrial and technological base which results in massive importation of machinery and raw materials for industries.

➲ An economy that has unemployment, underemployment, and a lot of unskilled manpower.

➲ An economy with food shortages, inadequate infrastructure, and basic utilities.

➲ An economy whose population growth rate is higher than its rate of economic growth.

The Obasanjo, Shagari and Buhari governments made unsuccessful attempts to solve the problems. Buhari's attempt was more bold than that of either Obasanjo or Shagari. He concentrated on:

❑ improving administrative efficiency (WAI[1]);
❑ fostering financial discipline;
❑ reducing overall fiscal deficit; and
❑ reducing the volume of imports and eliminating the accumulation of further external arrears.

His measures, well-intentioned as they might be, were nevertheless rather negative in that they were directed at controlling demand whilst what was required was increased production, supply and export. It was Babangida who introduced the required fundamental changes when he announced the following policies:

❑ Restructuring and diversifying the productive base of the economy in order to reduce the dependence on the oil sector and imports.

❑ Achieving fiscal and balance of payments viability in the medium term.

❑ Reducing the dominance of the public sector, and tapping the efficiency and growth potential of the private sector.

---

[1] War Against Indiscipline. This was an aggressive campaign to make discipline and orderly conducts part of the country's ethos.

He promised to implement the policies by stimulating domestic production and broadening the supply base of the economy, adopting a realistic exchange policy, adopting appropriate pricing policies especially for petroleum products, reducing complex administrative control with greater reliance on market forces, and encouraging the privatisation of public sector enterprises. This pronouncement is the background to the introduction of recent policies like the ban on the importation of rice and wheat, the removal of the subsidy on petrol, abandonment of import licensing, privatisation, and the now much talked about Second-Tier Foreign Exchange Market (SFEM). Therefore, in discussing SFEM, we should see it as part of the package for restructuring the economy.

SFEM

One of the greatest obstacles to the revival of the Nigerian economy was the overvaluation of the naira, and the refusal of successive Nigerian governments to devalue it. You are all aware that the main reason for rejecting the IMF loan was its insistence on devaluation. Government objected to devaluation for two reasons. The first was the social and political repercussions of the announcement of such a decision. The second was the difficulty of determining the correct value of the naira. In 1983, the IMF suggested 60% devaluation but government thought that it should be 20%. Under SFEM, the value of the naira is being determined, not by government or the IMF but by the market forces of supply and demand.

It is expected that the introduction of SFEM will bring about an efficient and competitive economy. In the past, the success of many companies did not depend so much on the sound economic decisions of their management teams but rather on the ability of management to lobby through the Ministry of Commerce and the Central Bank, sometimes at a price. Now, it is expected that management will be able to spend its time in planning and managing the company instead of shuttling between the Ministry of Commerce and the Central Bank. Again, the overvaluation of the naira brought about price-cost distortions which resulted in huge profits to distributors. With the purchase of the naira at its market value, the days of huge profits are gone and any distributor or manufacturer who attempts to make the profit of yesteryears will price himself out of the market. Already, consumer resistance to price increases is setting in and manufacturers as well as distributors have to be very competitive in order to remain in business. We are now entering an era of the buyers' market. All along it had been the sellers' market. We will soon have a similar situation that exists in Ghana, where goods are in the shops but no money to buy them. Already the cash squeeze is affecting the liquidity of commercial banks.

Companies that will experience great difficulties under SFEM are those that have substantial foreign debts, and industries that depend on over 50% of imported raw materials. So also will companies that are starting for the first time. They will need a lot of naira outlay especially where machinery and other inputs are to be imported. Having invested so much, they will find it difficult to compete with other local or imported products. The success of SFEM will depend on how far the market will be adequately funded. Sources of funds include the World Bank, the Central Bank and the domiciliary account of individuals. For example, the value of the naira was able to appreciate during the seventh week of the auction because the funds available went up from 75 million to 86 million dollars. The dollar went down from 4.7775 naira to a dollar in the sixth week to 3.8525 naira to a dollar in the seventh week. Last week the naira gained a further 25 kobo when it exchanged for 3.61 naira to a US dollar. Another condition for success is whether the proposed tariff will provide adequate protection to manufacturers. Unless there is an adequate differential between the duty on finished goods and that on imported inputs, the manufacturer will find it difficult to compete with traders. In some cases, the differential in the proposed tariff does not provide adequate incentive to manufacturers.

Another important area of concern under SFEM is the continued practice of bankers to debit the account of their customers with additional payments on transactions for which the customers had made due payments to their banks. The additional payments are in respect of shortfall arising from:

a. depreciation in the value of the naira;
b. interest charges arising from delayed payments to foreign suppliers.

In this 1986 budget, President Babangida said, among other things, that the burden of delayed payments arising from currency depreciation cannot fall on importers who had earlier fully settled with their banks as may be required by regulations. In spite of this statement, the banks have continued to debit the accounts of their customers with such charges. An example is that of a manufacturer whose transactions were executed and payments duly made to the bank in 1982, but who is now being debited with a huge sum of money that can cripple the company. You may wish to know that the question of providing adequate tariff protection to industries, and that of additional bank charges for completed transactions are being taken up with government by the Manufacturers Association of Nigeria.

I must, however, stress that the SFEM is a temporary measure which will cease when the market price and the official rate of the naira converge. Such a convergence will eliminate price-cost distortion, discourage smuggling, currency trafficking and the overinvoicing of import bills. It will also encourage the export of agricultural and industrial goods.

Having said all this, one must warn that the SFEM is neither a panacea nor an end in itself. It constitutes, along with other measures such as privatisation and the removal of subsidies and other controls, necessary steps towards the restructuring of the Nigerian economy. The test of success is the establishment of an efficient and competitive economy, which encourages savings, investment, production and export.

The silver lining of the oil glut and challenge to engineers

From the foregoing, it is clear that the oil glut has had an adverse impact on the Nigerian economy. But from a positive angle, it can safely be said that the oil collapse is not an unmitigated evil after all. From hindsight, well-meaning Nigerians can see some redeeming features in it. For the first time since independence, the governments of the federation are bracing up to the challenges of restructuring and reconstructing a structurally defective and collapsing economy. For the first time, the need for financial discipline is beginning to be appreciated. Peoples' tastes and consumption patterns are being forced to change towards home-grown goods and services.

Before now, the agricultural sector had been allowed to remain stagnant with increasing food imports. The manufacturing sector, defectively structured, has been completely dependent upon imported inputs to survive. A wasteful and inefficient public sector has left a legacy of inefficient services, corruption and poorly executed projects whose costs have been grossly inflated. Today, the nation has been shocked into the realisation that all these must change. Perhaps, without the collapse of the oil market, Nigerians would still today be basking in the glory of phoney wealth, wasting their resources with nothing to show for it except what economists have described as immisirising growth, i.e., growth without development. The country now has the opportunity to lay the foundation for a strong and viable economy. As engineers, you have a critical role to play in realising that objective.

Government has announced a number of far-reaching measures to restructure the economy. They include revitalising the agricultural sector and reducing the excessive reliance of the manufacturing sector on imported raw materials and other inputs. In this regard, industry is being called upon to integrate backwards and source their raw materials locally. Responses from manufacturers have been enthusiastic, but they have come face to face with certain defeating realities—most of the available local raw materials are in their raw state and must first undergo processing before industry can use them. Again, many of the existing machinery have been found to be incapable of handling the local materials. In some cases, the machines have suffered damage from local raw materials.

To a large extent, success in local sourcing of raw materials will depend on Nigerian engineers. New machines must be fabricated. New processes must be developed. Existing machinery can be adapted. Facilities to process the available raw materials into intermediate products must be created. By virtue of the nature of our soils, our agriculture cannot be sustained on a technology of tractorisation. There is a need for more appropriate, intermediate technology. All these are what the nation expects her engineers to find answers to. This is the challenge thrown to our engineers by the oil glut. As we go from here today, let it be on record that the success or failure of the drive towards restructuring of the Nigerian economy depends, to an important degree, on Nigerian engineers. That is a challenge you cannot afford to run away from.

25

SAP and the Crisis in the Industrial Sector of the Economy✚

"Government's reaction to our representations has been sympathetic but its sympathy has not been matched with positive action. Sympathy is not enough for a patient in danger of death. What he wants is relief not sympathy. We are all aware that many a post-mortem reveal how delays in providing the correct and timely treatment to the patient contribute to the patient's death."

Introduction

Gentlemen of the Press, I welcome you to this press briefing. The purpose is to draw your attention to the present crisis in the industrial sector of the Nigerian economy. The crisis is caused by the implementation of some aspects of the Structural Adjustment Programme (SAP). As a result, the very existence of the industrial sector is seriously threatened.

Two years ago, it was estimated that industries operated at 50% of installed capacity. Last year, it was approximately 30%. Today, for some industries the figure is even lower and some companies have had to close altogether. Even companies like Lever Brothers and Michelin that produce essential commodities such as Omo and motor tyres are no longer in production because of the counter-productive effects of the misapplication of some aspects of the Structural Adjustment Programme.

I will, however,like to state at the outset that when the federal government announced its Structural Adjustment Programme last year and then proceeded on September 26, 1986,to introduce SFEM as the main plank of the adjustment programme, we, in MAN, declared our support for the government. We did so because we fully appreciated and endorsed the overall objectives of the SAP which were:

✚ Speech presented as president of the Manufacturers Association of Nigeria during a press luncheon, February 19, 1987.

a. to effect a reallocation of resources in favour of the productive sector of the economy;
b. to stimulate local production in agriculture and industries in order to reduce inflation;
c. to reduce dependence on imported raw material and food items; and thereby
d. reduce and redress our unfavourable balance of payment.

As far as these broad principles of the Structural Adjustment Programme are concerned, our support for the government's strategies remains unshaken. Nevertheless, the application of the following aspects of the SAP is causing us grave concern and threatens our very existence:

1. the interim tariff
2. the stringent restrictive monetary policy; and
3. the devastating damage arising from the demand of banks for extra payments of transactions concluded long before SFEM because of the depreciation in the value of the naira.

We have, through formal channels, invited government's attention to these areas of concern. Government's reaction to our representations has been sympathetic but its sympathy has not been matched with positive action. Sympathy is not enough for a patient in danger of death. What he wants is relief not sympathy. We are all aware that many a post-mortem reveal how delays in providing the correct and timely treatment to the patient contribute to the patient's death.

By the time we end this briefing, I am sure you will also be able to find the explanations of two matters that are constantly on the minds of many Nigerians, namely, unemployment and the high cost of Nigerian-made goods.

The interim tariff

When SFEM was introduced in September 1986, the minister of finance promised that there would be a review of the customs and excise tariff in order to give protection to local industries against unfair competition from foreign importation of finished goods. But when the interim tariff was released, it became immediately clear that rather than protect local industries, the tariff placed them at a distinct disadvantage vis-à-vis imported finished goods. Whilst there was a reduction in the duty on imported raw materials, the reduction on imported finished goods was even greater. When you take into account that the local manufacturer has to pay excise duty, the net result is that it is cheaper to import than to manufacture goods locally. A few examples will illustrate the predicament of local manufacturers. Take the case of motor tyres for example. Last year the duty on imported tyres was 50%. Shortly after SFEM, i.e, in October, it was reduced from 50% to 20%. This year, after the budget, it was again reduced to 5%. On the other hand, various raw materials like steel wires and carbon black used in tyre manufacture attract a duty of 20% and 25% respectively. In addition, the local manufacturer has to pay another tax known as excise duty at the rate of 5%. You can then see that it is more profitable to import a tyre at 5% duty than to manufacture it at 20% or 25% import duty on raw materials, and later pay excise duty of 5%. Other examples are:

a. Corrugated iron sheets:

Tariff No.	Old Rate	Proposed Internal Rate	Budget Rate
73.13	40%	30%	15%

Raw materials for local manufacture attract a duty of 10%, plus excise duty of 5%.

b. Primary cells and batteries:

Tarrif No.	Old Rate	Proposed Internal Rate	Budget Rate
85.3	30%	10%	25%

Raw materials for local manufacture attract duties ranging between 25% and 40% plus excise duty of 5%.

Last, but not the least, is the case of vehicle assembly plants. Last year a car of 1800cc paid a duty of 70%. Now the duty has been reduced to 40%. On the other hand, CKD[1] for the same

---

[1] Completely Knocked Down parts.

size of car last year attracted a duty of 35%. Today, that duty is reduced to 30%. In addition, the assembly plant will pay a duty of 5% on its selling price which is equivalent to 10% on C & F.[2] The burden is heavier when we consider that these plants are currently working at a low percentage of their productive capacity.

Under these conditions many local products cannot compete with their imported counterparts. The net result is a return to the former colonial days of trade economy. We are importing unemployment along with the goods. Eventually, we will become the dustbin and a dumping ground of cheap European and Asian goods. This defeats one of the principal objectives of the Structural Adjustment Programme, which is the stimulation of local production in industries. It will also negate our strive to control inflation, our desire for self-reliance and self-sufficiency, not to talk of employment generation.

Severity of the restrictive monetary policy otherwise known as "Cash and Credit Squeeze"

The liquidity squeeze started when the Central Bank took away from commercial and merchant banks all deposits made by their customers against foreign transactions. This amounted to about ₦3 billion. Again, the trading in foreign exchange under SFEM took out a further ₦4 billion from circulation. As if that was not enough, there was an increase in the bank's prime lending rate, which now stands at 15%. A ceiling of 4.4% was also imposed on the growth of aggregate bank credit. The naira in circulation is estimated to have reduced by over 50%.

This restrictive monetary policy has been introduced to curb inflation by mopping up excess liquidity, with a view to curbing consumer demand. While the need to bring inflation under control is necessary in present circumstances, greater attention should also be given to the need to ensure growth through increased supply of goods. One of the practical effects of

---

[2] Cost and Freighting.

government's economic policy of demand management under the SAP, is that the supply side of the economy has not been given equal attention. The cash and credit squeeze on the manufacturing industry is of such severity that it has imposed an intolerable burden on local manufacturers, some of whom have been forced to close down. Industries are dying because of an overdose of government's restrictive measures. Not only has access to bank credit become increasingly difficult, if not impossible, but the sharp decline in consumer demand has aggravated the liquidity situation of local manufacturers.

Virtually all the manufacturing companies now hold excess stock, which they are unable to dispose of, owing to a fall in consumer demand. This in turn means even lower capacity utilisation— one of the anomalies which the SAP was intended to correct. But the practical effect of the liquidity squeeze is that the cost profile of the manufacturing industry is now on the upswing. It is true that in its 1987 budget government gave some measure of relief to the manufacturing industry such as the reduction of company tax from 45 to 40%, the reduction of advance payment of duty to 25%, the amendment of capital allowance, and the abolition of 30% import levy. But these measures, though appreciated, are not enough to reduce the escalating cost of production.

Devastating bank debits on concluded trade transactions

A major source of concern to the manufacturing industry is the present practice by commercial banks of debiting their customers with the shortfall on delayed payments arising from the depreciation of the naira. This is contrary to the assurance given in his 1986 budget statement by the president that manufacturers would not be made to bear the burden of these additional bank debits for transactions which had been completed long before the introduction of SFEM. In spite of strong representations to the government on this matter, the Central Bank proceeded on December 18, 1986, to issue guidelines which, in effect, chose the exchange rate prevailing on September 26, 1986, as the cut-off rate for the settlement of all such outstanding transactions.

This decision is totally unsatisfactory as it means imposing additional financial burdens on local manufacturers. Equity and fair play demand that for all the outstanding transactions, the settlement rate at the first-tier market should be that prevailing when the transactions were undertaken, that is, the date of the opening of the Letters of Credit. The inequity inherent in the CBN guidelines is evident from the following considerations:

i. Full payments at the prevailing exchange rate were made by the importers.
ii. The payments by customers were utilised by the banks.
iii. The goods produced from such imports were sold at prices dictated by costs determined by the prevailing exchange rate.

To now ask manufacturers, as the commercial banks now do, to make additional payments on the basis of the September 26 cut-off rate is doubly punitive, and is definitely unacceptable. The magnitude of the problem can best be perceived when it is considered that, on the average, the additional bank demands are about 300 - 400% of the original payments made to the commercial banks. Where, one may ask, does the CBN expect importers to get the additional funds from? This matter is very urgent, for if nothing is done, many companies will go into bankruptcy.

Another potential source of bankruptcy is with respect to the rate at which debts arising out of suppliers credit will be paid. Some of these debts are spread over three to five years, and some of them run into several millions of naira, and unless they are paid, either at the rate of exchange prevailing when the debts were incurred or at worst at the rate prevailing on September 26, 1986, several of the debtor companies will be unable to pay the debts at SFEM rates. Companies that paids 4,000,000 naira every six months pre-SFEM will now be required to pay above ₦10, 000,000 every six months. Hardly can any manufacturing company survive under such a heavy financial burden.

In conclusion, I would like to state that while MAN still supports the general thrust of government's economic policies and strategies, we are firmly of the view that the objectives of the

Structural Adjustment Programme will be vitiated unless the issues raised in this address are urgently dealt with by the government. Failure on the part of government to act promptly can only worsen the plight of the manufacturing sector, with more bankruptcies and unemployment. Is it not worrying that the appointment of receivers in bankruptcy has now entered into the industrial vocabulary of this country? A decision has got to be made whether industries are wanted or not. This decision must be made as quickly as possible for the patient might die whilst the experts are consulting. If the answer is, hopefully, in the affirmative, then the government should, without delay, formulate, after consultations with the organised private sector, a comprehensive long-term strategic industrial policy which should be consistently implemented if it is to enjoy the confidence of present and future investors.

26

Manufacturing in Nigeria: Problems and Prospects✛

"The industrial base is small, so there is still a great scope for expansion. Even the available industrial goods are of the low technology type, like beer, soft drinks, cigarettes, cotton, textiles, soap and detergents, cement and cement blocks, assembling of cars and trucks."

Introduction

When I received a request to make a ten to fifteen minute presentation on manufacturing in Nigeria, I discussed it with two American friends. They were unanimous in suggesting that my presentation should bear the American private investor in mind. I disagreed with them, arguing that as far as the investment of private capital is concerned, there is little or no difference between an indigenous and a foreign investor. They both operate in the same environment; they both come under the same government control regulations, and suffer the same frustrations arising from the inadequacies of underdevelopment.

You may not be aware of it, but the Manufacturers Association of Nigeria, which I represent, is made up of indigenous and foreign manufacturers. In fact, foreigners are in the majority, and one of the two vice presidents of the association is an Englishman who incidentally is also the deputy managing director of United African Company — a member of the UniLever Group of Companies. In the time allowed, I intend to concentrate on the problems and prospects of manufacturing in Nigeria.

✛ Paper presented to a conference on the Nigerian economy and the relationship with the USA, sponsored by the African-American Institute and the National Bank of Boston, June 21-23, 1983.

Problems facing the manufacturing industry

In spite of the various directives and incentives provided by the government, a manufacturer, whether indigenous or foreign, still faces several constraints. Among these are:

☐   inadequate basic infrastructure, especially water, electricity and telecommunications;
☐   weak raw materials base;
☐   lack of technológical know-how;
☐   strong competition from imports, including smuggling;
☐   excessive reliance on the external sector for capital goods and raw materials;
☐   strong competition for resources from other quick and high yielding sectors;
☐   institutional and administrative bottlenecks;
☐   delay in making payments for raw materials, and in the repatriation of profits and dividends.

Concerted efforts are, however, being made by both the government and organised private sector to remove the constraints. For example, the Manufacturers Association of Nigeria holds a meeting once in every two months with the minister of industries mainly to discuss the problems facing manufacturers. One result of such meetings is a decision to hold a seminar next month on the development of raw materials. Another is the recent reactivation of IDCC. This is a committee which has been moribund for years. Its job is to co-ordinate the various approvals necessary before an industry is established. These include approved status, expatriate quota, and approved user license.

Relationship with the USA

I would like to say that compared with the British, French and Germans, there is very little American investment in Nigeria, particularly in the manufacturing sector. This is quite surprising, especially when one considers the similarities between both countries. Not only have we adopted the American-style system of government, but Nigeria, like

America, is a country where private enterprises thrive, and where almost every citizen aspires to be a capitalist. American investments are also especially welcome because we won't like to put all our eggs in one European basket, especially given the fact that the American economy often acts as a locomotive to other economies. But the crucial question is: Do the Americans really want to invest in black Africa? In this connection, we will like to know the outcome of six bilateral talks between Nigeria and the USA. These talks started in 1977, and have been held at the highest levels of government. We are yet to see the results of the talks in terms of American investment. The last rounds of talks was held in 1981. Again, in January 1982, the Reagan administration sent a powerful mission to Nigeria which was led by the secretaries of commerce and agriculture. We are still waiting to see on the ground the results of that mission.

The prospects

I would like to emphasise that in spite of the present difficulties, which are largely caused by the global recession and the world oil glut, Nigeria remains the strongest and most democratic economy in the continent of Africa.[1] It is the only country in black Africa that has no political prisoner. Again, it is one of the few countries in black Africa that has a multiparty system. Business-wise, it is an economy of 100 million dynamic people. Anyone who has been to Nigeria will testify to this dynamism which is evident everywhere. One feels it is in the air which seems to vibrate and pulsate.

The strength of the economy lies principally in the country's natural resources, foremost of which is oil. At present, Nigeria is the sixth largest oil producing country in the world. She is the second largest supplier of oil to both the United States and France. Apart from oil and substantial reserves of natural gas, Nigeria is also endowed with other minerals and natural resources. These include uranium, manganese, columbite, limestone, coal, tin, salt,

---

[1]   At the time the speech was made, Nigeria was a multiparty democracy under Shagari's regime.

marble, iron ore, lead, bauxite, silver, silica sand and phosphate. There are also such agricultural products as groundnuts, cocoa, rubber, palm produce, cotton, and timber. For a developing country of the size and potential of Nigeria, industrialisation is essential if it is to achieve rapid economic and social development. Industrialisation is also imperative, for, in the world of today, every country is pursuing a policy of self-reliance and self-sufficiency. After all, development is nothing other than ensuring that maximum use is made of available mineral and vegetable resources for the benefit of the citizens of the country. Manufacturing in Nigeria is, however, still at an infant stage. It accounts for only about seven per cent of the Gross Domestic Product. The industrial base is small, so there is still a great scope for expansion. Even the available industrial goods are of the low technology type like beer, soft drinks, cigarettes, cotton, textiles, soap and detergents, cement and cement blocks, assembling of cars and trucks. There are also two petroleum refineries that process about 150,000 barrels of crude oil a day for gasoline and fuel oil. There is hardly any production of capital and intermediate goods.

Another feature of the manufacturing sector is its over-dependence on imports for the supply of raw materials and spare parts. There is no single industrial product in which the country is entirely self-sufficient. On the average, about sixty per cent of the total raw materials consumed in the manufacturing sector is imported. One of the consequences is that the country's import bill is dominated by the cost of raw materials and spare parts for industries. This explains why the present economic stabilisation measures[2] designed to conserve foreign exchange have affected industries most adversely. Many factories have reduced their scale of operation and labour force and some have closed down. Many more face the real danger of closing down unless there are immediate prospects of foreign exchange being made available for essential raw materials. In the circumstances, government has announced that in the future, only industries that are prepared

---

[2]   The economic stabilisation measures introduced by the Shagari regime in 1982.

and capable of developing raw materials locally will be allowed to establish.

The above considerations must have been in the mind of government, when, in the fourth National Development Plan, it specified the following industries as priority areas for private investment.

i. Building materials industry—cement industry, roofing sheets, ceiling materials, ceramics and floor/wall tiles, door locks, carpet tiles, plumbing materials, steel pipes, window and door frames, and fittings.

ii. Engineering and transport industry—components for automobile industry, machine tools and plant maintenance industries, metal working, aluminium roofing, metal working and extrusion.

iii. Chemical industry—downstream petrochemical industry, industrial chemicals, nitrogenous fertiliser manufacture, pharmaceutical products, manufacture of film mouldings and extrusion for the plastic industry.

iv. Electrical and electronics manufacturing as distinct from the assembly of components, switches, fuses, switch boards and transformers.

v. Scientific instruments—school and medical laboratory equipment.

vi. Telecommunications equipment manufacturing—telephone cables and receivers, exchange engines, intercom outfits.

vii. Household equipment and furniture—cookery and kitchen ware.

This list of possibilities is by no means exhaustive, but it illustrates some of the opportunities that exist. One can see from the list that government has reserved for itself what is generally referred to as the commanding heights of the economy. These include such industries as iron and steel, petrochemicals, liquefied natural gas, fertilisers, and refineries. They are considered basic and strategic and therefore not suitable for control by private enterprises. Some of us in the private sector do not share government's view on this, especially given the poor performance of public enterprises. Most of these are not managed on commercial principles, and as a result, they are often costly and inefficient. If we are to lay a solid foundation for an industrial take-off in the shortest possible time, private capital should participate in these industries. The best arrangement, in my own opinion, would be a tripartite syndicate of government, foreign capital and indigenous capital. Foreign participation would ensure expert management, and indigenous partners would provide extra guarantee for the stability and security of investment. I am pleased that the government, in a recent publication, has assured investors that,

> ...apart from the defence industries, no specific area will be reserved exclusively for government. Private investors will be encouraged in all lines of activity, provided they conform with guidelines to be issued from time to time by government.

The present guidelines expect manufacturers to:

i.   strive to maximise local value added. This they should do, through the use of local raw materials, linkages between one manufacturing industry and another, backward integration, and the training and use of indigenous manpower. There is provision for excise duty reduction for increases in local value added.

ii.   establish research and development units for improvement of the quality of products, efficiency of the production process, and increases in local inputs. Expenses on research and development are tax deductible.

iii.   satisfy both local and export demands. Industries that are export-oriented will be exempted from both import and excise duties.

iv.   generate employment and not be concentrated in a few urban areas. Industries that are established in less disadvantaged areas will be refunded part of their infrastructural expenses.

(27)

The Plight of Manufacturers under a Fluctuating Naira ✤

"A combination of operating factors in Nigeria would argue for the erection of a high tariff wall of protection for Nigeria's infant industries. They include general infrastructural deficiencies and the high start-up and operating costs arising therefrom, low volumes of operation and other related costs, including administration-induced costs."

Introduction

I have the pleasure to welcome all of you to the 16th Annual General Meeting of the Manufacturers Association of Nigeria. A year ago, at the 15th Annual General Meeting of this association, I drew attention to the anxiety and lamentation of industrialists about the uncertain future of their manufacturing establishments. This uncertainty is the result of continuing sad experiences of depressed industrial activities since the collapse of the world oil market in 1982. Following the world oil glut, Nigeria's economic fortunes worsened. The internal and external finances of the country went into severe crisis, which is still with us today. Faced with strained financial resources, the government introduced a regime of import licensing. The licensing system was aimed at rationalising the allocation of scarce foreign exchange. In the scheme of things, industry was supposed to be accorded high priority.

Piteously enough, the bureaucratic, inefficient and nepotic administration of the licenses often led to meagre and pitiable allocation to manufacturers. Corruption became, therefore, the order of the day, and the bulk of the license went to non-manufacturers. One of the results was the complete or partial closure of a number of manufacturing plants. Those that managed

---

✤ Address delivered as President of MAN at the 16th Annual General Meeting of the association held at the Federal Palace Hotel, Lagos, March 3, 1987.

to remain in operation experienced severe underutilisation of capacity, with average capacity utilisation standing at about thirty per cent. The attendant reduced turnover and earning, as well as the inevitable labour retrenchment, were among the sorry experiences that industry passed through in the period 1983-85.

Then hope was raised when President Babangida, at MAN's Annual General Meeting in March 1986, announced arrangements for a more rational allocation of the 1986 import licenses. Earlier in his 1986 budget, the president had indicated government's intention to ensure that industries achieved fifty-five per cent capacity utilisation. Unfortunately, as MAN was gearing itself up to embrace the promise of a brighter 1986, the vagaries of the international oil market conspired to frustrate that hope, with the price of oil falling from $20 to $10. The ensuing cash crunch, and the late issuance of the 1986 import licenses, as well as the difficulties in securing Confirmed Letters of Credit aggravated the fate of industries. By June, fresh spates of industrial closures started on a more serious dimension than in the past years.

Meanwhile, the commercial and merchant banks continued to debit their corporate customers with the shortfalls on delayed payments arising from the depreciation of the naira. There were also cases where the accounts of manufacturers were debited by their banks with interest charges on such delayed payments. These additional charges were on transactions that were executed even as far back as 1982, and for which manufacturers had made due payments as stipulated by regulations. Naturally, these additional charges — the result of a floated naira—only served to aggravate the plight of the already cash-strapped manufacturing sector.

The era of SFEM

This was the state of affairs when the Second-Tier Foreign Exchange Market (SFEM) was announced. The Manufacturers Association of Nigeria welcomed it for several reasons. At least, there was the feeling that it would be an improvement over the corruption-ridden import licensing system. However, SFEM, which came into operation on September 26, 1986, has not been free of certain limitations. In the first place, as the major element of the Structural Adjustment Programme (SAP), SFEM was accompanied by trade liberalisation which on the ground means inadequate protection of local industries. One of the results is that the expected beneficial effect of the SAP to stimulate new industrial investments (foreign and local) might well become elusive by virtue of this lack of protection. Disquieting revelations have emerged from our contacts with visiting prospective foreign investors and those who already have businesses in Nigeria, about their perception of the investment climate in the country since the inception of SFEM. In their evaluation, which is difficult to controvert, the new structure of customs and excise tariff introduced under Decree, 1986, offers no protection to industries and, therefore, has no attractions for investment. If anything, it has made importation and sale of finished goods easier, more profitable and attractive.

A combination of operating factors in Nigeria would argue for the erection of a high tariff wall of protection for Nigeria's infant industries. They include general infrastructural deficiencies and the high start-up and operating costs arising therefrom, low volumes of operation and other related costs, including administration-induced costs. All these represent a strong case for substantial tariff differentials between imported finished goods and industrial inputs (raw materials, machinery and spare parts) for the local manufacturing industries. Such differentials constitute the only shield against unfair competition and dumping of goods from the highly industrialised and low-cost producing countries of Europe, America and Asia, especially when the cost of production has been aggravated by more than the three times SFEM-induced increase in the naira cost of raw materials and other imported manufacturing inputs. By failing to provide this necessary protection, the new tariff structure can only succeed in stifling new investments. Of course, it is easy to imagine the dangerous implication this will have for employment generation and the overall growth and development of the Nigerian economy. Happily, the government, in the 1987 budget, has given an indication that it would review the whole tariff with a view to eliminating any anomalies.

Another development that has followed closely on the heels of SFEM is liquidity squeeze. While we understand the need to curb inflation, the squeeze has been too severe and is capable of strangulating industry in particular and the economy in general. For industry, it has created multi-dimensional problems; it has made access to credit difficult ánd more costly. This increased cost of capital represents another element of production cost increases with which manufacturers are now confronted. Equally disturbing is the fact that firms are finding it difficult to sell their products because of the liquidity squeeze. As a result of severe restrictions on the money in circulation, consumers have little cash in hand to exercise effective demand in the market. Unless something is done to loosen the noose of the squeeze, the danger is real that the economy might be forced into a deep economic depression.

As if all these problems are not enough, the Central Bank of Nigeria has further stiffened the burden of manufacturers by its December 18, 1986, release of guidelines for the settlement rate of outstanding pre-SFEM transactions. By these guidelines, the exchange rate on September 26, 1986, was chosen as the cut-off date for the settlement of all such outstanding transactions, provided the documents relating to them had been submitted to the CBN before that date. It is our view that this decision is far from satisfactory as it has complicated the problems of manufacturers. MAN feels that these guidelines contradict the logical interpretation of the provisions of section 15 of the Decree on SFEM, which they were supposed to clarify. Equity demands that for all the outstanding transactions that satisfied the provision of that section of the Decree, the settlement rate at the first-tier market should be that prevailing when the transactions were executed. This is only logical considering that they were the basis on which importers programmed their orders and entered into definite commitments.

In circumstances where the naira was subjected to accelerated downward fluctuations since 1985, it is difficult to rationalise the cut-off rate of September 26, 1986, for the settlement of all post-1983 outstanding transactions. The inequity inherent in this decision is clear from the following facts:

i.   The manufacturers duly made full payment to the banks when the orders were made and the goods imported.

ii. The banks themselves benefited from the deposits by doing profitable business with the money so deposited.

iii. The goods produced from such imports had since been sold at prices dictated by costs and rates of exchange prevailing at the time of production and sale, i.e., before September 26, 1986. To now ask manufacturers to make additional payments on the basis of the September 26 cut-off rate is putting them under double disadvantage. Inevitably, this can only accentuate the woes of the badly battered manufacturing enterprises.

From what I have said so far, it should be evident that the manufacturing sector in Nigeria cannot survive without prompt and positive action by the government to deal with the problems highlighted above. The sector has been under siege for the good part of the past four years and, therefore, requires some relief. The five per cent reduction in company tax announced in the 1987 budget is a welcome start. We commend the government for that. However, government should go further to make industrial activities under SFEM less burdensome and less unattractive. In this regard, it should have another look at the CBN guidelines on the settlement rates of outstanding pre-SFEM transactions. In our view, the applicable rates should be those prevailing at the time the contracts were entered into with suppliers and the imports executed. The banks should also be made to refund all additional payments or cancel debits against the accounts of their corporate (manufacturing) customers in respect of shortfall or interest on delayed payments for all 1982-1983 transactions, as section 16 of the Decree on SFEM provides that they should be subject to the relevant refinancing scheme already established. More importantly, a fundamental review of the Customs and Excise (Miscellaneous Provisions) Decree 1986 should be undertaken to provide adequate protection to the fledgling local industries. Finally, we expect that appropriate steps will be taken to loosen the corset of the present liquidity squeeze without sacrificing the objective of curbing inflation. Unless this is done, the growth anticipated in the 1987 budget stands the risk of being frustrated.

28

Manufacturers Association of Nigeria: Role, Problems and Prospects ✦

"... Government tends to class manufacturers with traders under the common appellation of 'businessmen', forgetting that there is a world of difference between the businessman who creates something by dirtying his hands in a factory floor and the smartly dressed itinerant briefcase-carrying businessman who often operates from a hotel room."

Introduction

Your Excellency, Distinguished Guests, Ladies and Gentlemen. I welcome you all to the 129th meeting of the National Council of the Manufacturers Association of Nigeria which is being held in the historic city of Calabar. I welcome, in particular, the Military Governor of Cross River State, Colonel Dan Archibong and his entourage. It is our custom to hold one meeting every year outside our national headquarters in Lagos. This year we chose Calabar for three reasons:

One, out of over 800 members spread throughout the length and breadth of Nigeria, only 12 or 1.5% come from Cross River State. It appears that the majority of the people in Cross River State are not fully aware of the existence of MAN or what it stands for. We have, therefore, decided that, "if the mountain does not go to Mohammed, Mohammed will go to the mountain".

Two, Calabar, the capital of the state, is not only an important seaport, it is also a major industrial centre with an enormous agricultural hinterland. By coming to Calabar, industrialists will not only see which industries are already here but will, in particular, assess the prospects of further investment in the state.

Third, our visit is planned to coincide with the final ceremonies of the Obong's coronation anniversary, and the commencement

---

✦ Speech presented at the National Council Meeting of the Manufacturers Association of Nigeria, MAN, at Calabar, December 3, 1984.

of the Calabar Trade Fair. You will agree with me that there could not have been a better time to come to Calabar than when her people are in such a festive mood.

What is MAN all about?

I will now say a few words about the Manufactures Association of Nigeria, MAN. Briefly, the Manufacturers Association of Nigeria is an organisation, the main purpose of which is the rapid development of Nigeria through industrialisation. We believe that the quickest and surest method of bringing about lasting development is through the establishment of industries. Development means ensuring that the resources of a country — human, animal, mineral, vegetable, etc.—are put to the best use for the citizens of that country. When this is done, something new comes into existence, employment is generated, wealth is created, and the process gives rise to a related number of economic activities. Wealth created in any other way is marginal and parasitical; it is wealth that is not broadly and firmly rooted in the economy; and that gives rise to progress without development.

Problems

Having outlined our role, let me briefly describe the constraints under which we operate:

The first is the apparent lack of appreciation by the government of the crucial role private industries play in overall development. We say this because government tends to class manufacturers with traders under the common appellation of 'businessmen', forgetting that there is a world of difference between the businessman who creates something by dirtying his hands in a factory floor and the smartly dressed itinerant briefcase-carrying businessman who often operates from a hotel room. The one has come to stay, the other is a bird of passage. The one is putting something into the country whilst the other is taking something out of it. The one is an investor, the other is a sucker.

Our second difficulty is the lack of proper appreciation, again by the government, of the historical causes of the present industrial predicament. Historically, industrialisation started in Nigeria with the wrong foot forward. It was industrialisation in a reverse process. Instead of starting with agricultural expansion and processing, we took the easy way of bringing everything — raw materials and machinery — from outside and putting them together here; instead of starting from the areas of our strength we started from areas of our weakness; instead of starting with basic industrial tools (machine tools, foundries and light engineering) we started with the importation of sophisticated machinery in addition to raw materials. Our industrialisation was, therefore, an assembly-type of business. One of the results of this is that our industrialisation policy is boosting other countries' economy rather than ours.

No doubt the wrong industrialisation policy was due to the import substitution policy adopted by the colonial power as well as by the post-independence Nigerian governments. Unfortunately, after twenty-four years of independence, the wrong approach is still with us, and instead of taking steps to correct the errors of the past, we prefer to visit the sins of the past on the present generation of industrialists. Instead of all concerned sitting down to devise corrective policies and programmes, we prefer either to pass the buck, or to point accusing fingers at each other.

Prospects

I am, however, pleased that recent statements by the head of state, and the chief of staff, indicate that they are now fully aware of the problems of industry. This is very encouraging, for once a problem is correctly diagnosed, its solution becomes easier. My plea is that manufacturers should now sit down with the government, universities and research institutes to work out a practical programme of industrialisation that will be beneficial to the greater number of Nigerians. It should be a programme that is broad-based, and one that maximises our economic strengths. It should be a programme where all concerned—manufacturers, government, the university and research institutes — have each a part to play in the achievement of the desired results.

In conclusion, let us hope that our meeting here, and the recent statements by top government officials, will constitute a turning point in the desired co-operative effort between government and industry.

(29)

MAN and the Question of Backward Integration✢

"There will be no solution to the raw materials problem as long as government and industry continue to point accusing fingers at each other, and as long as they indulge in passing the buck. A solution will come as soon as both sides accept the need for serious dialogue and co-operative action."

Introduction

In suggesting that this quarterly luncheon meeting should discuss the development of local raw materials for industries, we, the organised private sector, believe that the time has come, indeed it is overdue, when instead of pointing accusing fingers at each other, government and industry should actively and meaningfully co-operate in finding acceptable and workable solutions to this intractable raw materials problem. Both government and the private sector agree that there is an urgent need to eliminate the high dependence on external sources for raw materials. We also agree that until this is done, industries will be unable to make maximum contribution to the economy. There is also agreement that in view of the rapidly dwindling foreign exchange, the present import restrictions will have to continue. I hope that we are also agreed that the present unsatisfactory situation arose mainly from our colonial past, and the import-substitution policy adopted by successive post-independence governments. The first and second development plans extolled it as a good policy.

What appears not to be generally agreed, however, is the nature and dimension of the problem as well as the responsibility for its solution. But it is important that we remove any

---

✢ Opening address as president of MAN at a quarterly luncheon meeting between the government and the private sector, November 13, 1984.

misconceptions which may lead to wrong policies and strategies being adopted. Misconceptions are likely to arise in three areas: The first is in the definition of raw materials for industries. Raw materials mean either primary products in their raw state or processed and intermediate products which are used by other industries for the production of a final product of another industry.

The second area of misconception concerns responsibility for the production of raw materials, sometimes referred to as 'backward integration'. The view seems to be held in certain government quarters that it is the responsibility of the end manufacturer to backward integrate to all his raw materials. This is not always possible or desirable. A tyre manufacturer may be able to produce the natural rubber for his tyres but he may be unable to produce the steel wire or carbon black that go into the making of a tyre. So also can a cigarette manufacturer be able to produce the tobacco that forms over 50% of his raw materials but he may not be able to produce the wrapping paper or the cork tip that forms an indispensable part of a cigarette; nor may he be able to produce the cartons for packing the cigarettes. Someone else may be in a better position to produce them more efficiently and economically. What goes into the manufacture of a single product are so many that it requires careful planning to bring about the necessary linkages in the production process.

The third area of misconception is the volume and composition of imported raw materials. These account for less than 40% of the total imports by the manufacturing industry. The balance of 60% is made up of machinery and spare parts. Again, agricultural raw materials (palm oil, sorghum , wheat, malt) account for about 33.5% of raw materials imports. The balance is accounted for by semi-processed industrial raw materials. Therefore, whilst it is possible to develop our agricultural raw materials base, we should be under no illusions that this would solve all our raw materials problem.

MAN's contributions

Having outlined the nature and magnitude of the problem, let me briefly state what we ourselves have been able to do. In July

1983 the Manufacturers Association, in partnership with NISER[1] and the Ministry of Commerce, organised a national workshop where officials of the government and the private sector had a full dialogue on the issues involved. The report of the workshop has been published and circulated by MAN. I will like to draw your attention to the recommendations at pages 4 and 5 of the report. MAN has also gone further to initiate action towards the implementation of the recommendation about a raw materials council by establishing a Raw Materials Development Committee. The government, industries, universities and research institutes are members of the committee. Its terms of reference are at pages 2 and 3 of our memorandum. The committee is at present collecting and studying the data on raw materials now used in industry.

Some companies have also expanded their research and development units, and gave them the responsibility for finding alternatives and/or substitutes for the agricultural raw materials they import. Progress is being made, but the companies are experiencing several difficulties. The first is the difficulty in obtaining land from state governments. Some state governments are known to ask for exorbitant compensations and for rents, as high as ₦100 per annum per hectare! At the federal level there is need for appropriate positive incentives to induce investments into the development of raw materials and other inputs. Such incentives should include tax concessions and preferential treatment in the allocation of licences. This is important because companies must be kept reasonably alive whilst they are researching into local raw materials.

The role of petrochemical and machine tools industries

A discussion of raw materials for industries will not be complete without reference to petrochemicals, machine tools, and the need for our steel plants to produce flat steel which is used by industries in addition to producing round rods for construction companies.

---

[1] National Institute for Social and Economic Research.

Petrochemicals form at least 40% of raw materials at present imported by industries. Since the project has been on the government drawing board for sometime now, we want to know the present position of the project, and to be assured that the timetable for its implementation has not changed.

The importance of a machine tools industry cannot be overemphasised. It will produce some of the spare parts now imported from abroad. It will also strengthen the technological capability of the nation. Priority should, therefore, be given to this industry either by encouraging state governments that planned such industries or by providing appropriate incentives to private investors to induce them into this line of activity.

Before I take my seat, I would like to raise one or two urgent matters, though not related to the subject-matter under discussion, but which are causing our members anxiety. The first is the need to extend the life of 'Form M' for spare parts from six months to one year. The reason is that most spare parts are tailor-made and are not available on shop counters. The second matter is the unreasonable amount of management time that is spent in chasing import licences, in establishing 'Form Ms', and in shopping around for a bank with a line of credit. Is it impossible in future to centralise all these procedures, as I understand is the case in India, Zimbabwe and Kenya? This will require designing one comprehensive form and setting up a single committee under the minister of commerce and industry. The Central Bank, and representatives of commercial banks and industries should be included in the committee. What I have in mind is something similar to the Essential Commodities Committee which worked very successfully during the early days of this administration.

Speaking on licences, companies would like to know as early as possible what value of licences they are likely to expect during 1985 to enable them make their production plans. Also, as much of the licences as possible should be issued before the end of the year.

Let me conclude as I began. There will be no solution to the raw materials problem as long as government and industry continue to point accusing fingers at each other, and as long as they indulge in passing the buck. A solution will come as soon as both sides accept the need for serious dialogue and co-operative action. Let this meeting be the beginning of this much needed dialogue and co-operation. Let this meeting be where the buck stops. The country and its workers are watching and waiting for a solution. We must not fail them.

30

Developing Local Raw Materials for Nigerian Industries✦

"Raw materials for one industry may be finished goods of another. It will, in most cases, be impossible for a manufacturer to backward integrate all his raw materials."

Introduction

I would like to begin by complimenting you, Honourable Minister, for organising this workshop, this dialogue between the government and the private sector, for the purpose of finding a mutually acceptable solution to the problem of developing local raw materials for our industries. This is what the organised private sector has been asking the government to do. This request for dialogue and consultation is often misunderstood and misinterpreted as an attempt to hijack the decision-making powers of the government. But what the private sector asks for is not a take-over bid, but a prudent and democratic request that before the government exercises its right and responsibility of decision-making, it should consult those who either have practical experience of the problem area or are ultimately going to be responsible for putting the decisions into practical effect. I go further to suggest that in all problem areas where a Nigerian talent is available, full use should be made of such a talent. For example, in the oil industry, there are several Nigerians who have acquired considerable national and international experience of the industry who would willingly put their expertise at the disposal of their country. But another cause of the present misunderstanding is that some persons in the public sector

---

✦ Opening address delivered as president of MAN to the "National Workshop on Raw Materials for Nigerian Industries", at the Administrative Staff College, Badagry, July 4, 1983.

assume that they are more patriotic than their neighbours in the private sector. This is unfortunate, and I can only advise that in the prudent and careful search for talent, every Nigerian should be presumed patriotic until the contrary is proved.

Honourable Minister, this workshop could not have come at a more opportune moment. It is being held at a time when the country is passing through a very difficult time. In fact, we are near a crisis situation. Today, our factories are closing down because of the shortage of raw materials and spare parts; workers are being laid off; consumer goods are in short supply; those available sell at prohibitive prices; local commercial banks on the other hand refuse orders for raw materials and spare parts; overseas correspondent banks refuse to confirm letters of credit emanating from Nigeria; and lastly but not the least, the Nigerian currency is being smuggled out and sold in Europe and America at ridiculous prices. Nigerians conspire and collaborate with dubious foreigners among us to cheat the nation. Our image in the international scene has never been so low.

This workshop is only to find an answer to one of the problems listed above. I hope that other government ministries and departments, especially the economic ministries of agriculture, commerce, finance, petroleum and energy, will follow the example of the ministry of industries and organise workshops for the examination of several problems under their respective ministries. Ladies and gentlemen, we have not come here to apportion blame for our present predicament. Rather, we have come to find solutions. If the session had been one of pointing accusing fingers, I am sure that if one finger is pointing at the accused, four will undoubtedly be pointing at the accuser.

I would like to suggest that in our discussion of the development of local raw materials we should pay attention to the following areas:

1. The importance of the manufacturing sector in our bid either for general macro-economic development, or the narrow micro policy of self-reliance and self-sufficiency.
2. Historical background of our present problems to enable us discover their root causes.

3. A clear perspective of what we mean by local raw materials.

4. Consistent short and long-term planning which will assign roles to the government and the private sector , bearing in mind that whilst the private sector reacts promptly to economic incentives, it is also very sensitive to unpredictable stop and go policies.

I will now briefly elaborate each of the above points.

Importance of the manufacturing sector

For a country of the size and potential of Nigeria, industrialisation is essential if the country is to achieve rapid economic and social development. This means ensuring that all the mineral and vegetable resources are put to maximum benefit for the citizens of the country. And this can be done through industrial processing or the making of finished products out of the raw natural resources. This cannot be achieved unless the country puts the right emphasis, and recognises the importance of manufacturing. Unfortunately, Nigeria is so addicted to trading that many are incapable of distinguishing a trader from a manufacturer. Both call themselves businessmen. But there is a world of difference. A trader is very often a bird of passage. Some of them are 'flight by night fast buckers' who have no interest in the country except to make a quick profit. Consequently, they have no need to invest any money in the country. Very often, their only investment is in a single hotel room. They are by and large portmanteau investors. A manufacturer, on the other hand, invests in a feasibility study, in machinery, land, buildings, and training. Above all, he has faith in the future of the country. His relationship with the country is like a marriage between husband and wife, whilst that of the fast buckers is like the relationship between a man and his mistress. That being the case, the manufacturer, like a wife, should be treated with due care and attention. To treat him and a trader alike will amount to non-recognition of the economic advantages of manufacturing, such as employment generation, transfer of technology and the conservation of foreign exchange, to mention just a few.

Historical background of our present problems

The present absence of resource-based industrialisation can be traced to three historical causes:

a. Our colonial past.

b. The import substitution policy introduced during the colonial era and adopted by successive post-independence governments. The first and second development plans extolled it as a good policy.

c. Government reservation to itself in the second and third plans of such industries as iron and steel, petrochemical, and liquefied natural gas which would have hastened the development of local raw materials had private capital been allowed to participate in those projects.

A clear perspective on what we mean by local raw materials

When we speak of raw materials for industries, we mean primary products in their natural state as well as processed and intermediate products, which are used by other industries. Raw materials for one industry may be finished goods of another. It will, in most cases, be impossible for a manufacturer to backward integrate all his raw materials. A tyre manufacturer may, for example, be able to produce the rubber for his tyres but he may not be able to produce the steel wires or carbon black that go into the making of a tyre. So also can a cigarette manufacturer be able to produce the tobacco that forms over 50% of his raw materials but he may not be in a position to produce the wrapping paper or the cork tip that forms part of a cigarette; nor may he be able to produce the cartons for packing the cigarettes. What goes into the manufacture of a single product are so many that it requires careful planning to bring about the necessary linkages in the production system.

Consistent short and long-term planning

This is necessary if we are to bring about the necessary linkages that make for a successful resource-based industrialisation. Such planning will provide for:

a. an inventory of the type and quantity of raw materials used in Nigeria;

b. an inventory of those immediately available;

c. those not immediately available but can be developed from available forest and mineral resources in the country;

d. feasibility studies on those under (c) above, and then encourage investment in those areas;

e. determination of the critical raw materials that are needed by strategic industries but which are not available in the country, and arrange for their importation;

f. the adoption of a deletion programme for CKD parts and attract investment in the manufacture of the parts deleted;

Let me say, for the avoidance of doubt, that the Manufacturers Association of Nigeria supports the idea that the country has to shift to resource-based industrialisation. In other words, we have to seek out those resources — forest, mineral and animals — that can be processed into finished or semi-finished goods, and then set up industries or give incentives that will direct private investment into those areas. But saying that manufacturers should use local raw materials is not the same thing as saying that they should also develop them, i.e., that cocoa industries in Nigeria should go and grow cocoa, or that West African Milk Company should develop a ranch, herd the cattle and milk the cow before producing evaporated milk. There are a few areas, however, where this is possible, but in a majority of cases, someone else just has to take it as his business to produce what others further 'downstream' will need as their own raw materials.

Honourable Minister, Ladies and Gentlemen, I do not want to start anticipating the outcome of the workshop or what will be said in the many papers that will be presented. I, however, hope that the recommendations of this workshop would be acted upon, and not confined to the ministry's archives. I hope also that the recommendations will point the way to our economic survival, and most importantly, that there should be a national commitment and political will to make such economic survival a reality. Let me end by emphasising the need for institutionalising a system of dialogue and consultation between government and the private sector on all major matters affecting the economic destiny of Nigeria.

(31)

Trade Fairs should be substituted with Agricultural Shows ✢

"Trade fairs originated in Europe, for the exhibition of new advances in machinery and technology by their manufacturers. The fairs were not trade marts for the sale of existing products."

Introduction

On behalf of the Manufacturers Association of Nigeria, I salute Your Excellency, and thank you for the stimulating opening address. I thank you also for the contribution of your government to the fair. Its success, I am told, is largely due to your personal interest and the high degree of enthusiasm and devotion shown by the staff of the Ministry of Commerce and Industry as well as by other members of the Trade Fair Committee.

We are all aware that this fair is taking place at a time when the country is experiencing a great recession which is due mainly to the shortage of foreign exchange for the importation of essential industrial raw materials and spare parts. This has resulted in factory closures, mass retrenchments, and all round scarcities. The companies that have taken up stands at this fair are victims of the depressed economic situation. They are all operating well below their installed capacities, with a severe drop in production, increased costs, and declining profits, if any. Their willingness to participate in the fair, despite all the constraints, is a demonstration of their faith and confidence in the future economic recovery of this country. I admire and salute their courage and determination to survive.

✢ Speech made as president of MAN at the Calabar Trade Fair, December 4, 1984.

Are trade fairs really relevant now?

This year, there has been a number of trade fairs in different parts of the country. I believe that the time has come, indeed it is overdue, when we should review, and reassess the whole purpose of these fairs. Trade fairs originated in Europe for the exhibition of new advances in machinery and technology by their manufacturers. The fairs were not trade marts for the sale of existing products. They were specially organised shows for the exhibition of specialised machinery, such as new printing machinery, new food processing machinery, or new automobile designs. The organisers took pains to invite their overseas and local distributors and customers.

In the case of Nigeria, we built the gigantic and expensive Lagos Trade Fair Complex for the purpose of inviting overseas machinery manufacturers to come and show us their wares. We woo them to come and advertise their wares to Nigerians. Again, our trade fairs have become more or less market bazaars and jamborees where swarms of people come to buy and sell. At the recent Lagos International Trade Fair, it was disturbing to see swarms of women and school children buying goods from toys, pots, and pans, to milk, palm oil and orange. It was reported that ₦50 million was realised in sales at the fair. Similarly, the sum of ₦5 million was reported to have been realised at the Bauchi Fair. I have a feeling that at this fair, what will be realised will most likely exceed the amount realised by Bauchi. But is this what we really want to achieve by these trade fairs? I think that we should ask ourselves the following questions:

❑ Are our trade fairs not helping other countries to promote their own products and solve their problems?
❑ Should we not use our trade fairs to solve our own pressing economic problems especially in the fields of agriculture and industry?

Although I fully appreciate the need for a made in Nigeria fair as a means of showing progress in the nation's policy of self-reliance and self-sufficiency, nevertheless, such shows should not assume the character of market bazaars. I appeal to the governments of the federation to scrap the present trade fairs as presently organised and in their place substitute two types of shows, which are more relevant to our present problems:

a. The first should be agricultural shows arranged in sectors to cover food production and cash crops, poultry and livestock. Prizes should be awarded for the best exhibits in order to boost agricultural production.

b. The other type of show should be exhibitions on the development of industrial raw materials which is one of the most critical problems now confronting the Nigerian manufacturing sector. Such exhibitions should be used for displaying advances by manufacturers, research institutes, and universities, in the development of local raw materials. The whole purpose of such shows and exhibitions would be to encourage Nigerians to be more innovative and enterprising in the solution of these two economic problems.

The Manufacturers Association of Nigeria will give both material and moral support to the organisation of such re-organised and more meaningful shows and exhibitions.

Government and the Private Sector should work as Partners

"It is generally said that government and the private sector are partners in progress in that whilst the government calls the tune it is the private sector that plays the pipes..."

Introduction

On behalf of the organised private sector, I thank the Chief of Naval Staff for the challenging address delivered on behalf of the Chief of Staff, Supreme Headquarters. I promise that we will at subsequent meetings take up the challenge one after the other and come up with solutions.

It is generally said that government and the private sector are partners in progress in that whilst the government calls the tune it is the private sector that plays the pipes; and we all know that there can be no melody unless the commander and players co-operate. We of the private sector often wonder if the importance of this co-operation is fully appreciated by the government. This is because whilst we are stretching the right hand of fellowship, government appears to be looking the other way and at other interest groups. I will not mention names, but will give the example of the ousted administration that had more dialogue with trade unions and student unions than they had with either NACIMA[1], NECA, or MAN. If ever there was a time for co-operation between government and the private sector it is now that the economy is passing through a very critical time. The private sector has considerable knowledge and practical experience of the working of the economy, which it can put at the disposal of government. And let me make it

---

[1] Nigerian Association of Commerce, Industries, Mines and Agriculture.

abundantly clear that in asking for dialogue and co-operation our intention is not to hijack the decision-making powers of government. The responsibility for governing and making policy decisions are squarely those of the government, but before it decides on economic matters, it will be fruitful to consult those who either have practical knowledge of the problem area, or are ultimately going to be responsible for putting the decision into practical effect.

Consultations with the organised private sector are a regular feature of democratic economies. The president of the United States is regularly in touch with leaders of American industries. Only ten days ago, Margaret Thatcher[2] scheduled a meeting with the Federation of British Industries. Unfortunately, she had to cancel it because it clashed with the funeral of Mrs. Indira Ghandi.[3]

An example of our lack of co-operation is in the negotiations regarding the re-scheduling of our short-term trade debts. When you think about it, it is the private sector that incurred much of the debts in the first instance. Their members are also more familiar with the creditors with whom they had been doing business over the years. And yet when our government was conducting the negotiations, it did not occur to it to consult or include in its team some representatives of the private sector. Our knowledge of the details of the negotiations is usually through information from our trading partners and overseas newspapers. Our desire is that this quarterly meeting be institutionalised and structured with precise membership and agenda. More importantly, however, is that recommendations and decisions reached should be promptly implemented and not confined to the archives of the ministries or the secretariats of the organised private sector.

---

[2] Former British Prime Minister.
[3] Indian Prime Minister who was shot dead by her body guards.

The Challenges facing Agro-Businesses in Nigeria ✢

"In outlining what the government can do to assist farmers, let me quickly acknowledge that government is already providing considerable assistance. Unfortunately, the assistance doesn't reach most farmers because of bureaucratic delays and abuse by unscrupulous intermediaries between government and the farmers."

Introduction

Your Excellency, the Governor of Anambra State, I salute you. Your Excellency, the Governor of Imo State, I salute you. Your Grace, the Archbishop of Onitsha and Metropolitan of Eastern Nigeria, I bow. Your Highness, the Igwes of Anambra State and Ezes of Imo State. The Chairman, Ihiala Local Government Council. Distinguished Ladies and Gentlemen.

Some of you may not be aware, that for sometime now I have advised myself to reduce my public engagements and speeches. The reason is that I believe the time has come when I should step aside and make room for the up and coming generation. I have sometimes made exceptions, and today I also make an exception for three reasons:

First, it is an opportunity for me to pay my due respect to Your Excellencies. Second, Chief Gilbert Ekwenugo Okeke and I are age-long friends. We were together in the Zik and Okpara administrations of the 1950s and 1960s, and today we are both engaged in agro-allied industries in the Ihiala Local Government Area; he in cassava starch, and I in agro-rice cultivation and milling. Third, I feel that being here is also an opportunity to alert those contemplating to go into agro-industries of the difficulties and problems that will confront them.

✢ Speech presented at the special launching of the expansion programme of the Nigerian Starch Mills, Ihiala, March 15, 1991.

275

The problems are real

The reality of the problems require little proof. One only has to inquire why the agricultural policies of the successive Nigerian governments have failed to produce the expected results. Here, I am referring to the National Accelerated Food Production project of the Gowon administration, the Operation Feed the Nation of the Obasanjo regime, the Green Revolution of the Shagari administration, and the current Directorate for Food, Roads and Rural Infrastructure of the present government. In spite of these well-intentioned policies that span almost a quarter of a century, Nigeria is still unable to feed herself. Something must, therefore, be responsible for the failure of its agricultural policies. Permit me to point out, what, in my humble opinion, I feel is at least partly responsible for this.

Let me start by saying that my observations are based primarily on my four years experience agro-business, and are, therefore, made without prejudice to the opinions of those who have been in the field for a longer period. My first observation is that past agricultural policies seemed to focus excessively on the peasant farmer. By a peasant farmer, I mean the man with a hoe and a machete. For some valid reasons, including a desire not to disturb the prevailing land tenure, the policies tended to fight shy of mechanised agriculture. I feel, however, that unless our agriculture is mechanised, it will be impossible to feed a population of 100 million that is growing at the rate of three per cent per annum. Furthermore, there is little evidence that the policies take cognisance of the fact that peasant farmers are fast disappearing in the wake of free primary education and urbanisation. Urbanisation in cities like Lagos, Onitsha and Aba grow at the rate of about 20% per annum. The present reality is that a peasant farmer with a hoe and a machete can hardly feed his family, let alone have a surplus to feed the nation. A recent United Nation's study on Malawi, for example, revealed that forty per cent of her peasants never produce a surplus. Another forty per cent can only do so during a good season and only twenty per cent have food to spare (see *African Farmer*, No.

2, 1990, page 7). A similar study for Nigeria, I believe, will reveal a gloomier picture.

I believe that there are two main ways by which we can feed the teeming population of the nation. We have either to increase the number of farmers and the area they cultivate, or increase the capacity of the few farmers to cultivate more land. To increase the number of farmers will invariably mean attracting educated men and women. To do this, we must not only relieve agriculture of some of its physical drudgery but must also demonstrate that it is a profitable venture. Neither of these can be satisfied without the use of modern farm methods, which include mechanisation. But mechanisation is capital intensive and can only be successful under certain conditions. One of these conditions is that funds must be available at affordable rates for the purchase of machinery and other inputs. Today, a tractor costs a million naira and a harvester 1.5 million naira. A farmer borrowing 2 million naira from the bank to purchase these machineries will pay interest at the rate of 21%. Until recently, the rate was 28%. Payment of 28% interest means a payment of ₦560,000 interest every year. 21% is ₦420,000 yearly. No farmer working with a tractor and a harvester can generate enough profit to be able to pay such interests. His overheads will be such that he can hardly break even, let alone service the loan. To be able to service the loan and produce a profit, he must cultivate no less than 400-500 hectares of land. This would require additional three tractors and at least an extra harvester. In other words, adequate funds must be available, and at special interest rates, because a farmer cannot compete with a trader in an open and deregulated loan market.

Next to the provision of soft loan capital is the importance of an assured price and market. If a farmer knows before hand the market and the price at which he will sell his crops, he will devote all his energies in raising the crop. This is why tobacco farmers in the North and West are successful farmers, because the Nigeria Tobacco Company provides a ready market at a previously agreed price. The non-availability of ready market was also one of the reasons why the wheat project was a failure in spite of the huge sums spent by the government in encouraging the farmers in Bornu to grow the crop. Government fixed a price but when the crop was ready, there was no ready market because the farmers were left to bargain with the millers who considered the government price too high.

The above are some of the problems that almost every agricultural entrepreneur is facing in Nigeria today. I am almost sure that the Nigerian Starch Mills has also been grappling with similar problems for the past ten years. I hope that they have documented their experiences.

How the government can assist farmers

In outlining what the government can do to assist farmers, let me quickly acknowledge that government is already providing considerable assistance. Unfortunately, the assistance doesn't reach most farmers because of bureaucratic delays and abuse by unscrupulous intermediaries between government and the farmers. Let me briefly mention the problems surrounding government's assistance in the areas of fertiliser and plant hire. For example, a farmer at , say, Ihiala requiring bags of fertilisers for his farm has to go to Enugu[1] at least four or five times before he can get an allocation. Only one woman can give allocation and there is always a long queue when she is available. On getting an allocation, the farmer has to take the allocation paper to Onitsha for payment and later go to either Ihiala or Atani to collect the fertiliser. You can imagine the cost and time consumed by these journeys. For successful farm results, the application of fertiliser must be made at the appropriate time in the life of the crop. This timing is often missed because of bureaucratic delays.

Regarding plant hire, unless the machinery are well-maintained, and their use well-supervised, the laudable objectives of providing them cannot be achieved. Quite often, deposits are made for hiring some machinery but the hires are not effectuated because of constant breakdowns. Today, the

---

[1] At the time the speech was made, Enugu was the capital of Anambra State.

Anambra State government is owing farmers several thousands of naira for deposits made in 1990 for hiring machinery but which were not effectuated. Plant hire cannot be successful unless there is serviceable machinery, a good workshop with trained operators and supervisory personnel as well as an adequate supply of spare parts. I believe that success in agriculture will continue to elude us until the problems surrounding its financing, interest rates for agricultural loans, prices and markets are sorted out.

Let me conclude by saying that one of the greatest problems facing Nigeria today is low productivity not only in agriculture, but also in industries. This low productivity is partly responsible for all our ills — from inflation to deficit financing and from depreciation of the naira to unemployment. I believe that with increased productivity, we will be able to export more than we import which will improve our balance of payment, help shore up the value of the naira, stem inflationary pressures and increase employment opportunities. Increased productivity is one of the secrets of the greatness of Europe and America. It is also one of the secrets of the wealth of Japan and Germany.

The Importance of Limited Liability Companies and the Stock Exchange ⬥

"When a company depends on equity and reserves to fund development, you know that that company has arrived."

Introduction

I have been requested to speak on the importance of limited liability companies and the role of the Stock Exchange. These are two separate but related subjects, none of which can be discussed fully as an after lunch address. I shall, however, touch briefly on each subject and allow you to ask questions on areas that are of interest to you. Let me say immediately that one cannot discuss limited liability companies without first discussing unlimited liability companies. There are two types of unlimited liability companies. These are single proprietorships and partnerships.

Single proprietorship

All businesses start with an idea by someone known as the *entrepreneur*. He is the man with an idea. He is the man or woman who perceives an opportunity for making money, and marshals out resources in terms of men, money and materials with which to translate the idea into a successful business. Entrepreneurship is the father of capitalism, it is also the father of wealth and development. Consequently, the degree of entrepreneurship in a nation determines the level of that country's development. The US, Japan and Germany are examples of countries with a high degree of entrepreneurship. They illustrate that it is not government but individuals, either singly or in companies, that are mainly responsible for progress and development. A single

---

⬥ Speech delivered at Nnewi, October 11, 1990.

proprietor owns everything and whatever profit he makes at the end of the month is his. Even before the end of the month he can take whatever amount of money he wants. If there is any loss it is also his. If he fails to pay his debts the creditors can make him pay with his other personal assets. In law, the single proprietor has *unlimited liability* for all debts contacted by the business. All his property is legally attached to meet the debts. Single proprietorships are common in retail trade and service industries like hotels, laundry, transport, repair shops and petrol stations.

Some difficulties faced by sole proprietors

Even if the business is doing well, a sole proprietor will have difficulty in expanding his business. Reputable banks will hesitate to give him a term loan, or even an overdraft because of the risks involved. The banks' refusal will most likely be because of the absence of a track record of success and /or the absence of a proper book of accounts. In the absence of proper accounting, there is no way of knowing the exact state of the business. In other words, the business cannot expand beyond a certain level because of lack of capital. Furthermore, a one-man business suffers in case of the proprietor's illness or absence, and in many cases the business dies with the proprietor. Ojukwu Transport is an example of a sole proprietorship. So also are the businesses of the retail traders at Onistha and Nkwo Nnewi. I am sure that Hotel De Universe has a sole proprietor.

Partnership

Partnership is when two or more persons own a business, i.e., they jointly provide both capital and labour. Unusually, they draw up a partnership agreement either orally or in writing. It is, however, more businesslike to have it in writing. The partners share the profits in proportion to their capital. One of the reasons for partnership is that it is a method by which a sole proprietor can provide more capital for his business in the absence of bank support. As the business expands, it needs more capital which can be provided by bringing in more partners. An example of a business partnership is G.M.O. Group of Companies (G.M.O). Even though it is incorporated as a company, for all intents and purposes, it is a partnership of three persons.

Disadvantages of partnership

Whenever a new partner is accepted, the partnership agreement has to be redrafted. In some countries like the US, there is no limit to the number of partners one can admit. It can be as many as 100. In Nigeria, the limit is twenty. Partnership can be dissolved whenever any partner finds the existing arrangements unsatisfactory and wishes to withdraw. The partnership law prohibits a withdrawing partner from selling his shares to a third party. Each partner is liable without limit to the full extent of his personal properties for all the debts contracted by the partnership. If a partner owns one per cent, and the business fails, he will be called upon to pay 1% of the debts and the partner with 99% will pay the rest. But if the owner of the 99% cannot pay, the owner of 1% will be called upon to pay. The liability of each partner is, therefore, unlimited. It is single and several. This is why partnerships tend to be confined to small personal enterprises like law firms, accountancy firms, medical practice and engineering consultancies. In such firms, each partner has powers to act as an agent to commit the whole partnership. Therefore, unlimited liability and the method of ensuring continuity are the main disadvantages of partnerships.

Limited liability companies

The problems of continuity, finance for expansion, and limitation of liability are taken care of by the formation of companies. In the first place, a company is a legal person quite different from its shareholders. It can do everything that a human person can do such as owning property, borrowing money, hiring and firing staff, and suing and being sued to court. In a way, a company is more than a human person because it never dies. Unless dissolved, it can last for centuries. Some 17th and 18th Century companies are still in existence. UAC is the successor of the Royal Niger Company of the 19th Century. A company can also mobilise capital easily. Because of the publicity attached to companies and the books of account it has to keep, its status and progress are easily ascertained by banks. Furthermore, the liabilities of shareholders are limited to the extent of their equity. A shareholder cannot be called upon to use his other properties to pay for debts incurred by the company.

There are other advantages that companies have. By forming a company, a founder or sole proprietor can diversify his investments rather than putting all his resources in one business. By providing shares to other persons, he minimises his risks. In a company, ownership is divorced from management. The latter is in the hands of professionals and experts who ensure profitability. In this regard, even if the sons of the owner of substantial shares are not interested in the activities of the company, the company survives its founder or promoter. Professionalisation of management ensures expansion both vertically and horizontally. Company status helps to improve the image and standing of the business in the eyes of the public.

There are, however, a few unpleasant features of company status. The first is the loss of control by the founder. Once management is professionalised and ownership divorced from management, control is also surrendered. But loss of control is the price the founder has to pay in return for expert management. I would rather have 5% of a well-managed company than 90% of one that is inefficiently managed. The most unpleasant aspect of a company is double, or even triple taxation. If it is a manufacturing company, you have to pay excise duty, then company tax which can be up to 45% of profit, and lastly tax on your dividend! Sometimes it appears as if the company is working for the taxman. Some companies try to evade tax by having two sets of accounts, one for the taxman, and the other for the shareholders. Others do so by padding the expenditure items in order to reduce tax liability. A company that has a record of clean business and efficient management can make good profit irrespective of the heavy burden. In the long run, honest business pays. Once everyone — taxman and other public officials — know that you are not prepared for any improper dealings, they respect and refrain from making illegal and improper demands from you.

Private and public companies

Before discussing the role of the Stock Exchange, I must say a few words about the two types of limited liability companies — private and public companies. A private company is restricted to fifty shareholders. Also its share capital must not be less than ₦10, 000. It must not invite the public to subscribe to its shares, and any shareholder wanting to sell his shares must first of all offer them to other shareholders. A public company has no such restrictions. There is no limit to the number of shareholders. Companies like Nigeria Breweries have up to 4,000 shareholders. UAC and NTC have even more than that. The share capital of public companies must not be less than ₦500, 000.

The role of the Stock Exchange

It is surprising that many businessmen are not aware of the role of the Stock Exchange. The Stock Exchange is a house where securities are sold. It is a market where only authorised persons are allowed to buy and sell. These persons are known as *stockbrokers*. They buy and sell on behalf of their clients — companies and individuals. What they buy and sell is only securities. A security is the common name for any well-printed and decorative document that is evidence of ownership of part of the equity of a company. It can also be a document that is evidence of debt owed to the holder and which entitles him to the payment of interests at regular periods before the payment of the principal. Shares of a company or bonds issued by a government are examples of securities.

Besides being a market, the Stock Exchange is also a financial institution where money can be cheaply raised, not from banks, but from the public, in the form of shares and debentures. Now that interest rates are very high, sometimes as high as 30%, the servicing of bank debts can cripple a business. But equity funds are permanent and cannot be recalled at short notice, as is the case with bank overdrafts. In this sense, the Stock Exchange is a financial institution which companies use for raising funds for their expansion. But not all companies can raise money through the Stock Exchange. It is only public companies that are on the list of the Stock Exchange. Such public companies are referred to as quoted companies, that is, companies whose shares are quoted on the daily list of the Stock Exchange.

The Stock Exchange has some conditions which a company must satisfy before it can be put on the list of companies entitled to use the Stock Exchange either for raising money or for sale of their shares. The requirements are:

A. It must be a public company — equity not less than ₦500,000. No limit or restriction as to who can be shareholder.
B. Must offer not less than 25% of its shares to the public.
C. Must produce its financial statements, i.e., audited accounts for the last five years.
D. The company must publish its accounts in the newspapers every six months. These conditions are designed to safeguard the investing public.

Security and Exchange Commission
This is a body that monitors, on behalf of the government, the performance of the Stock Exchange. It is its responsibility to fix the price at which shares will be sold on their first appearance on the Exchange. It also supervises the allocation of shares after a public offer for subscription.

Importance of commercial banks
Since bankers are among the audience, I shall say a few words about the importance of banks to companies. Banks are indispensable allies of companies. Not only do they provide capital, they also provide operating expenses. Sometimes what they provide is three or four times the equity of the company. The ratio of debts to equity is known as *gearing*.

The amount of money a bank can lend to companies depends

on the quantum of its deposits and savings. Without deposits and savings, there can be no loans. One of the reasons why bank loans are expensive is that they have to pay interests to their depositors. Sometimes the interest on loans is so burdensome that a company virtually works for the banks. This happens where nothing or very little is left for the shareholders after servicing the debts. The situation is similar to that between developing countries and the IMF, the London and Paris clubs. Developing countries use up to 75% of their foreign exchange earnings in debt servicing. For these reasons companies should try to build up reserves so that they can finance expansion without recourse to banks. When a company depends on equity and reserves to fund development, you know that that company has arrived.

Besides the provision of funds, banks also act as facilitators of business transactions especially one that involves two countries with different currencies. They receive in one currency and pay in another. This has often led to problems between banks and their customers especially in a period of fluctuations in the rate of exchange between the two currencies. In such a situation, there may be a need for the Central Bank to clarify the situation in the interest of harmony between banks and their customers.

35

Nigerian Industries: Which Way Forward? ✦

"The private sector is always poised and ready to follow government guidelines as long as they are clear, unambiguous, and consistent. This is particularly so if such clear statements of policy are backed up with appropriate incentives."

Introduction

Mr. Minister, Your Excellencies, Ladies and Gentlemen. I welcome you all to the 14th Annual General Meeting of the Manufacturers Association of Nigeria. I must first and foremost apologise for the short notice of the date of the meeting. It was to enable the minister to be present. Mr. Minister, the people before you are the chief executives and representatives of over 700 manufacturers from all over Nigeria. They have come with one, and only one question in their minds, and that is, the future of Nigerian industries.

In the past, our annual general meetings were occasions for letting the government know how its policies affect the manufacturing industry. Today, we are not going to complain about this or that policy, nor ask for any concessions, be they licenses, foreign exchange, expatriate quota, reduced excise, change in tariff or other taxes. Our only concern today is whether industries are to be or not.

After the traumatic experiences of 1984 which was characterised by operating at less than half of installed capacities, shutdowns, redundancies, and higher operating costs, we find

---

✦ Speech delivered as president at the 14th Annual General Meeting of MAN held at the Nigerian Institute of International Affairs, Lagos, March 1, 1985. This speech was delivered during the era of terrible foreign exchange scarcity and foreign exchange rationing.

ourselves at the crossroads with no idea of which way to go. We are, therefore, in desperate need of government's guidance in clear and unmistakable terms. To us, the day's of treating every industry alike is gone, and time has come when we must be told which industries government, under the prevailing circumstances, is prepared to support, and those it cannot. We know that all industries are desirable, if not important. And that must be why they each got the permission to establish and be registered in the first place. But since the country can no longer afford the foreign exchange required for the survival of all the presently established industries, the need for rationalisation and prioritisation becomes imperative. The question then arises: on what criteria should government base such policies of prioritisation and rationalisation?

As far back as two years ago, we in the MAN advised the government on a set of criteria to be used in examining the claims of manufacturing companies for import licenses and foreign exchange allocation. Our recommendations were watered down by the plethora of criteria evolved in the ministry, and which resulted to very little being given to every company. And this left everyone dissatisfied.

Our suggestion now is that government should adopt two levels of classification — a primary classification based on the strategic importance of industries, and a secondary classification based on how individual industries within a group satisfy national goals and aspirations. The suggested primary classification is as follows, in a descending order of priority:

❑ Basic and core industries.
❑ Essential industries.
❑ All other industries

Basic and core industries

These include iron and steel, petrochemicals and infrastructure, i.e., power, communication and water. These industries have a great multiplier effect. They are strategic, indispensable, and form the bedrock of industrial growth. Because of their strategic and capital intensive nature, government should take the lead in establishing them. Private capital should, however, and with proper safeguards, be invited to participate in their management and equity. Every facility should be placed at the disposal of these industries, and the private sector must be poised to take off from those bases.

Essential industries

Next in importance to the core and basic industries are those industries that relate to food and drugs, transportation and construction. Food and drugs are essential for human existence and survival, whilst transportation and construction are essential for economic growth. Industries in this category should receive adequate facilities by way of licences, foreign exchange allocation, expatriate quota, etc., to enable them operate efficiently.

All other industries

All other industries should receive whatever is left after the claims of the basic and essential industries have been met.

Further sub-classification

Within the above three classifications, there should be a further sub-classification and prioritisation on the basis of:

❑ the extent to which a particular industry uses local raw materials;
❑ the extent to which a particular industry is export oriented;
❑ the extent to which a particular industry generates employment;
❑ the extent to which a particular industry generates revenue;
❑ the extent to which a particular industry creates linkages with other industries.

Weight should be assigned to each of these criteria. I strongly believe that such an objective categorisation will clear present doubts and uncertainties. It will also go a long way in stimulating the right type of industrial development, and steering the private sector into the types of manufacturing that are in line with national goals and aspirations, and away from the present consumer taste type of industrial development. The private sector is always poised and ready to follow government guidelines as long as they are clear, unambiguous and consistent. This is particularly so if such clear statements of policy are backed up with appropriate incentives. I have no doubt in my mind that if government comes up with such a clear-cut and well-articulated policy, it will be only a question of time before Nigeria, with its extensive market, will become the industrial hub of West Africa. And if adequate infrastructure could be added to this bargain, we could become the regional industrial centre of the West African sub-region. Similarly, with some progressive planning in agriculture, Nigeria could as well become the granary of West Africa.

A discussion of the future of Nigerian industries will not be complete without reference to the local sourcing of raw materials. The head of state, in his 1985 budget speech, stated that "government will continue with the drive to get manufacturers to develop and make greater use of local raw materials." Unfortunately, the budget speech did not spell out any concrete government policy on the issue. We expected such a detailed statement of policy, for to us local sourcing is not merely an expedient of the current recession, it is also a fundamental change in industrial policy and strategy. For this, I feel that there ought to be a comprehensive government policy statement which should, among other things, set down timetables, targets and incentives for the different industrial sectors. That will be the most practical method of making "our industries to shift from their present dependence on imported raw materials and spare parts to an increased utilisation of local raw materials and local fabrication of spare parts."[1]

Mr. Minister, we are pleased and encouraged to learn that your ministry is already busy working out a programme of raw

---

[1]   Statement made by the Chief of Staff, Supreme Headquarters in late 1984.

materials targets and incentives. We humbly suggest the need for regular consultation with manufacturers during the formative stages of such an important change in policy.

In conclusion, let me say that MAN is anxiously awaiting the new industrial policy. It is going to be our "bible," and as such, we expect it to be clear and categorical in stating which industries government is going to support, and on what conditions. On local sourcing of materials, we expect a timetable of targets, together with supporting incentives which will direct both manufacturers and others into the business of local sourcing.

Finally, the success of any industrial policy depends on how far the industrialists who will ultimately implement the policies understand them as well as consider them workable. In this regard, the need for regular consultation cannot be overemphasised. Once again, Mr. Minister, I thank you for finding the time to be with us in spite of the heavy pressures which you and your ministry are under at this time. Your presence is, therefore, very much appreciated, and I have the honour now to invite you to address the 14th Annual General Meeting of the Manufacturers Association of Nigeria.

Index